THE PELICAN LATIN AMERICAN LIBRARY

General Editor: Richard Gott

The 20 Latin Americas: 2

Marcel Niedergang is a regular correspondent on *Le Monde*, and also spent ten years on *France Soir*. His particular expertise is the continent of Latin America, where he has spent the greater part of his journalistic life; his articles on Latin America in *Le Monde* have achieved world-wide fame. The present two-volume survey has been built out of his experience on the continent.

The 20 Latin Americas

VOLUME II

Marcel Niedergang

Translated by Rosemary Sheed

Penguin Books

Penguin Books Ltd, Harmondsworth,
Middlesex, England
Penguin Books Inc., 7110 Ambassador Road,
Baltimore, Maryland 21207, U.S.A.
Penguin Books Australia Ltd, Ringwood,
Victoria, Australia

Les 20 Amériques Latines published in France by Plon, 1962
Revised edition published in France by Editions du Seuil, 1969
English translation published in Pelican Books 1971

Made and printed in Great Britain by
Hazell Watson & Viney Ltd, Aylesbury, Bucks
Set in Linotype Juliana

Contents

CHAPTER 1

Chile

STATISTICS

Area: 292,257 square miles
Estimated population in 1967: 9,000,000
Population density: Nearly 31 per square mile
Annual rate of population increase: 2·5 per cent
Annual increase in average per capita *income from 1960 to 1966:* 2·1 per cent.

PRINCIPAL PRODUCTS

Copper (world's third largest producer), nitrates, gold, silver, iron.

From the pier at Arica, the first town one comes to on crossing the Peruvian border, to the port of Antofagasta where the nitrate cargoes are loaded, the Chilean coast faces the cold waters of the south Pacific in a series of hostile and oppressive yellow cliffs, bare and inhospitable. This is a land of salt, rock and iodine. Occasional streams, and clusters of frail palm trees lead one to believe that there may be green and pleasant valleys behind this fortress of a coastline. But in fact there is only an almost total desert there, burning under an ever-present sun, from the shores of the Pacific to the icy peaks of the Andes.

According to the rain-gauges in Chile no more than 2·5 millimetres of rain fall on Iquique per year. The minute green specks of strange oases in the two provinces of Tarapaca and Antofagasta, in the Norte Grande, result more from falls of dew than any generosity from the clouds.

South of Antofagasta the two provinces of Atacama and Coquimbo present the monotonous appearance of long stony steppe-land; the Chileans call it the Norte Chico to distinguish it from the Norte Grande, but the aridity there is barely less total. There is hardly any more rain there than in the Norte Grande, and the great drought years are as disastrous to the harvests of the farmers there as are falls in the prices of copper and nitrates to the miners in the Norte Grande.

Five per cent of all Chileans live in the mining settlements of the Norte Grande, and just under 6 per cent are settled in the Norte Chico. The real, populated Chile only begins as one gets near the port of Valparaíso, more than 2,000 kilometres distant, on the southern border of this long strip of land between the Pacific and the Andes.

The Spanish conquerors, having come by way of the northern deserts and over snowy passes anything up to 3,000 metres high, found in central Chile the climate they had left behind in Andalucía, and they gave the name of Valley of Paradise, *val paraíso*, to this lovely strip that ran down to the sea.

The five largest towns in the country are all in an area bounded on the north by Aconcagua, and on the south by the Bío-Bío river, where poplars, weeping willows and the famous vineyards recall both the temperateness of Europe and the invigorating warmth of the shores of the Mediterranean.

South of the Bío-Bío a new kind of country starts, and for a long time this marked the frontier between the Spanish newcomers and the proud Araucano Indians who wanted to be subject neither to the Incas nor to the envoys of Charles V. The town of Concepción, by the mouth of that great river, was up to 1851 Santiago's traditional rival. It was also the fortress of the army and of their opposition to the judicial notions of the politicians who held sway in the capital.

*

The provinces of Arauco, Bío-Bío, Malleco and Cautin contain the coal mines, the afforestation projects, and extensive agriculture. Colonies of German immigrants brought to this favoured piece of south American land the same habits, skills and ways of living as their compatriots brought to Paraná and Santa Catarina in Brazil. Chileans of German descent did a great deal towards this conquest of the southern lands. They also brought and are still bringing their own special contribution to political life. It is certainly the presence of so many officers of German descent that explains the established traditions of energy and discipline in the army, navy and air force of Chile. Puerto Montt, Osorno and Valdivia look like German towns, and German is spoken in them as well as Spanish.

The three southern provinces, Chiloé, Aysén and Magellanes, are inhabited by only 3 per cent of the people. This part of Chile alone is half the size of France. It starts more or less with the large island of Chiloé, and ends at Cape Horn. Hundreds of islands, some tiny, keep silent watch over this tongue of land, punctuated by the few final humps of the Andes, and by lakes through which passes the still disputed border between Chile and Argentine Patagonia.

*

The arid desert of the Chilean far north is balanced in the far south by another, this time icy, desert, merging into the green waters of the ocean. Despite – or perhaps because of – these difficult conditions, the people of Chiloé have deep-rooted traditions which go right back to colonial days. It is hardly surprising that this disconcerting juxtaposition of climates and landscapes, one following another over a distance as long as that between Timbuctu and Copenhagen, should have been the subject of contradictory and often exaggerated descriptions.

The regular earth tremors in the Andes for a long time forced town builders to be content with very low houses. From 1520 till the present day there are records of no fewer than 311 medium or severe earthquakes, and the town of Santiago alone has had 32. The permanent risk of quakes, and the sense of isolation which is produced so easily in this unstable land have, paradoxically enough, combined to make Chileans philosophic, cheerful and even carefree.

All those who have braved danger to make contact with the people so happily settled on this wall of land rising out of the sea have always been enormously admired. One still hears echoes of the exploits of those who pioneered the air mail services, the Mermoz, the Guillaumats and the Godoys. Two expeditions in particular have been singled out for admiration and compared with the crossing of the Alps by Hannibal or Napoleon. Both were of great historical significance: the first was that of Almagro, lieutenant and rival of Francisco Pizarro, the conqueror of the Incas; the second the crossing of the Andes by the troops of San Martín.

Diego Almagro left Peru in 1536 with fewer than 500 Spaniards and 15,000 Indian mercenaries recruited in the Cuzco valleys. Almost half his troops were lost in the ice and snow of the Andes – literally petrified, turned into macabre and Dantesque statues beside their frozen horses. Six months later the rest of the Spanish army, disheartened by the resistance of the Indians, had to go back past the bodies of their dead companions. Five years later the attempt was made again, by another Spanish captain from Estremadura: Pedro de Valdivia. This expedition succeeded in getting across the Andes and the deserts of the north without great losses, and founded the city on the edge of the world, Santiago del Nuevo Extremo.

Unlike Peru, Chile had not a lot to offer the conquistadors:

its rivers held little gold, and its Indians were far less amenable. Valdivia's small force had to face their bad luck with fortitude, and do battle with the Araucanos.

*

The conquest of Mexico by Hernán Cortés took two years, from 1519 to 1521. Francisco Pizarro landed at Tumbes, sooth of the Equator, in 1531, and in 1533 the execution of the Inca, Atahualpa, marked the fall of the Cuzco empire. In Peru, as in Mexico, it took only two years to annihilate a magnificent pre-Columbian civilization. It was to take seventeen to complete the conquest of Chile.

The Araucanos held their 'inviolable' line along the Bío-Bío with a tenacity and courage which astounded and maddened the Spaniards. Valdivia paid for his victory with his life; captured by his former Araucano page Lautaro, now a military leader, he was dismembered alive by his captors. Araucano resistance did not really end until the mid-nineteenth century. And one may agree with the anthropologists that, ultimately, alcohol and sickness did more to contribute to the relative pacification of this fierce people than any military operation.

Today there must still be something over 200,000 Araucanos, who have in theory the same rights and duties as any other citizens. Around Temuco they still live in huts made of leaves, and their traditional chieftains ensure that the customs of the past are kept up. But since the land reserved to them is not enough to provide for their subsistence, they very often take jobs as domestic servants in the towns, or go to work in the copper and nitrate mines. What is significant about this episode of the conquest is the proof it gives of the pride and hardihood of the Araucanos, qualities inherited by the Chilean mestizos who form over 60 per cent of the population.

The greatest of all Chilean writers, Pablo Neruda and Gabriela Mistral (who won for Chile the first Nobel prize ever given to a Latin American), have made a point of drawing on Indian sources when trying to show what they consider to be the genuine nature of the country, though of course such a return to Indian traditions is not something peculiar to Chile. Pablo Neruda, magnificently evoking those primitive times when 'man was earth, mud, an eyelid winking from the soil, a clay shape, a Carib pot, a Chibcha stone or lump of Araucano quartz', climbed up the mysterious and exciting ruins of Machu-Picchu, near Cuzco, to find both the splendour and the poverty of the Indian people.

The Chileans' achievement of independence at the beginning of the nineteenth century was characterized by their grandiose geographical setting and their fighting spirit. The Army formed and prepared by San Martín near Mendoza in 1817 counted 4,000 men. They managed to cross the Andes by following steep mule tracks; and they maintained an order so perfect that their famous exploit has been lauded quite lyrically by historians. San Martín decided that eighteen days was what it would take to get all his men, horses and artillery through. And eighteen days after the first column had set off, led by General Las Heras, the main body of his army reached the appointed stop in the Aconcagua valley. On 5 April 1818 the battle of Maipú was fought: it took six hours and sealed the independence of Chile, 'separated for ever more from the Spanish throne'. Only the archipelago of Chiloé was to continue resisting for a few more years.

At first sight, there must have been little likelihood of this 'country at the end of the world' becoming a strongly centralized state. Yet its recent history is comparatively straightforward, and we do not find in it the endless series of *coups d'état* which have disturbed the political life of so many of its neighbours. The craziness of its geography seems to have given birth to a political wisdom: after the two dictatorships – by Generals O'Higgins and Freyre – presidential terms of ten, and later of five, years have given Chile, since 1830 and for over a century, the peaceful appearance of a nation that has overcome the teething troubles of independence.

*

The discovery of nitrates was made quite by chance, and at first was not thought to be of any major significance. The story is told of groups of Indians crossing the Atacama desert who stopped one evening to set up camp on a spot near what is now the María Elena mine. They gathered grey stones to build their fire on. Suddenly the ground began to crackle, and sparks flew into the dark like fireworks. The Indians thought it must be the devil, and they quickly packed up their camp and went to tell their story to the Spanish priest of a nearby village. The priest decided to get some ashes from the camp-fire and have them analysed. The experts were not interested, but this mysterious powder, which the priest finally flung out into his garden, produced surprising results: his maize grew to twice its usual size.

The nitrate industry has had its ups and downs. There was a spectacular boom at first, and thousands of men flocked to the Chilean deserts. From 1880 to 1920 production rose fantastically, from an average of 200,000 tons per year to over 3 million. Exports were over a million tons by the end of the century, owing to a heavy demand from the explosives industry; and during the First World War the increased demand for saltpetre led to a new wave of prosperity. Nitrate production employed up to 100,000 workers during 1917 alone, and Chile earned 30 million dollars. Then, with the coming of peace, the boom ended.

In 1914 the development of manufactured nitrates struck a new blow against Chilean nitrates. In 1932 there were 83 factories producing synthetic nitrates – in Germany, the U.S.A., France, Japan, Belgium, Holland, England and Italy. All together that year they produced 3,500,000 tons, while exports from Chile fell to 610,000 tons, and a year later to

60,000. Many firms closed, and thousands of workers trailed back along the roads of the *Norte Grande* to sell their labour in the *estancias** of the coastal and central areas. The extraction of nitrate was then undertaken with more well-planned and scientific methods, and thus recovered to some extent, but nitrates no longer play the lead in the Chilean economy.

With a production of 657,000 tons in 1966, Chile is the world's third copper producer, and it is its ambition to reach first place by 1971 as a result of the cooperation agreements made by the Frei government with various north American companies intending to invest considerable sums and increase production substantially. With 12·2 million tons in 1966, iron ore is the country's second largest natural source of wealth. And nitrate, though on the decline, is still produced in large enough quantities to make Chile the world's largest source of this natural product, the average production being in the region of a million tons per year.

*

Geologists have not yet satisfactorily explained the formation of saltpetre deposits in the deserts of the north. The mineral beds which contain among other things the famous nitrate lie on the surface of depressions once filled with water. Those beds are an average of 30 centimetres or less in depth, and thus easy to work.

The installations of María Elena and Pedro de Valdivia, which provide 70 per cent of Chile's total production, are unique in the world; indeed there can be few mining undertakings anywhere that have demanded such efforts and sacrifice in conquering natural enemies. The daily miracle of the green lawns and pools of María Elena is due to the building of aqueducts and reservoirs which were anything but easy work. The only river worthy of the name in the area is the Río Loa; it comes down from the Andes and flows into the

*Large estates.

Pacific north of Tocopilla but it almost vanishes as it winds across the desert. Alongside it stands Calama, the largest natural oasis in the Atacama desert; but further on the Loa, which for no apparent reason takes on new power, hurtles down into a canyon so narrow that its sudden rushing waters disappear from view. Along this shore the creeks and sheltered spots are so unsafe that boats have to give it a wide berth, and the landing of goods or people is always a complicated operation.

The workers' housing estates and the lawns of María Elena rose literally from nothing, beginning in 1926. And where today stand the *oficinas* of Pedro de Valdivia, there was until 1930 nothing but empty steppe-land. That María Elena and Pedro de Valdivia are paying propositions is largely due to investment by foreign firms during the early years, which enabled a modern infrastructure to be established. And the directors of those firms have naturally tended to stress this fact in their disputes with the Chilean government. Nitrate is to Chile what oil is to Venezuela or tin to Bolivia: a cause for permanent discord. The Santiago government is all the more determined not to yield an inch because it cost the country a war to gain possession of this desert.

The battle for nitrates saw the Chileans ranged against the Peruvians – who got sporadic support from Bolivia – from 1879 to 1884. This was the Pacific War which, though it certainly was not as scandalous as the Chaco War, had deep-rooted causes and long-term consequences of an almost identical kind. The Santiago government considered that all the land south of the 23rd parallel belonged to Chile. The Bolivian government declared that its rule extended as far as the 25th parallel. The exchanges of notes and the arguments which went on for at least fifteen years finally ended with the landing of Chilean troops in the port of Antofagasta on 14 February 1879. Fifteen months later Chilean soldiers wiped out the Bolivian and Peruvian units in Tacna, and in January

1881 they occupied Lima. The peace treaty gave Chile the lion's share – the contested province of Tarapaca. Bolivia lost her only access to the sea. The Pacific war left a bitterness in the hearts of Bolivians – and, to a lesser extent, of Peruvians – which still persists. The railway opened in 1913 from the high plateaux of Bolivia to the port of Arica hardly provided adequate compensation to a country totally enclosed by its own mountains ever since that unfortunate war. The government in La Paz has always continued to claim a 'legitimate access to the sea', and General Barrientos, who came to power in 1964 after the *coup d'état* which overthrew the Paz Estenssoro regime, actually put the phrase at the head of his claims upon the other American states. It was an irony of fate that just as the Bolivian government was establishing a large-scale campaign on this demand for *la salida al mar**, the appearance of guerrilla *focos* in the Nancahuaza forced the authorities to turn their attention once more to this eastern area so close to the Chaco of dismal memory. Bolivia's claim to a natural access to the Pacific in fact made it impossible for her to take part in the summit conference of heads of state of members of the OAS at Punta del Este in April 1967.

*

Three powerful foreign firms control and profit from the production of Chilean copper: Braden Copper Company, Chile Copper (a subsidiary of Anaconda) and Andes Copper Company. Braden first appeared near Santiago in 1911. The mines of El Teniente, 2,000 metres up in the Andes, still had a certain dangerous glamour about them, and tourists interested in economics and statistics would make a point of going up to the very peak of El Teniente. A 'roller coaster' of a railway links the mines with the town of Rancagua. Chile Copper followed Braden in 1915, but chose an area

* Outlet to the sea.

more to the north. It opened its first *oficinas* in nitrate deserts only twenty kilometres from the oasis of Calama. It was thought at first that the deposits of copper ore in the region prospected by Chile Copper were something like 53 thousand million tons – in other words, the largest copper deposit yet found anywhere.

Chile Copper invested a large amount in its efforts to develop this, and the result appears most clearly in the achievements of Chuquicamata: this artificial town in the middle of the desert rose up alongside the largest open-cast copper mines in the world. Seen from the air, Chuquicamata looks simply like a narrow crater, 3 kilometres long by 1 wide; it resembles a greenish-grey funnel, cut into ridges along which convoys of miniature trains run endlessly; a gaping wound from which rise great columns of dust.

One's first agonized reaction is that Chuquicamata is either an inhuman folly, or perhaps a futurist city only kept in being by the rigid laws which enable it to survive: everything is determined, decided and organized by the company – work, wages, leisure activities, the lawns, the pools. The electricity used there is carried by cable from the port of Tocopilla, 150 kilometres to the west. Water is brought down by canals from high up in the Andes. But what no statistics can explain in this enclosed world is the nature of human relationships. In 'Chuqui', Chilean workers and American engineers watch one another, judge one another, envy one another or hate one another, from street to street, from ridge to ridge. For all the excellent reasons for lassitude on the part of the *gringos* and for resentment on the part of the Chileans provide more than adequate fuel for interminable disputes. It has been said of Chile that it is a laboratory for social experiment; if so, then Chuquicamata is certainly one of the areas in which the opposing attitudes of Americans and Chileans are in the most intense conflict.

The Andes Copper Company, which, starting in 1927,

chose to develop the area round Portrerillos, is also a subsidiary of Anaconda. There are various other firms around Santiago or in the Andes of the Atacama desert; but they are pygmies in comparison with the three giants which among them control the copper industry. This predominance of north American trusts, and the fact that Chile's foreign resources depend essentially on copper – which brings the country 70 per cent of its foreign credits (and 33 per cent of its foreign currency) though it represents only 6·9 per cent of the GNP – explains the issues at stake in the incessant negotiations between the Santiago government and these huge foreign companies. Copper, which is capitalized by the Americans, has overtaken nitrates (which was capitalized by England), but it employs an estimated work force of only 50,000 miners, whereas the nitrate industry, up until the First World War, employed some 100,000. Of course the Vietnam war led to some expansion in the Chilean copper industry, but since the spring of 1967 prices have tended to drop.

Agreements with the trusts were drawn up in 1964 by the Frei government, and adopted by the Santiago legislature in April 1966. They stipulated that the state must have a share in the developments being made: 25 per cent in Anaconda, 49 per cent in a subsidiary of Anaconda, 51 per cent in Kennecott, and 25 per cent in the Cerro Corporation. The total investment of capital was estimated at 416 million dollars, quarter of this to be provided by Chile. The country's capacity for refining 'copper blister' was to be increased from 270,000 tons per year in 1968 to 700,000 tons by 1970. This 'Chileanization' of the copper mines was looked on as a great success by the Christian Democrats in power in Santiago; it seemed to them that 'you cannot make revolutions on all fronts at once', and that 'one must take capital wherever one can find it'. The left-wing parties, on the other hand, dismissed the whole thing as a farce, and pointed out that all these agreements to cooperate had not 'fundamentally changed the omnipotence of the copper monopolies in Chile'.

In effect, the ups and downs of the price of a pound of copper on the international market continued to have decisive and, at times, catastrophic effects on the political situation in the country.

Thus Santiago has regularly felt the temptation to sell more to the countries of the communist bloc, especially China. Torn between the need to sell to the highest bidder, and the wish not to displease the U.S.A. too much, the Chilean authorities will undoubtedly continue to vacillate in their policies as long as they fail to free the Chilean economy of the bonds which have held it fast since the beginning of the century.

*

Hostility to the *gringos* is naturally at its keenest in the mines, and in the universities where Chilean engineers and other experts are trained for work in the mines. The different salaries paid to north American and Chilean engineers doing the same work in El Teniente or Chuquicamata, the almost total absence of any personal relationships between the north American and Chilean staff, the difficult work and conditions and relatively low pay of the workers – all these are so many reasons for the anti-American feeling and consequent success of communism in Chilean working-class circles.

The temptation to take complete control of the copper industry by nationalizing foreign firms has often struck the Chilean leaders. That they have resisted it, up to the present at any rate, is because the structure of the industry is so fragile. Certainly the trusts do make enormous profits, and at least half of those profits are made in Chile. But nationalization would not achieve much, for copper has not only got to be produced – it must also be sold.

The threat of nationalization has been brandished many

times during electoral campaigns, and has sometimes even figured in the inaugural speeches of presidents of the Republic. But the financial and technological power of the foreign firms has got such a grip that this desperate measure would ultimately seem to be more dangerous than effective. However, the sense that Chile is being outrageously exploited by the north American trusts is deeply rooted in public opinion, and the big firms are attacked for having for so long forced the country to sell its copper below the world market price. The trusts defend themselves by presenting convincing accounts of the problems they face: they stress the exorbitant duty they have to pay on all the equipment they import, and add to that the amount they have to spend on housing, canteens and social services.

For over a quarter of a century the monotonous accusations of Chilean politicians and economists against the United States have simply highlighted the impossibility of emerging from this absurd situation without making certain revolutionary decisions. Meanwhile hostility to the copper trusts continues to grow – verbally at least – and is something the Chilean leaders will be forced to reckon with.

*

For the past thirty years Chile has been making strenuous attempts to diversify its economy. A national industry has grown up, which the government does everything possible to assist. Perhaps the name that best symbolizes this wish for independence is Huachipato – Chile's version of Brazil's Volta Redonda. Built near Concepción and its coal mines, the Huachipato steelworks was opened in 1950. Within two years its production had already reached 248,000 tons of cast iron and 246,000 of steel – far more than the home market could use.

By 1965 the production of steel was 51·5 kilos per head. The *Corporación de fomento** has worked to achieve ever-

* Development Corporation.

increased industrialization: a copper foundry has been built at Paipote, and an oil refinery at Concón. In 1966 Chile produced over a million tons of cement and 60,000 tons of newsprint; and with nearly 600 million litres, it is the major wine-producer of Latin America. Its processing industries supply all the needs of the home market for tinned fish, textiles, and beer. But Chile still has to spend 150 million dollars a year on food, and this can only increase. The country is poorly cultivated because of its archaic property structure – only slightly improved by the Frei government's agrarian reforms.

Industrialization has resulted in a concentration of population in the cities. According to CEPAL statistics 60 per cent of all Chileans were living in urban areas by 1960. In 1968 a quarter of the whole population lived in Santiago alone. But Valparaíso, Concepción (which is on the way to becoming the country's major industrial centre) and Arica (benefiting both from the exodus of the nitrate workers, and the results of efforts to decentralize) have all expanded spectacularly. The population of Arica tripled in three years.

Since the 1865 census the population of Santiago has doubled regularly every twenty years: in 1968 it had 2½ million inhabitants. This fantastic growth is partly due to the increase of births over deaths and partly to the constant influx of people from the countryside to the towns. For agriculture is still the poor relation in the Chilean economy. Though Chile has more arable land or grassland per head of the population than California, Sweden or Switzerland – all places with similar climatic conditions – its agricultural production is half that of Switzerland, and only a third that of California.

The main cause for this is the agrarian system inherited from colonial times. Vast holdings – *fundos* of 5,000 hectares and *haciendas* of 100,000 – are the rule. It is estimated that 600 Chileans own 60 per cent of all the country's arable land.

Yet this tiny body of wealthy landowners are not interested in farming, and prefer to live in the capital. In this archaic and inefficient system of the colonial *fundo*, the labour is provided by *inquilinos* who live on the proprietor's land in adobe huts, and have a patch of ground allotted to them. *Inquilinos*, small farmers and agricultural workers in the normal sense, together make up some half-million men. Their average wage is between 50 and 70 (American) cents a day (20–30p). They are tied to land that is being inefficiently farmed and which they do not own.

From father to son, they work the same piece of land, in conditions of the utmost poverty. Infantile mortality is enormous – one in every three children dies in the first year of life. Obviously it is essential to reform this anachronistic system inherited from the sixteenth century; but every attempt at reform so far has come up against the determined hostility of the landowner class. Dr Eduardo Frei's reformist government met with as much opposition as any other: his plan for agrarian reform, the boldest ever put forward in Chile, had to overcome innumerable obstacles before being finally accepted by Parliament on 21 February 1967. In theory the reform applied to all properties containing more than 80 hectares of irrigated land, and two state bodies were given the job of putting it into effect: the CORA was to purchase land and manage what had been bought, and the INDAP was to prepare the peasants for the changes and technological developments upon which the new structures depended. The government urged small farmers and the new landowners to form cooperatives. There is no doubt that this reform had made major changes in the old system in 1968: by then 1,200,000 hectares had been expropriated. Though the reform was attacked by the conservative right as a 'communist threat' and by the revolutionaries of the left as 'appallingly inadequate', it was none the less thought by the leader of the left wing of the Christian Democrats (though with reservations) to have made certain irreversible changes.

Indeed there can hardly be any doubt that the appearance on the political scene of a rural proletariat demanding their rights has disturbed the balance of power. As yet farm workers are not very politically conscious, and trade unions are only beginning to be formed. But the addition of an organized body of peasants would certainly provide a powerful new weapon for the Chilean extreme left wing.

*

The communist movement in Chile has long been thought to be one of the most active in all Latin America, since the trade unions in the copper and nitrate mines have so long a tradition of struggle behind them. Chile can certainly be proud that, with Uruguay, she has one of the most progressive bodies of social legislation in South America. But Cuba stands as a reminder to the Santiago government that the combined pressure of anti-American nationalism and the demands of vast numbers of farm workers is enough to produce a surge of unrest from below that nothing can serve to repress.

There already exists one link between the backward peasant of the Chilean *campo* and the specialized worker of the Santiago suburbs: the *roto*, a character unlike anyone else in South America. The *roto* is someone who has left an *estancia* to become a mason, an artisan, a miner, or perhaps an electrician. He is lively, courageous and sharp-witted; and Chilean caricaturists have recognized his qualities by giving him the role of Everyman, mocking and wise, in the form of 'Verdejo' – a ragged and simple-seeming little fellow who makes ironical comments on political events.

Geographically Chile is like California turned upside down, but politically it is more like France than anything. The two countries are alike, not only in the multiplicity and complexity of their political groups, but also in the way those groups have evolved. The Chilean political spectrum shows a pattern including every possible tendency, from communist to neo-fascist by way of conservative. Chileans themselves declare that there are only three major political groups in their country: left, centre and right, though each, it is true, is subdivided into three sub-groups. But in fact the shades of opinion are infinite.

For convenience of analysis it is usual to divide the map of Chile into three. Ricardo Cruz Coke, one of Chile's finest sociologists, divides the political movements of his country into nine major chapters; this makes it possible for him to give a brilliant description of the chronic instability of Chilean politics. According to him such instability is common to all western democratic regimes in which the three majority parties can never agree at the same moment on the following three basic points: education, the economy, politics. That such an analysis, applicable to the great democracies of Europe and the west, should apply equally to the republic of Chile is in itself evidence of the high degree of political awareness that exists there.

Chile was the first country in Latin America to have a Popular Front government. This significant event took place in 1938, only two years after the same thing happened in France. It was the period when *caudillos* were ruling a great many South American countries; but in Santiago a coalition of all the movements of the left and the centre reached agreement in a *Frente popular*, making their slogan, 'Food, a roof, a shirt', one which could not fail to delight a nation weary of the complacency of the outgoing President, Alessandri, towards the conservative landowners.

*

President Aguirre Cerda, leader of that *Frente popular*, died in 1941, before he had had time to carry out his plans for agrarian reform. Cerda had been elected with the support of the communist vote. In 1946 González Videla triumphed in the presidential elections with a majority of 50,000 – 40,000 of whom were quite clearly of the extreme left. During the municipal elections a year later the communists with 91,204 votes – 16 per cent of the whole – swung the balance. But the three communist ministers in González Videla's first cabinet held their portfolios for less than two years.

In 1948 the communist party was made illegal, and for fifteen years Chile was in the curious situation of having the officially 'banned' communists in the forefront of public life. Yet the law which banned them was called the 'law for the defence of democracy'. It was in part his promise to repeal that law that got General Carlos Ibáñez del Campo re-elected president in 1952.

His return to power may seem somewhat surprising. From 1927 to 1931 he had been in office, and Santiago had no very happy memories of that period, for during those four years he earned a reputation for being a rigid and insensitive dictator. In one sense he was a forerunner of Perón: elected in 1927 with a leftist programme, and by a large working-class vote, Ibáñez, who had been Minister of War in the previous government, soon took to using the most authoritarian methods. He restricted the freedom of the press. The prosperity resulting from the international situation combined with loans from America certainly made it possible for him to launch a vast programme of public works, but his mistakes, his extreme authoritarianism, and the first echoes of the depression finally led to a popular uprising in 1931. Legend has it that the General was forced to flee on mule-back across the Andes to his refuge in Buenos Aires.

There he stayed for ten years, which gave him time to form some very useful political friendships, and he then came back unobtrusively to Santiago, where he spent another ten years in complete silence. When he felt that the Chilean people had forgotten the dictatorial nature of his first term of office, remembering only the prosperity it had brought, he offered himself for election and was elected (though by a tiny majority) by those who looked back nostalgically to the thirties, by the communists, and by the extreme right-wing nationalists who hoped to establish a form of Peronism in Santiago. In fact it seems probable that secret gifts of money from Perón contributed to Ibáñez' victory.

But miracles never take place twice. The Ibáñez of 1952 lacked the energy and determination of the Ibáñez of 1928; at 75, he certainly looked a likely saviour figure, with his military bearing preserved intact by regular exercise, and his cold eyes behind thin steel-rimmed spectacles – but the people soon realized that he had not moved forward as fast as they had.

At first he gave the appearance of wishing to form links with Perón's Argentina: he met Perón in Buenos Aires, signed a trade agreement with Argentina, and in his speeches made frequent allusions to the need to 'put an end to the rule of the oligarchs and plutocrats' – language far more redolent of Buenos Aires than Santiago. Even Eva Perón had her counterpart in Chile, in the person of María de la Cruz, a doctor and a highly excitable senator.

But Ibáñez's Peronist tendencies did not last for long. The barrier of the Andes, though dominated by a statue of the redeeming Christ as witness to the eternal friendship between Chile and Argentina, remained as solid as ever. This became obvious when the beginning of Peronism's decline coincided with Chile's return to its traditional policies. Ibáñez had let it be understood that he would abrogate the treaty of military aid with the United States and restore diplomatic relations with the Soviet Union which had been broken off in 1948. But he did no such thing; nor did he repeal the law for the defence of democracy, and the communists, who had supported his election in September 1952, were having second thoughts by 1953.

In the end Ibáñez adopted a policy of the centre which was not notably different from that of his predecessors. There was one reason, and one only, that made it imperative: the need to negotiate new agreements with Washington for the sale of copper. Rossetti, his Finance Minister, undertook this delicate mission – a labour of Sisyphus as far as the Chilean government was concerned.

This was indeed conclusive proof that the clear-cut demands of the Chilean economy were more powerful than all the good will or reforming purpose of governments, whether right-wing or left.

Chronic inflation is an evil with which all Chilean governments have had to deal with varying successs since the end of the last century. All one can say is that the end of the battle is still not in sight. The inability of the Frei government, even in 1966, to hold down salaries and prices, led to a fresh burst of inflation, and in 1968, the Christian Democrats themselves were forced to admit the serious long-term consequence of this.

*

Every government in Chile for the past fifty years has begun its career by promising to raise the standard of living of the masses: then each time galloping inflation and rising prices have forced it to pursue the policy dictated by conservatives and businessmen to check the process.

The two-part story of General Ibáñez del Campo is a perfect example. It is far from being unique. When demand from the workers becomes too overwhelming, there always remains one last resort: the armed forces. In 1958 the army made it possible for Ibáñez to complete his term of office in spite of all opposition. The elections of September 1958 saw a confrontation of the major classic political groupings: conservatives, socialists and radicals. Jorge Alessandri, a conservative, and number one on the electoral list, was the son of the Alessandri who had himself begun as a left-wing president, and been the first Chilean leader to concern himself seriously with the problems of the *rotos*.

Especially during the first years of his term he had established the foundations for a very progressive system of social security which made Chile the most advanced state in Latin America. Then economic necessity forced him to make more large-scale promises to the country's businessmen. But he was well remembered, and his son profited from the fact. However, as the owner of a network of large paper, metal and textile firms, and chief shareholder in various banking and insurance concerns, Jorge Alessandri was under no illusions. He was the classic man of the right and presented himself as such. His electoral slogan was simple: 'Our country does not need revolutions or magic, vote-catching cure-alls. What it needs is good government.'

His platform was: defence of free enterprise, non-intervention in the economy, anti-communism at home, and a resolutely pro-American policy abroad. The electors knew exactly what they were being offered: they could be grateful to Alessandri Junior for his frankness.

His victory was by a small but adequate margin. He got 386,192 votes as against 354,000 for his closest opponent, the socialist senator Allende. The economic situation which faced him on coming to power was anything but good: copper had gone down by 50 per cent in price during 1958 alone; debts abroad had reached 600 million dollars. Faced with the demands of the blue- and white-collar workers and the civil servants, Jorge Alessandri had to govern with the support of the armed forces and the propertied classes.

From 1930 to 1960 the political battle between left and right had changed into a struggle between the centre-right and both left- and right-wing extremists. Under Jorge Alessandri's presidency Chile recovered its traditional complex and reassuring image as a nation whose political development was advanced enough to exclude the likelihood of any dramatic upheavals. It would be too much to say that this 'land at the end of the world' lived in total happiness, but relative peace looked like continuing until the end of Alessandri's term of office.

The communists continued to make regular progress. In the 1958 elections, they achieved 155,000 votes, and it became clear that their traditionally firm hold in the mining areas (Chuquicamata, Portrerillos, Sewell, Iquique and Lagunas) was now extending to the southern part of the country. Up to then they had never posed any real threat, despite their long history. Back in 1919, the FOC (Chilean Workers' Federation) could muster 100,000 people for a meeting in Santiago. Chilean communists have always directed their activity towards gaining control of unions, and today they are still one of the most powerful elements there.

In fact the Chilean CP was not much affected by the 'law for the defence of democracy' which forbade it any overt action. A fundamentally bad social situation and the rapid growth of the working class made it possible for the Party to do its fighting on a terrain where it naturally had all the weapons it needed.

The continual development in processing industries (textiles, foodstuffs, metals, plastics), together with the formation of state enterprises (Huachipato, the National Electricity Company, the National Oil Company, and sugar refineries) had, during recent years, largely compensated the CP for the loss incurred through the run-down in the numbers of nitrate mining workers who had been their major traditional support during the twenties and thirties. Here again one cannot really describe the evolution of the Chilean CP better than by comparing it with certain European Parties, especially the French one. The Chilean CP, having made common cause with the FRAP socialists (Front for Popular Action) against the Christian Democrats has, ever since 1964, regularly adopted more 'reasonable' and 'moderate' positions than those of the socialists and young revolutionaries who identified more or less with the Cuban revolution. The Chilean CP, hostile to the policy of armed struggle set out in Havana during the solidarity conference of Latin American nations in August 1967 and faithful to the policy of peaceful coexistence supported by Russia, found itself on the eve of the major electoral battles of 1969 and 1970 rather closer to the position of the radicals than to that of some of its own left-wing 'allies'.

Between those extremely left-wing forces – becoming increasingly more powerful – and the upper middle class of businessmen, there stands a large, intelligent, forceful and demanding middle class. Electorally speaking, they are a somewhat floating mass, who will often decide their allegiance at the last moment, thus making it hard to make any exact forecasts. The existence of this unpredictable element is a force to be reckoned with.

But it was also that middle class so concerned with their own living standards who were the first to indicate disquiet in respect of certain elements of the Christian Democratic programme for 'revolution in liberty'. The relative atrophy of that programme since 1966 is due more to resistance on the part of the higher echelons of the middle class, than to the classic delaying action of the large landed proprietors' pressure group.

The popular landslide of 7 March 1965 astounded all observers, even the young leaders of the Christian Democrat party. The electors had to choose the 146 deputies for the new Chamber, and 21 of the 45 senators in the second house. Frei's party – he had been elected president on 4 September 1964, and took office the following 4 November – won 82 seats in the Chamber, thus adding 59 to its numbers there, so that for the first time in the country's history one party had an absolute majority. In the senate the twelve Christian Democrat candidates won by such a huge majority that one may feel sure that had it also been totally renewed, it too would have presented Frei with an absolute majority. On the evening of that triumphant day for Chilean democracy, thousands of the president's supporters massed outside the ancient and ugly palace of La Moneda. Eduardo Frei, beaming, wearing the well-worn university gown he was so fond of, raised his arms aloft, and shouted: 'Now we can really begin. Chile will be an example for all of Latin America...'

*

Six months earlier, outside that same palace, the same supporters had sung to celebrate the little professor's victory in the presidential election. 'Latin America will be Christian Democrat...' But the triumph of this son of German Swiss emigrant parents had a certain ambiguity about it. He had, of course, won by 1,463,535 votes, thus defeating by over 500,000 votes the FRAP candidate, senator Salvador Allende – a doctor, who had only lost to Jorge Allessandri by a few thousand votes in September 1958. Allende, misleadingly described by conservative and liberals, obsessed with fear of any possibility of a return of the popular front, as 'Moscow's man', seemed doomed to take second place to everyone. In fact the FRAP won 975,670 votes – far more, proportionately, than the old style popular front of 1938. Frei's victory was thus not due to any sudden collapse of the left block, but to a failure of nerve on the right: conservatives, liberals and radicals, fearing a possible victory by the Marxist candidate, had instinctively rallied to vote for the Christian Democrats. This did not mean that the traditional ruling classes of Chile supported the policy of economic and social reforms of Senator Frei (agrarian reform, 'Chileanization' of copper, increased power for the government, fiscal reform, the fight against poverty, workers' participation in the profits of industry). And from November 1954 to March 1965, with the risk of a new popular front gone, the right-wing deputies showed tremendous obstinacy in opposing the Frei government's every attempt to achieve reform.

But those elections of 1964 and 1965 were significant: it could scarcely be denied that the reactions and attitudes of the Chilean electorate, whether of the right, the centre or the left, were very similar to those of a sophisticated European electorate; and from this point of view, Chile once again proved beyond doubt that it was considerably in advance of other Latin American nations, where the voting is still so often dependent on the will of the military.

For the first time in Latin America the Christian Democrats were in power and were able to exercise it effectively. This was not just a chance: the Frei party had been advancing steadily ever since the municipal elections of 1963. In the provincial election of Curicó, in March 1964, it got 27 per cent of the votes, almost wholly overturning the traditional support of this mining area for Gonzáles Videla's old radical party. The alternative between 'communism' or 'Christian democracy' was clear even then. The elections of September 1964 and then of March 1965 did no more than confirm the tendency of previous years.

The reasons for this are equally clear: the Christian Democrats were no new group in Chile. As long ago as 1920, a group of young academics centring round R. P. Vives and Eduardo Frei had founded the National Front, the first beginnings of the party that was to triumph in 1965. But up to the end of the Second World War, progress was slow, laborious, and marked by setbacks and failures. Eduardo Frei, born in 1911, went to the Catholic university of Santiago, and for his doctoral thesis in law chose the subject of 'the rule of the wage-earner'. He was an active Catholic and lived a very austere life; he had no private means, and never moved out of the modest bungalow in the Hindenburg district where he went to live in 1937, on the day he married María Ruiz Tagle.

The beginning of his active career in politics coincided with the end of the war. In 1944 he joined the Ríos cabinet as Minister of Public Works. He became senator for Norte Chico in 1946, was re-elected in 1957, and in 1958 he stood for the presidency, but came a poor third after Alessandri and Salvador Allende.

Frei was a Christian reformist but did not believe it possible for Chile in 1965 to stand out directly against the all-powerful United States (though of course there might be minor confrontations arising out of the dishonesty of the big north American copper companies). In September 1964 the U.S. publicly proclaimed their delight over the victory of Frei over Allende; it may well be that the State Department's reasons were similar to those of the Chilean landowners and the industrialists of Santiago and Valparaíso. When it became clear that the will to act of the Frei government was totally paralysed by the twofold opposition from both right and left in Congress, the U.S.'s 'enthusiasm' for the Chilean experiment waned considerably. Frei was blamed for his 'ultra-conservatism' and his 'inability to act' – as though that could possibly have come as a surprise when it was known that the new president could expect unconditional support only from the twenty-eight Christian Democrat deputies. America, having decided to give way in theory to the principle of the 'Chileanization' of copper – in order to avoid having later to become involved in a dangerous trial of strength over 'nationalization' as demanded by the leaders of the FRAP – would obviously have preferred to keep the whole of its huge economic advantage in Chile. According to the 'Survey of Current Business', U.S. investments in Chile rose in 1967 to 1,268 million dollars – including 887 million in the mines, 191 in public services, and 27 in the manufacturing industries.

Che Guevara had warned the Chilean government back in 1964: 'You will not succeed if you try to make deals with American imperialism, if you come to terms with it instead of fighting it....' In 1970, six years after the Christian Democrats had begun their first attempt to overthrow the system while respecting basic human freedoms, and, after the election of Allende, it would be rash to say that they had totally failed.

It was, however, clear that the great hopes – not only in the country itself but all over Latin America – aroused by Frei's spectacular victory were considerably dashed. The Christian Democrats' experiment of 'revolution in freedom', which had been put forward in November 1964 and again in March 1965, as the 'decisive' answer to the 'Cuban challenge' for every country in the sub-continent, had, by the end of 1968, two years before Frei's term as president was to end, come to look just like another attempt at reform. It was undoubtedly more determined, more definite and better worked out than any other attempt had been, but all that was open to doubt was how much good or harm it had achieved – not whether it was really 'revolutionary' or not. 'Where is the revolution we have been promised?' asked the Christian Democrat senator Rafael Gumucio, president of the party until 1968 and one of the chief leaders of the so-called 'rebel' wing of a movement which had in 1964 claimed to rally all the country's dynamism and force for renewal. Such leading economists as Jacques Choncholl, formerly a CEPAL expert and inspirer of the content of the government's plan for agrarian reform, were bemoaning the experiment's 'slide to the right', and Choncholl himself chose to resign from his job as director of the INDAP.

The Christian Democrat 'rebels', supported by a considerable part of the rank and file and of the youth groups in the party, as well as of the younger clergy attracted to the revolutionary theories of the non-communist radical left, insistently demanded a 'dynamic' fresh start to the movement for 'revolution in freedom'. In terms of concrete action what they wanted was a speeding up of agrarian reform, a genuine reform of the economy, measures to put an end to the virtual monopoly of foreign companies (American and Japanese) in iron mining (iron being the second largest export), and a less conciliatory policy towards the copper companies.

'Faster and farther' : such was the impatient slogan of these 'rebels', and Frei's reply was, 'It is I who will determine the rate'. But everything combined to show that his anxiety not to fight on too many fronts at once, to avoid possible unforeseen consequences both at home and abroad, was almost inevitably leading him to join forces with the right wing and the conservatives.

Communist and socialist leaders, for their part, were asking what had happened to freedom, noting that the Frei government had, on two occasions (March 1966 and November 1967) called on the armed forces to put down strikes in the mines, 'just like any other middle class government ...' During the incidents of November 1967 and the general strike, six people were killed, and dozens of others wounded in the streets of Santiago.

Yet according to the figures – both those given by the government and those issued by international bodies – the first results of the Christian Democrat experiment were not negligible. Agrarian reform, the core of the programme which aroused most hostility, was certainly nothing here in comparison to the wholesale agrarian reforms in Cuba; the need to allow for the opinion of Parliament, and a review of the original estimates of the cost, were two major handicaps. But the system of *asentamientos* which allowed for collective agricultural projects, did help to create a new mentality in the peasants who were still all too easily convinced by the self-interested arguments of the paternalist landowners. Indeed several occasions were noted when peasants, spurred on by them, actually fought to resist change. And starting in 1968 there were serious incidents between the police and groups of landless peasants supported by students who belonged to the

MIR (Movement of the Revolutionary Left), demanding direct action. But, all in all, this reform was one of the most profound attempts ever made to change traditional Chilean social patterns. Peasants not actually given their own land could to some extent share in the profits of collective farming. The *ley de sindicación campesina** in 1968 affected almost 600,000 peasants – something like a quarter of the working population. A new union was founded, the Confederation of agricultural workers of Chile, comprising almost 50,000 workers, independent, in theory, of the traditional mainstream of the unions.

In the three years from 1964 to 1967, 242,000 new jobs were created – a satisfactory increase compared with the past, but still not enough given the fact that the population was growing at an average of 2·5 per cent per year (with a birth rate of 36 per thousand, and a mortality rate of only 13. In May 1968 the proportion of unemployed was estimated as less than 5 per cent, whereas in 1963 it had been almost 7 per cent. Laws were passed to ensure the part-payment of wages during the first six months of unemployment, and to prevent anyone's being dismissed without good cause.

During that same three-year period, almost half a million more children started school, thanks to a big increase in educational spending, and the number of students at university was expected to rise sharply (from 35,000 to 48,700). Two major earthquakes, in 1960 and 1965, destroyed nearly a hundred thousand houses, which did nothing to ease the already serious need for buildings; but none the less almost a million people were housed or re-housed between 1964 and 1967. However, despite the increased state aid given to building community housing (reckoned to be some 70 per cent more than in 1964) the problem was still, in 1968, one of the most serious the country had to deal with. The average annual rate

* Law permitting peasant organization into unions.

of construction rose to 22,000 homes, though the Coporación de Fomento had estimated that 444,500 more would need to be provided from 1961 to 1970.

To these statistics proclaimed by the Frei government the 'rebel' Christian Democrats and the opposition leaders responded by giving other statistics to illustrate the new burst of inflation (which looked like reaching 35 per cent in 1968), the undeniable rise in the cost of living, the inadequacy of wage increases, the proliferation of foreign business interests with a lot of new north American consortia on the scene (Cerro Pasco, the Bank of America, American Cables, Continental Coppers, Ralston Purina, Dow Chemical). The intervention of the IMF, advising here, as elsewhere in Latin America, a restrictive financial and economic policy to stifle inflation, from which the standard of life for the mass of workers would be bound to suffer, was denounced – not without justification. The cost of living had increased by 25 per cent in 1965, 17 per cent in 1966 and 22 per cent in 1967; and because of the continual fall in the value of the Chilean *escudo*, the whole economy was in a very bad state, despite the relatively high price of copper.

Significantly, the plan providing for a revision of wages at the end of 1967, combined with the setting up of a Fund for National Capitalization, and restrictions on the right to strike, produced rage on both right and left; the plan was withdrawn in January 1968 and the government re-shuffled. A new plan for wage review worked out by the new Minister of Finance, Rául Sáez, a liberal economist, was received in many circles with almost equal dissatisfaction. The National Party (a coalition of the Liberal and Conservative parties) feared an increase in taxes; radicals, socialists and communists spoke out against it; and the CUT, the big central workers' organization, began organizing strikes. However, discreet and direct negotiations between the Christian democrat headquarters and the communists resulted in the acceptance of the plan with some modifications – though socialists, radicals and the National Party still opposed it.

This kind of bickering made clear at the beginning of 1968 the increasing difficulties the Frei government was having to face within the country. Wage demands rose from postmen, teachers, electricity workers and miners. The Christian Democrats were certainly still the largest party in the country with about 35 per cent of the votes but a local election in some of the southern provinces in December 1967 resulted in the government party's being badly defeated there. However the chances of the 'officialist' wing of the Christian Democrats in the legislative elections of March 1969 and the presidential election of 1970 did not look hopeful. Frei's supporters' hopes lay, in fact, in the ever-deepening divisions of all the other groups, apart from the communists – who were trying to increase their influence and their representation in parliament by a policy of prudence based on compromise. The socialists, though split into two divisions – one led by Salvador Allende, the other by Rául Ampuero – refused to take part in any coalition including the Christian Democrats, and some of their more militant members dreamt of carrying out the theories of 'armed struggle' evolved in Havana. The communists certainly remained aware that their uneasy alliance with the revolutionary and pro-Castro socialists still represented 30 per cent of the electorate, but Russia's friendly policy towards Santiago involved urging them to have a greater 'understanding' of the government. In April 1968 a Soviet minister was in Chile negotiating the sale of industrial plant worth 42 million dollars, and President Frei's invitation to visit Moscow was renewed.

Thus the Chilean spectrum, from the communists to the conservatives, was very different from that at the time of the previous election. Realizing the mounting danger Frei began a campaign tour of the country, and Radomiro Tomic, the former ambassador to Washington, spoke in favour of a new 'social pact' appealing to communists, socialists and 'all people of good will' to launch a definite attack 'against the intolerable reality of under-development'. It was really a re-phrasing of the 1964 slogan, 'revolution in freedom', and the fact that one of the leading figures in the party could speak in such terms was an admission that the promised revolution had yet to take place. There could be little doubt that the Frei government would have to deal with a much less amenable parliament in 1969 than they had in 1965. This being so, it was essential that the Christian Democrats work out their strategy for the 1970 election with great care. Should new alliances on the left be sought for, and possibly on the extreme right, as the idealist Radomiro Tomic (a close friend of Robert Kennedy) seemed to think, or would it be better to come to terms with the moderate right, which really was more natural to the Christian Democrat movement, as the new president of the Party, Jaime Castillo, suggested? Electoral arithmetic certainly supported Tomic, but the return of Jorge Alessandri as the probable, and formidable, candidate of the national party for 1970, supported the 'officialist' point of view.*

One thing was clear: Chilean Christian reformism had not succeeded as was hoped in making any radical transformation in social structures over the past few years. Yet despite everything that could be said against it, new advances had been achieved by this nation which had almost always been ahead of any other in the sub-continent. Though mutterings had begun to be heard from the armed forces (which Frei stifled by appointing an officer as Minister of Defence in May 1968), it remained highly unlikely that there would be a military coup in Chile. And the voice of this modest country of nine million people was always listened to with special respect in international gatherings and in the OAS; indeed Chile's diplomacy played the decisive role in the Punta del Este conference

* This comment was written prior to Allende's electoral success.

in April 1967. It was the Chileans who brought the notion of the need for an economic integration of Latin America out of the area of specialist discussion into politics. And the creation of the 'Andean group' (Chile, Peru, Ecuador, Colombia and Venezuela) was the first step towards the formation in South America of regional organizations dedicated to breaking the circle of selfishness and ignorance which has worked to set one nation apart from another since the heroic days of Bolívar.

CHAPTER 2

Bolivia

STATISTICS

Area: 424,162 square miles
Estimated population in 1967: 3,801,000
Population density: 9 per square mile
Annual rate of population increase: 1·9 per cent
Annual increase in average per capita *income from* 1960 *to* 1967: 4·6 per cent.

PRINCIPAL PRODUCTS

Tin (14 per cent of the world's total), mercury, copper, zinc, wolfram, nickel, gold, silver.

The Altiplano of Bolivia is, on average, 4,200 metres above sea level. It is some 1,000 kilometers long and 250 wide, with a line of mammoth Andean peaks on either side, and is 6,000 metres at its highest. It is like a South American version of the Pamirs, enclosed in the snowy peaks of Indian mythology. There are no trees, apart from a few clumps of eucalyptus. There are resiniferous bushes and sparse patches of grass: the sky is an unbearable, unchanging blue by day, but in winter nights the thermometer often goes down to $-20°$ C. At 5,000 metres, on the slopes of the Andes, this *puna*, as it is called, becomes almost totally desolate, and is known as the *puna brava*. Flocks of llamas run wild in this desert, and great slabs of gleaming, copper-coloured stone indicate the presence of metal ore breaking through to the surface. Turquoise lakes reflect the glaciers above and the huts of the men who work in the tin or antimony mines. At night, on the rough trails which lead from the southern shores of Lake Titicaca to the terrifying ravine where the first Spaniards established the foundations of La Paz, men trot along behind one another like Marathon runners. Short, with bright-coloured ponchos over their broad torsos, their pointed woollen hoods flying in the bitter wind of the steppe, these strong silent descendants of the Aymará people are hurrying to their now invisible villages. In the blazing daylight these are revealed as being made up of huts of stone and mud, windowless and dusty-looking. The people of these high plateaux have cheekbones patterned with tiny purple veins, and the flat, yellow-tinged faces of Asians. They are always chewing coca leaves, and their monotonous chewing accentuates still further the sense of perpetual motion in their thick, green-stained lips. The poverty of those who live on the Altiplano is the worst among any South American peasants, and it is exacerbated by the rigours of the climate, the barrenness of the soil, and *soroche*, or mountain sickness. The only remedy the Indian of the high plateaux can find either for *soroche* or for his constant hunger, is the poisonous and destructive coca. In the isolated villages where he lives, one hears no sound but the moaning of the wind; he was forced by the colonists to work in the mines, and he is still doing so today – still for an outrageously inadequate wage. Other Indians farm, or live in native communities in the *ayllus*.

*

These communities are intensely patriarchal in structure. They used to be, and still to some extent are, the basic cells of Indian society in the Andes. The *ayllu* is a threefold unit: religious, family, and economic. Each *ayllu* or clan chooses its own sign; this may be some formidable animal, such as the condor, or a phenomenon looked on as supernatural, such as the rainbow; clans are based on blood relationship, and have traditionally venerated their own domestic gods. Finally, all work implements and ground are the collective property of the *ayllu*. Inside the community the individual barely has a separate existence: he merges into the anonymous mass which at once protects him, absorbs him and gives him meaning. The Indians drink *chicha*, a beer made of fermented maize, and eat dishes made out of frozen potatoes, sometimes with llama meat, but since llamas are their faithful and proud companions, this only happens when an animal has died of old age. It is a monotonous and austere life, studded with solemn, mystical or carnivalesque feasts in which pagan and Christian rites are intermingled. It is hard to believe that their ancestors who lived in this same wild landscape were subjects of the Incas whose boast was that they had got rid of the word 'hunger'. All that remains of that vast empire is an occasional fortress, the ruins and temples over which the conquerors built their cathedrals and the parallel lines left by the old terraced farm-land.

The Indian is a sad man, and this is reflected in his music, played on reed flutes: 'I was conceived in a night of suffering. ... The rain and wind were my cradle. ... No one pities my suffering. Cursed be my birth. Cursed the world. Cursed myself ...' These laments sung in moments of despair are scarcely any gloomier than the dance music on feast days which is used to reduce men and women to a state of utter exhaustion which happily enables them to forget everything. For the Indian is resigned to his lot – he is anything but a revolutionary. The conditions in which he lives are so hopeless that he cannot ever imagine any improvement. He is apathetic and apparently indifferent; it is possible that he looks back with longing to the harsh but secure rule of the Incas. Who knows? He does not speak Spanish but the languages of his forbears, rugged Aymará or Quechua with its poetic intonations.

The Aymará–Quechua peoples, representatives of a pre-Columbian civilization of which we still know little, are far and away the largest group of Indians in Bolivia. Both in their homogeneity and their cultural development they are comparable with the group who live in the central plateau of Mexico, the Agusco, and the Chibchas of Colombia. They are the established inhabitants of the Altiplano, whereas those Indians scattered in the forests of the east and the low-lying parts of the *yungas*, the tropical valleys, which are still frequently inaccessible to outsiders, take almost no part in the life of the country. The Aymarás are mainly concentrated around Lake Titicaca, between Oruro in Bolivia and Puno in Peru. The Quechua area, strictly speaking, extends from the south of the Altiplano to well north of Cuzco, the one-time capital of the Inca empire. The Bolivians therefore often contrast what they call the Tiahuanaco civilization – whose most striking reminder is the Gate of the Sun south of lake Titicaca – with that of the Incas. And it is also extremely probable that the tremendously civilized men who built that fragile temple and created such magnificent ceramics were, unknown to themselves, the descendants of other, even more perfect and cultured societies which existed before the Incas established their supremacy high in the Andes.

The ruins of the Gate of the Sun bear witness to builders of outstanding quality: huge blocks, some four metres high, are fitted together with a precision comparable only to what we see in Egypt. Where did these Tiahuanaco people come from – Egypt, India, Sumeria or China?

We still cannot give any dates to this pre-Inca history, and the details given by specialists remain too contradictory to be of much scientific use. Certainly the Aymarás, the tribe most primitive, fierce, secretive and hostile to the advances of the white man, have remained as the real lords of these desolate highlands.

*

Officially the capital of Bolivia is Sucre but its real capital in practice is La Paz. The city was founded by Pedro de la Gasca, a monk, silent, sinister and coldhearted, sent by Charles V to Peru to stop the fratricidal wars between the supporters of Pizarro and of Diego Almagro. This special envoy of the emperor's must certainly have felt at home in the austere landscape in which he found himself: this extraordinary area is crossed by the La Paz river, a tributary of the Río Beni and ultimately of the Amazon, as it runs down the humid eastern slopes of the Andes, carving out one of the most spectacular gorges in the world. Going along the ridge, from peak to peak, the gorge is not more than 19 kilometres wide, but about 4,000 metres below the spine of the mountains, the river falls through a narrow passage with vertical cliffs on both sides. It would be hard to imagine a less likely-looking spot on which to build a city. The Indians considered this deep gorge facing the mountains as uninhabitable; but to the Spaniards it offered the twofold advantage of being a convenient stopping place on the main route across the colony, and of being protected from the cold winds of the Altiplano. That route from Lima to the silver mines in the highlands of Bolivia went past Titicaca on the south-west side, where there were fewer and gentler peaks than to the north east. From there it went along the eastern edge of the Altiplano and then on towards the south. When the first railways were laid La Paz became a junction. But the climate was still to be reckoned with: sharp changes of temperature, and an altitude at which breathing is difficult for those not acclimatized and which only the most placid of temperaments can bear for long without suffering great nervous tension.

Today the first houses in the Bolivian capital stand at a

height of 300 metres below the plateau where the highest landing strip in the world has been laid at 4,000 metres above sea level. The sharply eroded edges of this 'lunar' crater look on the point of total collapse beneath the snowy Illimani mountain rising above it to 6,800 metres. La Paz has over 400,000 inhabitants. In the centre, around the 16 de Julio and Camacho Avenues are modern hotels, smart shops and the university buildings. Further down are the comfortable residential districts. Here wealth and social standing do not vary as between the west and east ends, but between low and high. The poorer suburbs stand above the town. Despite the altitude Bolivians throng cheerfully along the narrow and precipitous streets of their city; the roads up to Chijini have been turned into permanent markets. The Indian women wait motionless, their children wrapped in blankets knotted behind their shoulders, squatting with their colourful but dirty skirts spread out around them, their straight hair emerging from the round black hats stuck low down on their foreheads. The typical hat worn by Indian women and *cholas** in Oruro, Sucre and round Potosí is more like a bowler than anything. In Cochabamba, only 2,800 metres above sea level, and comparatively the most soft and delicious climate, the hats are more cylindrical and snow-white. The unusual headgear is almost the most characteristic symbol of this country of 4,300,000 people of whom 63 per cent are pure Indian and 30 per cent mestizos of varying hues (CEPAL estimates).

Bolivia, right up against the Andes, and with no outlet on the sea, does not present the kind of startling contrast one sees in Ecuador or Peru, or to a lesser degree, Colombia, between coast-dwellers and those living on the *sierra*. From La Paz you must cross the eastern Andes, pass over the lush plain of Cochabamba, and go down pretty well as far as that dark green and impenetrable carpet where the Mato Grosso

* Half-breeds.

of Brazil appears, before you find a town with no significant number of Indians: Santa Cruz de la Sierra. It is the only one. With an area of 424,162 square miles Bolivia is the fifth largest country in South America; but its population is relatively small and the scattered nature of the Indian communities in the valleys and hollows of the eastern Andes, and along the cultivable strips beside Lake Titicaca or east of the inhospitable banks of Lake Poopó, provide an additional obstacle to the creation of any real national unity.

Bolivia is thus, like Mexico, a country in layered terraces; but the stairways linking the terraces are peculiarly steep and narrow. To the Indians the political border which passes through the lake between the Peruvian town of Yunguyo and the Bolivian Copacabana is an unreal abstraction. Every year the *indiecitos* and their womenfolk converge from both sides of the border on a sharp peak above the cold blue waters of the lake to beg favours of 'nuestra Señora de Copacabana' in her primitive shrine.

*

In the twentieth century the Indians appear as little moved by the rumours and upheavals of the world as they were by the battles and greed of the conquistadors. But the major problem every Bolivian government has had to face is simple: they have got to get the mass of Indians to take some part in the national life.

As in Ecuador or Peru, illiteracy is a tremendous obstacle on the difficult path towards enfranchisement for these people. There are certainly not enough schools; teacher training colleges only began to exist in 1920 – though Bolivia's universities, especially those of La Paz and Sucre, have a long tradition that goes back to the years of the conquest, and a past of which they can be proud. It is clear that an effort similar to that found so successful in Mexico some years ago is needed in Bolivia. Only thus can Bolivia obtain her rightful place in the sub-continent. In 1950 a census, ordered by the Ministry of National Education in La Paz, revealed that 68 per cent of Bolivians aged 5 and over were illiterate. A further study showed that only one of every two children of school age went at all regularly to any kind of school. In 1965 official sources still estimated over two million illiterates in the population. In theory primary schooling is free and obligatory, but secondary teaching is rudimentary, and there are fewer than ten thousand students in the country's seven universities. On the other hand, there is a relatively large number of colleges run for foreigners, especially the Germans in Santa Cruz.

In 1956, a government decree declared that it was 'the duty of every citizen to learn to read and write', and that 'every student must instruct two illiterate persons every year if he was to be allowed to continue his own studies'. Up to now it must be admitted that these draconian measures have only really been applied in the towns. The vast mass of more than two million peasants continues to stagnate in total ignorance of the outside world, even though 40 per cent of the budget is now earmarked for education.

*

Unlike Mexico or Argentina, Bolivia has not suffered from the persistent and ridiculous clichés about sombreros, siestas, tangos and comic opera generals. What it has suffered from is total ignorance; and from that it suffers still. This astounding lack of interest on the part of Europe and the western world in one of the most exciting of all Latin American countries dates back to 1868. In that year Queen Victoria's representative in La Paz was summoned to a diplomatic reception by the then president, Mariano Melgarejo. He refused the invitation and the enraged president had him mounted on a donkey and forced to ride three times round the main square of La Paz in that ridiculous posture. When the incident became known in London the Queen wanted to punish the man who had so mocked her emissary, but a glance at the map made it clear that La Paz was not within the range of the guns of her Majesty's fleet. So the Queen seized a pencil, scratched out the map and decreed that 'Bolivia no longer exists'! Diplomats in La Paz still smile over the story, but in fact Bolivia did remain an almost unknown country right up to the beginning of the twentieth century. It was the number of tin mines that drew the world's attention to this part of the world, which, along with Malaya, contained the largest reserves yet discovered. But the fabulous fortunes amassed by the tin barons in a short space of time yet again pushed the real problems of Bolivia into obscurity.

Up until 1960 Bolivia was still, in spite of itself, associated with the adventures, trickery and scandals that grew up around the 'happy few' of the *rosca**, and the tin which simultaneously brought vast wealth to some and misery to the country as a whole.

The Altiplano is especially rich in veins of every kind of ore. In 1545 the Spaniards found an absolute mountain of silver, tin and tungsten – the *Cerro Rico*† at whose base they built the town of Potosí. It was incredibly easy to exploit these minerals, and for almost three centuries the magnificence of Potosí itself reflected that fantastic wealth, though the area as a whole was one in which living conditions were desperately hard for the gold-seekers from Europe. The decline of the Potosí silver mines naturally led to the decline of that splendid city: it had had over 150,000 inhabitants, but by the end of the nineteenth century it was just a sleepy small town at the foot of the Andes. Then came the start of the tin boom which gave it a new lease of life. In Potosí, as also in the areas of Uncía, Llallagua, San José, Milluni and elsewhere where deposits of tin were found, the total production

* Inner circle (of wealthy mine owners). † Wealthy Hill.

amounted to some 40,000 tons by 1912; but generally speaking, all the veins were quickly used up because they tended not to be very deep, nor were conditions such as to make the work any easier. And though a little gold was found in the alluvia of the streams which wound their way through the *yungas* and petroleum production was continually increasing, it was tin that remained the major product of the country.

The mines of Uncía alone, which belonged before nationalization to the Patiño group, produce half of Bolivia's tin, and 90 per cent of the country's total exports. But only 4 per cent of the working population is employed in the mines and consequently there is a serious imbalance. The development of Bolivia's prime wealth does not contribute to raising the living standards of most of the population. Furthermore, the production of tin has been diminishing since 1949, not because the mines have been exhausted, but because the merciless law of supply and demand has worked against Bolivia after several decades during which it caused a rapid rise in exports. In 1952 Bolivia's production was no more than 32,000 tons; it rose to 34,000 in 1953, but fell sharply in 1954. In 1957 it did not exceed the relatively low figure of 28,000 tons, and in 1958 a further fall reduced it to 18,000 tons. This desperate drop in production since 1953 is also partly explained by the effects of nationalization. The tin barons were investing abroad most of the profits they made in Bolivia – so that an underdeveloped country was exporting its capital assets. This paradox was put a stop to in 1952, but the Comibol (Mining Corporation of Bolivia) established by the State was soon paralysed by the conflicts between the various authorities concerned in the work. Poor discipline, a high rate of absenteeism and an unnecessary increase in ineffective adminstrative staff all added up to an increase in production costs and a lowering of productivity in the nationalized mines by an average of 14 per cent (26,000 miners worked in the nationalized mines, and about 15,000 in the smaller mines still run by foreign concerns – Americans, British, German, Japanese or Italian). The lack of capital for indispensible investment accentuated this downward trend. The continual plans for 'recovery' set on foot by first the Paz Estenssoro and then the Barrientos government since 1964 have generally resulted in major battles with the miners and their unions. Fierce armed repressions leading to the sheer massacre of civilians were mounted in 1965 and 1967.

Bolivia may have hoped that the formation of an international tin cartel would enable her to organize her production better in relation to international demand. In March 1931 the first such cartel was founded, consisting of Bolivia, Nigeria (then still British), Malaya, and the Dutch East Indies. Bolivia's quota was fixed at a maximum of 46,000 tons a year, out of an estimated world production of 162,000 tons. The agreement was renewed successively in 1934, 1937 and 1942, on practically identical terms. But in 1953 an international conference on tin met in Geneva to reconsider the facts about the world market. On 25 June 1954 an agreement was signed in London that was far less favourable to Bolivia's interests. But the real catastrophe took place in 1958. Given the ever increasing quantities of Soviet tin coming onto the market, the international cartel decided to stop keeping the price up artificially, and further reduced Bolivia's export quota by 30 per cent. It became clear, in addition, that no agreement could really protect Bolivia against the inevitable rises and falls in so sensitive a market. Averaging good years with bad Bolivia's production now represents about 20 per cent of all the world's tin – which is not a lot. The only real trump card held by La Paz is that the tin mines in their country are in the west and thus would become of major importance if there were to be a war. It is this that explains the relative complacency of the United States, and in fact since 1953 is has only been thanks to loans from America that Bolivia has been saved from total economic suffocation.

*

Until his death in 1947 Simón Patiño was the undisputed emperor of a curious dynasty. He was born in 1861 in Cochabamba, the second largest city in Bolivia. He bought a concession of four hectares, and began working there unobtrusively with his family. His wealth dated from the discovery of a vein of ore containing 60 per cent tin on his land. By the time he died this little Cochabamba *cholo* was undoubtedly one of the five richest men in the world. His annual income was far larger than that of the Bolivian government. The 'Patiño Mines Enterprise Company Incorporated' controlled 60 per cent of Bolivia's tin production. He also controlled – and his family still control – the tin foundries of the William Harvey Company of Liverpool, and the Lead National Company. He had bought interests in a number of other mining companies in Siam, Indonesia, Nigeria, and particularly in Malaya, chief of which was the Eastern Smelting Company. Thus not merely had Simón Patiño managed to build an all-powerful trust in Bolivia itself, but also indirectly to dominate the other sources of tin ore in the world, and to control the foundries, without which the nationalization of Bolivia's tin mines by itself was really meaningless.

This insurance against the fortunes of politics, which Simón Patiño took out long before he died, has made it possible for his descendants to wield a power quite out of proportion to their actual position, and they have ways of exercising pressure which the nationalist government of Victor Paz Estenssoro could do nothing to escape. For in fact half of Bolivia's production consists of a pure, easily smelted concentrate, which is sent to Liverpool to the William Harvey Foundry (i.e. to Patiño); the other half is a concentrate containing 20 to 30 per cent of tin, which could only be treated by one foundry in the world – Long Horn Foundry in Texas – until the Long Horn Foundry was shut down in 1956 because it was losing more and more money.

It was not enough simply to nationalize Iranian oil; it had still to be sold. And the nationalist wizard of Teheran still had to make a deal with an international consortium. Similarly with the tin mines of Bolivia; the Paz Estenssoro government had to do more than just nationalize them in order to free the Bolivian economy from one day to the next from the curse of a single-product economy.

Simón Patiño's ability to work, his flair and his commercial genius were beyond question. But it also took an exceptional situation to make it possible for him to create that State-within-a-State that his tin monopoly really amounted to. It called also for sweat, blood, and the systematic exploitation of one of the least known proletariats in the world.

*

Of course the Patiños met with reverses. The social and gossip columns in the big European and American papers frequently mentioned them. The first Simón, whose flattened, sculptured face betrayed his Indian origins, arranged for his children marriages with some of the grandest families in European society. His son Antenor married a niece of King Alfonso XIII of Spain. One of his daughters married a French nobleman, and another a Spanish grandee who had the tremendous privilege of being permitted to keep his head covered in the presence of the king. All these stormy unions, larded with divorces, reconciliations, breakings-off and lawsuits with endless complications, did more to make the name of the Patiños known throughout the world than all the unrelenting, perfervid but obscure hard work of their founding father. He personally also had diplomatic ambitions, and appointed himself Bolivia's minister in Paris – which gave him the additional advantage of not having to pay taxes. He had luxurious homes built in Biarritz and Nice, and purchased several estates, estimated at the time to be worth 30 million dollars. At his death his total fortune was reckoned to be some thousand million dollars.

The other tin barons were more unobtrusive both in amassing their wealth and in their personal behaviour. Mauricio Hochschild, a German by descent, could charter a special plane to take him from Recife, where he was stranded, to New York; but though this cost 1,500 dollars per flying hour, his name never achieved the scandalous notoriety of the Patiños'. As for the Aramayos, former proprietors of the La Paz daily, *La Razón*, their name has been almost forgotten, and Don Carlos Victor Aramayo, who inherited his father's business interests, has made his headquarters in Switzerland.

A Bolivian parliamentary commission of enquiry established that the Patiño Company had earned more than 5 million pounds sterling in five years, and that its social capital, estimated at 2,500,000 pounds sterling before nationalization, was larger than the entire Bolivian budget. 'Under Spanish domination' the commission's report concluded, 'Bolivian mines earned 21 million ducats, of which 5 million, roughly a quarter, remained in the country. Yet from 1941 to 1946 the mines of the Patiño company alone made a profit of 1,515 million Bolivian pesos* – thus tripling the initial capital invested – and during that period they paid no more than 307 million Bolivian *pesos* in tax. The Patiño mines took more out of the country than the Spanish did during the whole of their occupation.'

These figures are of academic interest only until we compare them with the size of the national revenue of Bolivia and the standard of living of her people. The UN and OAS statistics show that the standard of living of the Bolivian working class is one of the lowest in all of South America.

* 12 Bolivian *pesos* = $1 and 29 = £1.

Whereas Argentina annually consumes 119 kilos of meat per head, Bolivia only consumes 23. The Argentinians eat 152 kilos of bread a head per year, the Chilians 158, and the Peruvians 118: in Bolivia the figure is 23.

The living conditions of some 50,000 men working in the tin mines are in striking contrast to those of the tin barons. In the mine galleries it is so hot that the men in front cannot stand more than five minutes against the rock in the shattering noise of the pneumatic drills. Their bare torsos running with sweat in passages where the humidity often reaches 95 per cent, and almost suffocated by the dust, the workers emerge after eight hours into the rarefied air of the plateau 4,000 metres above sea level, where the temperature may well fall below zero during the night. In Milluni, up above La Paz at 4,600 metres, the streams in the galleries are frozen; tiny moving lights flicker in the impenetrable darkness, stopping occasionally against a wall to avoid the mine locomotive as it goes by – and for an instant one glimpses the wide brown faces of the men beneath their helmets.

On coming out of the mine the daylight seems blinding. At the foot of the mine enclosure, the camp, a collection of low huts with corrugated iron roofs, stands on the edge of a grey lake, reflecting the 6,000 snow-clad metres of Huayna-Potosí. Groups of Indians stand silently in front of the *pulpería*, the local cooperative store. Oil is used solely for cooking food and heating in the workers' camps is non-existent. In these circumstances it is hardly surprising that 60 per cent of Indian miners have tuberculosis; half also have syphilis, and one child in two dies during its first year of life. Those who survive babyhood in this hell have a life expectancy of thirty-five years at most.

In short, the average living conditions of the tin miners have barely improved since nationalization. Independent miners, or those who work for the small foreign companies, do not even have the very few social benefits granted by

Comibol. They earn at best four dollars a week, whereas a worker in the nationalized mines earns on average eleven cents an hour. To all of them coca is the pathetic remedy for their permanent hunger.

*

On 21 July 1946 a huge crowd of infuriated Indians and mestizos stormed and captured the governor's palace in La Paz. The president of the republic, Gualberto Villarroel, was dragged from his office despite fierce resistance by his guards. The rioters removed his clothes and hanged him head downwards from a lamp post right beneath the balcony of his residence. His aide-de-camp, Ballivián, a secretary called Uría, and two or three of his other colleagues were also killed and hanged in the same ignominious fashion from other street lamps in the Plaza Murillo.

Bolivians have grown used to the *pronunciamientos* and the sudden and bloodthirsty revolts of the *indiecitos*. Fifteen years after the revolution of April 1952 which brought Paz Estenssoro and the MNR leaders to power, diplomats still had a habit of listening to every sound as dawn broke each day – not for the milkman on his rounds but for the gunfire that so often heralded a change of government as it echoed around the vast and sinister gorge of La Paz.

From 1825, when it won independence, to the present time, Bolivia has had no fewer than 179 revolutions – approximately one every nine months. This makes it one of the most turbulent of all Latin American countries. However, the disturbances of July 1946 were to produce more lasting results, and the hanging of Gualberto Villarroel is significant from several points of view. It is still said in La Paz that press photographs of Mussolini hanging by his feet from a butcher's hook in a square in Milan were published in the Bolivian papers, and that they were the inspiration for the rebel crowd's choice of method in slaughtering the president and his assistants. Several months later the urchins of La Paz were still playing hangings.

The Minister of Finance in the Villarroel government was Victor Paz Estenssoro. He was a shy, cultivated man, and almost unknown; he managed to get away, and left Bolivia to take refuge in Buenos Aires. He was elected president of the Republic, and even installed for a second term in the same office which had witnessed so many scenes of violence. There was only one thing for him to do – to draw the curtains back from his window: in the corner of the Plaza Murillo the street lamp, so ordinary, yet so horribly effective, was still there. A commemorative plaque had been embedded in the ground nearby – at once a tactful call to order, and a homage to Villarroel who was a travelling companion in the National Revolutionary Movement in its first phase.

*

Historians have passed somewhat contradictory judgements on Villarroel. To some it was a cruel and stupid dictator who came to power following the *pronunciamiento* of 20 December 1943. Shortly afterwards promoted to Lieutenant Colonel, he was legally established as president by the national Convention which developed out of the elections of July 1944. It is true that during his two years' rule all rebel movements were put down with extreme force; and the Colombian liberal, Germán Arciniegas, in *The State of Latin America*, tells of the summary execution of a number of high-ranking officers and public figures in Oruro in November 1944 after the failure of an attempted putsch. But others, on the other hand, see Villarroel as a progressive and nationalist soldier, supported by the revolutionary intellectuals of the MNR, whose programme included the nationalization of the tin mines and agrarian reform. To them Villarroel was really a Bolivian Perón who failed nine years earlier than his counterpart in Buenos Aires.

These opposing views are understandable if one looks closely at how the MNR was created and developed. It must not be forgotten that the last years of the Second World War were characterized by a strong German influence in South America. Thus in Brazil, Chile and Argentina, nationalist movements, usually led by the military, took inspiration from the Axis powers. Perón, who was to take power in Argentina, was military attaché in Rome, and had a strong admiration for Mussolini's methods. The Brazilian integralists were so active as to encourage Getúlio Vargas to proclaim the Estado Novo in Rio de Janeiro. All over the sub-continent there were officers who made no secret of their wish to copy the methods of the totalitarian dictators, and Bolivia was no exception.

The German influence there was particularly long-standing and deep-rooted. From the beginning of this century Germany, looking for markets in Latin America, had fixed its eye on Bolivia. In 1908 the Berlin government was given what amounted to an economic *carte blanche* in La Paz, and provided with every favour and assistance. A German military mission was established in La Paz, led by Colonel Kundt and Captain Ernst Roehm. It was Kundt who commanded the Bolivian troops in the disastrous Chaco war against Paraguay. As for Ernst Roehm, Hitler's right hand man in the early years of Nazism, he, as we know, came to a terrible end. At the end of the war the German colony in Bolivia was some 8,000 in number, and there were a dozen German firms more or less dictating matters in Bolivian trade. Obviously the work of Nazi agents was made considerably easier by all this; Bolivian officers imprisoned in Paraguayan camps after the Chaco war returned to La Paz deeply embittered and determined to avenge their country's honour; several of them went to follow study courses in Germany and Italy, and at least one had the imprudence to confide the plans for a *coup d'état* to the German minister in La Paz. There can certainly be no doubt that the Nationalist Bolivian officers were in close contact with the German representatives in their country; and it is clear that the leader of this secret group in 1943 was Gualberto Villarroel.

But it would be going too far, indeed it would be quite unjustified, to suggest that the Germans were the only people who influenced the Bolivian MNR. The sympathies of Bolivian officers for Nazism did not survive the defeat of the Axis. Obsessed by the omnipotence of Washington and the U.S. mining monopolies in their country, they hoped to find a counterbalance by supporting the European totalitarian regimes which looked like winning the war; but the fall of Berlin marked the end of their hopes. In effect the MNR of Paz Estenssoro was formed in 1941 out of the bitternesses and frustrated hopes of a frustrated generation: young officers, lawyers, intellectuals and academics had a common longing to see their country escape from the stagnation it had sunk into after several decades of mishaps and failures. In Spain the loss of her colonies gave birth to the generation of '98; the mutilation of Bolivia's territory after several military defeats, and her total loss of any access to the Pacific, gave birth to the generation of the Chaco.

*

Bolivia, Paraguay's enemy in that vicarious war for oil, is also her competitor when it comes to national disasters. In 1879 the Pacific War against Chile ended with the wiping out of the Bolivian troops, thus forcing them to evacuate the areas of Antofagasta and Arica. The Chaco War left Bolivia in 1935 still more closely imprisoned in her mountains. This fresh defeat also marked the start of a particularly rapid succession of revolutions and counter-revolutions. In 1934 President Daniel Salamanca was replaced by Vice-President José Luis Tejada Sorzano. In 1936 there was a military coup against Tejada Sorzano, with Colonel David Toro taking power. In 1937 the military overthrew Colonel Toro, who was replaced by Colonel Germán Busch. In 1939 Busch committed suicide after a night-long orgy in the presidential palace. General Carlos Quintanilla followed him. The next general elections were won by General Enrique Peñaranda. In 1943, Peñaranda was thrown out by the military, and Commandant Gualberto Villarroel took his place...

Behind this bloody and breathless roundabout, however, something else was happening. Just at the moment when the Bolivians seemed to be most completely caricaturing the South American habit of revolution, one group was working out a coherent political line.

It was in fact the disasters of the Chaco which provided the framework for the National Revolutionary Movement (MNR). Paz Estenssoro, a refugee in Buenos Aires after the rioting of July 1946, was preparing to return. He offered himself in the May 1951 elections. He was forbidden to enter Bolivia and had to run his electoral campaign from his place of asylum in Argentina; he had no radio station, no newspaper he could count on – yet he defeated the government candidate by 14,000 votes. This easy victory was not just the success of the MNR: Paz Estenssoro had found a new ally in the Workers' Revolutionary Party (POR), composed of the most dynamic members of the mining unions. Their leader was Juan Lechín, a *turco* – i.e. an immigrant from Syria-Lebanon. Lechín, with his huge shoulders, powerful face, gift of oratory (in which he could be both dynamic and demagogic when occasion demanded) was described by Washington as 'the Paz Estenssoro government's time-bomb'. The alliance between the MNR and the POR did, in any case, provide a new impetus in Bolivian politics. The MNR as it was in 1943, with its fascist-minded military allies, had been replaced by a socialist-minded MNR; and the entry of the unions onto the political scene was undoubtedly the most important phenomenon of the decade in Bolivia. Without the tin miners, Paz Estenssoro would possibly never have won the presidency.

His victory in the 1951 elections in fact produced another *pronunciamiento*: in May 1951 a junta led by General Ovidio Quiroga seized power. From his retreat in Buenos Aires, Paz Estenssoro gave his apologia: 'I am neither pro-Nazi, nor pro-Communist, nor anti-American. I am simply pro-Bolivian ...' He and his supporters, however, had to wait until April 1952 and the revolution organized by the mining unions before actually taking possession of the office in the Plaza Murillo; it involved three days of fighting and 1,500 deaths.

The worker-fighters left Milluni to come to La Paz where street fighting was raging. The result still hung in the balance, but their intervention decided it.

*

What happened in the MNR was of interest not only in Bolivia, isolated and unknown as it was, miserably hemmed in by the Andes. The agrarian reform proclaimed on 2 August 1953 by the Paz Estenssoro government provided an example to the other Andean countries as well.

To the conservative opposition and the tin barons who had fled the country there could be no doubt that Bolivia was already communist, with private property on the way to vanishing altogether, religion persecuted, and thousands of political prisoners languishing in the wind-swept concentration camps of the Altiplano. That opposition, both internal and external, inspired (usually through the intermediary of the right wing movement of the socialist Falange) several coups which failed until 1964.

The nationalization of the big tin companies (Patiño, Aramayo, Hochschild), though determined immediately after the victory of April 1952, was not announced until the following October. The new revolutionary government was in two minds, and was only moved to act by the growing disquiet in the unions. The MNR (a varied association including a dynamic middle class, and workers' movements whose most active leaders were not Moscow-type communists at all but Trotskyists) was clearly afraid of being drawn into too rapid an acceleration of popular demands. But nationalization came at a bad time. With the Korean war coming to an end, the price of tin was falling. The mining corporation was given the job of administering the nationalized companies. Inflation began. The Bolivian working class had welcomed the nationalizing of the mines as a rightful release, for few firms anywhere in the world were as hated as the 'three giants' in Bolivia. The appalling exploitation of the labour force, the disregard of national interests, and the scandals attaching to the families themselves, had long made the Patiños, the Aramayos and the Hochschilds loathed and despised. The scale of their revenge matched that of the arrogance they had shown in their days of power: the companies removed all foreign technicians, and did everything they could to make trouble. Paz Estenssoro was forced against the grain to compromise to some extent with the foreign members of the companies. Comibol was obliged to go abroad for the sophisticated equipment it needed to continue to work veins of ore that grew ever harder to reach; 14 million dollars were granted to the Bolivian government by Washington in the financial year ending 30 June 1954. The American government promised to buy all the Bolivian tin ready for sale by 30 March 1954; this was not enough, since Bolivia would have needed at least 60 million dollars to get its accounts straight before 1958, and Washington was not disposed to offer so much. Paz Estenssoro could only save his country from total economic chaos by making certain concessions: 'To those who demand the nationalization of all our industries, I say that that would simply mean nationalizing poverty. We are making a nationalist revolution, not a communist revolution,' he declared on the day that Santa Cruz–Corumbá railway was opened.

Pressure from the unions had made the government nationalize the mines. Unrest among the Indian population pushed forward the proclamation of agrarian reform.

Up until 1952 most of the land in Bolivia belonged to owners of huge estates, some as much as 5,000 hectares in size. The status of farm workers employed by foremen working for a 'boss' who lived in the city was governed by the system of the *pongueaje* – similar to the *huasipungo* of Ecuador: three or four days' unpaid work every week on the estate, in exchange for the right to cultivate a small allotment – generally of not very good land. The law of 2 August 1953 did not change the basic property pattern. It allowed for three types of holding: small, medium and profit-making large-scale agriculture. This last category included the large farming estates. There the Indians were granted ownership of the allotments where they had been living, and unpaid labour and all forms of serfdom were abolished.

Only the small and medium properties (whose value would vary from one area to another – Altiplano, warm valleys, or sub-tropical regions) were untouched by the reform. Paz Estenssoro had grasped the need to move carefully in order to avoid disaster. However, the *peones* would not always wait. Around Cochabamba and Lake Titicaca they seized the *patrones*' land by force. There is no doubt that this reform did a lot to improve the situation of the Indian country people; one of the visible signs of this was the appearance of bicycles and sewing machines in even the most remote villages. It was reckoned in 1965 that 107,397 householders had been settled by the reform on 3,597,834 hectares. We may add to these the 40,000 families who profited from the stipulations already registered by the National Council for Reform. Undoubtedly this first stage of the reform was accompanied by a certain lowering of production – reaching its lowest point from 1954 to 1956. After 1956 production began to rise again and by 1962 had reached its pre-reform figure. But despite the average rise in the standard of living, it is clear that the vast majority of Bolivian peasants still live in conditions described by some of the clergy as 'sub-human': housing, food and hygiene have for most of them remained quite deplorably bad. Though the peasant population has begun to migrate from the high plateaux and upper valleys (Sucre and Cochabamba) either to the warm districts of the east, or to the farming areas of northern Argentina, the situation has hardly changed at all. The individualism and mistrust of the Indian peasant often prevent his telling his village neighbours anything of the experience he has had elsewhere. The true visible 'revolution' on the highlands of the Altiplano is really the transistor radio; it has at last brought some knowledge of the outside world into the closed lives of the Indians, and even in places become the substitute for the spinning wheel as the social focus of the women.

*

Paz Estenssoro's term as president ended in 1956. He had retained the modesty and quiet smile which he had brought with him from his old job as professor of political economy in Buenos Aires university. His programme was far from completed and before he left he summed it up in this way:

Political independence has been incomplete, because the peasants still live in the same conditions as they did in colonial times. That is why one of our major objectives was agrarian reform, so as to emancipate those millions of Bolivians who have lived almost like serfs on the fringes of the national community. In this the MNR may provide an example for all Latin American nations to copy. The nationalism of Latin American countries represents one and the same thing in each, because we all have common problems to face. We are revolutionaries because we believe that Bolivia cannot become a politically independent nation without social justice. We are not responsible for the fact that our economy depends totally on the state of the tin market; that is hardly the fault of the National Revolutionary Movement. But responsibility for that tragic dependence does rest with the oligarchy which has kept our country in the ridiculous situation of having a single-product economy....

It was impossible to say how the presidential elections of 1956 would go because the electorate had more than doubled – from 200,000 in 1952 to 500,000 in 1956. The candidate of the ruling MNR party was Siles Suazo, the *éminence grise* of the regime, and already Vice-President. Opposing the MNR the most formidable movement was still the socialist Falange, which represented all the opponents of the popular revolution of 1952, and could depend on financial support from the former tin barons living in exile. Siles Suazo won fairly easily; perhaps more flexible than Paz Estenssoro and certainly less dogmatic, he was equally intransigent as to the MNR's fundamental principles, and up until 1960 had to fight an exhausting battle on two fronts. First against the Phalange: right wing putsches followed one another thick and fast. One of the most serious revolts broke out in Santa Cruz: the Corporación Boliviana del Fomento, a semi-public body pre-dating the revolution, had opened a network of roads whose most magnificent highway went down from Cochabamba to Santa Cruz through all the sharp ups and downs of the last foothills of the Andes. Now that this tropical area of Bolivia was no longer isolated, and now that oil had been discovered there and sugar refineries built, Santa Cruz had achieved a new importance. The sugar plantations and cultivation of other tropical crops developed rapidly and by May 1958 the central government in La Paz hardly exercised more than a nominal authority over Santa Cruz. A local committee made the laws in this 'wild west' type Bolivian city, where idlers were strung up in the trees of the public parks and state officials simply had to come to terms with the committee. In June 1959 a fresh revolt shook Santa Cruz and once again snipers were hiding in streets corners and arcades; this was a particularly violent rising, and there were 150 people killed, among them a number of Falange leaders. Others went into hiding to continue the fight.

Thus jostled from the right, Siles Suazo was also criticized from the left. He had not been in office for a year when Vice President Ortiz publicly accused him of 'handing the country over to American imperialism'. A left wing had begun to form within the MNR during the last years of Paz Estenssoro's presidency, controlled by Juan Lechin, the miners' federation leader. Ortiz and Lechín, 'left-wing deviationists', drew support from the mass of the workers and the armed militia which Paz Estenssoro had perhaps unwisely enlarged (in 1956 it had 100,000 members). There were parts of the country where whole gangs, armed and quite undisciplined, ranged widely, and there were more and more incidents involving armed militiamen and orthodox *Pazestenssoristas*. Siles Suazo, a man of honesty and courage, still had enough prestige to re-establish apparent harmony by himself visiting the workers' camps. But his plan for economic stabilization ran into increasing hostility from Lechín's confederation of workers – and Lechín himself also had to cope with enemies on the left – communists and Trotskyists.

*

There are not many orthodox communists in Bolivia, but there is a hard core of Trotskyism in the POR. Having rejoiced over the coming to power of the MNR, communists and Trotskyists alike took up an attitude of total opposition. Despite Lechín's efforts at moderation their influence was part of the reason for his continually raising, so to say, the revolutionary stakes.

In June 1960 Paz Estenssoro was elected for a second term. He got 100,000 more votes than his opponents in the party, and the MNR controlled 75 per cent of the votes in the country. Eight years after the revolution the Bolivian people were thus indicating a quite remarkable consistency and fidelity. Juan Lechín was elected Vice-President. The National Revolutionary Movement therefore appeared more united than ever before and better prepared to take up the hopeless task of rescuing Bolivia. But it was only united in appearance. Paz Estenssoro carried on the same policy of prudence and austerity as Siles Suazo and he too, in the first weeks of his return to the Plaza Murillo, had to deal with a wave of Falange putsches. Furthermore in February 1961 he had to declare a state of siege in order to put down a coup officially labelled 'communist'. Though the Bolivian communist leaders were certainly involved in the conspiracy, it was equally certain that a great many non-communist left-wing elements (trade unionists and Castroist students, for instance) had followed their lead. What this left-wing putsch chiefly indicated was an increasing unease within the MNR, worn out by its years in power and forced to keep compromising with the U.S. to save the country from bankruptcy.

In 1960 Russia offered Bolivia a loan of 150 million dollars but Paz Estenssoro the moderate refused. He preferred to depend on loans from the Alliance for Progress. That was his main trump card; the second was oil. Drilling had taken place by Cochabamba, also near the Argentinian border, and even more in Santa Cruz province. A state body, YPFB (Yacimientos Petrolíferos Fiscales Bolivianos) had held the monopoly for extracting and exporting oil since 1957. Pipelines ran across the *sierra* from the Cochabama refinery to Oruro and La Paz. Bolivia was already exporting oil to Brazil. Tankers went down from Cochabamba to Santa Cruz by road, there the oil was transferred to rail transport, made possible since the opening of one of the most beautiful railway lines in the world – from Santa Cruz to Corumbá.

Paz Estenssoro came to power in 1952 with the support of the sub-machine guns of the workers' militia from the tin mines; twelve years later, in November 1964, he was overthrown by the fury of those same men. The fresh political storm raging in the high plateau of Bolivia and sweeping through the streets of La Paz was, as usual, brief, but violent and tragic. Within a few hours Paz Estenssoro had become a hunted man, an outlaw, only with the greatest difficulty managing to reach the international airport with the help of a few air-force units acting more from pity than conviction. Some hundreds of his supporters died in the fighting, in which they were faced with regular troops called up for the occasion, and for a short time the capital returned to the suffocating and agonizing atmosphere of the great days of the revolution.

*

Everything begins, everything is ultimately decided, in Cochabamba, which plays a role in contemporary Bolivian history completely out of proportion to its apparent unimportance as a sleepy provincial town lying against the rugged foothills of the Andes. From August 1964 Vice-President René Barrientos, a young paratroop general, then aged 46, repeatedly indicated his disapproval of the somewhat stagnant regime; his complaints were echoed on many sides, not only from the right, but from the left too. Both in fact were mainly worried about Paz Estenssoro's length of time in office. Could he – would he if he could? – follow the 'Cuban road' which the more leftist of Juan Lechín's friends would, though with reservations, have liked? Could he break once for all with the U.S. and seek aid from the communist bloc? How could Bolivia, in its Andean isolation, then have achieved the kind of total economic revolution which Cuba, with far more advantages on its side, had not managed to achieve perfectly or fully by the middle of 1965? There was no answer to these questions; the revolution of 4 November forced all such speculations to be put off until a later date.

Paz Estenssoro, moving gradually more and more to the

right, had naturally tended to lose more and more of his left-wing friends: the communists, then the Trotskyists, then Lechín's Federation of Miners, then the supporters of Guevara Arce, the former Minister of the Interior who founded the PRA (Authentic Revolutionary Party), and finally even the loyal and honourable Siles Suazo, who had been President from 1956 to 1960, his earliest comrade in arms, who also longed for that 'pure, hard revolution' which never came.

The tragedy for Paz Estenssoro – a classic one, a commonplace indeed with all reformists who are obliged to compromise their revolutionary dreams – was that his ever increasing loss of support from the left was not balanced by any new support from the right. The upper middle class who had suffered from the agrarian reforms and nationalization, would never forgive him for what he had done to them in 1953. By the middle of 1964 the only body to remain loyal was the peasant militia who had been reinforced in order to check the workers' militia who had gone over to the opposition along with their leaders of the left and the far left. Discontent was mounting in the armed forces.

General Barrientos, known for his North American sympathies, soon began to look like the new strong man in Bolivia: by September a trial of strength seemed inevitable. The official visit of General de Gaulle provided a respite, but everyone knew that the crisis was about to occur. The French head of state was met in Cochabamba on 28 September by a smiling Paz Estenssoro, flanked by his Vice-President Barrientos. The peasant militia provided a picturesque escort for the official motorcade, and the strains of the *Marseillaise* played on rudimentary Indian fifes and flutes rose from the square in front of the Prefecture. But the following day the expected storm broke.

Student unrest developed in the University of La Paz. Pitched battles took place between students barricaded in the various Faculties and the police, with the militia called to reinforce them. The tin miners took things a step further, and before long the whole area south of the capital was in a state of siege. Despite massive arrests (over 700 in La Paz) and intervention by the army, Oruro, the fortress of working class opposition, did not weaken. By the end of October chaos reigned everywhere. On 30 October the miners' federation declared an indefinite general strike. General Barrientos 'pronounced' against the government. Most troop garrisons, disliking having to intervene against the students and miners, soon rallied to their support. A final stand in the capital by the last few MNR activists achieved nothing: a provisional military junta led by General Ovando Candia, Chief of the General Staff, handed over two days later to General Barrientos, following a plebiscite among the opposition.

The honeymoon was not long-lived. The coalition was altogether too mixed: communists, Trotskyists, trade unionists, academics, former supporters of Paz Estenssoro. And it became clear, too, that the fall of Paz Estenssoro had done nothing to solve any of Bolivia's problems. The gulf between the military now in power and the leaders of the newly-formed left wing group grew ever deeper. Juan Lechín had fought Paz Estenssoro; in February 1965 he began to fight General Barrientos as symbolizing a regime with obvious authoritarian tendencies. The general elections were due to take place on 26 September 1965. Barrientos, going back on his earlier promises, agreed to offer himself for the presidency. Thus the fall of Paz Estenssoro and the somnolence of the MNR – which had achieved a real but incomplete revolutionary experiment – laid the path for a new military regime.

In May 1965 Barrientos decided to have a trial of force with the tin miners' leaders: he deported Juan Lechín and sixty other union leaders to Paraguay. Despite resistance by the miners the army occupied the Siglo Veinte pits in the Oruro district, thus making it possible for the government once again to take over the administration of this key industry.

One of the arguments used by the heads of the armed forces in November 1964 to justify their *coup* against the Paz Estenssoro government was the 'need to combat administrative waste and corruption'. Indeed it might well be considered that in twelve years in power the MNR had allowed the number of officials to multiply quite unreasonably. But this is not a failing peculiar to Bolivia; few Latin American regimes have avoided it. The need to satisfy voters where the government is constitutional and ensure that the key jobs are held by trustworthy men where the government is authoritarian make it easy to see how this happens – indeed it is not even peculiar to Latin America. The galloping inflation in the commercial sector over the previous ten years was one of the reasons for the serious social and political crisis in Uruguay – a country whose stability was envied and admired all over South America during the period after the Second World War. A regime as 'European' in nature as that of the Christian democrats in Chile was no better, between 1964 and 1968, at avoiding this excessive proliferation of state officials – the 'state' being commonly confused with the regime in power at the time. And it might similarly be thought in La Paz, in November 1964, that the administration of Comibol left much to be desired, and that it was essential to review the methods of work and to reduce the administrative staff. But the men who overthrew Paz Estenssoro, whether for lack of imagination or sheer incompetence, did not look as though they were acting in response to the real needs of the situation. Barrientos, impulsive but disorganized, with enormous physical courage and at times even foolhardy (it is said that he decided to parachute down to La Paz airport after an accident which had cost the lives of two young paratroopers), had little political experience and only the vaguest knowledge of economics; and he soon showed the extent of both his *sang froid* and his lack of political insight. He went to the mining district of Siglo Veinte, in order, in his own phrase, 'to talk to the miners and find out how they lived', and succeeded in disarming one worker who was carrying sticks of dynamite. But the military repression begun in May 1965 and continually increasing, showed the new regime's lack of sympathy with or understanding of the harsh and generous world of the workers on the Altiplano. Though it did not formally dismantle the nationalized structure for the mines created in 1952, the military regime did its best to limit its scope and change its purpose.

Some reorganization was certainly needed, but ultimately this was done against the real interests of the miners, and in such a way as, discreetly or openly, to invite foreign investment; and it became clear that the successors of the MNR were also often taking the easy way out. From 1952 to 1964 the miners' situation had only improved very slightly, and it was evident that Comibol was courting disaster by its inefficiency. Starting in May 1965 the direct intervention of the armed forces in the mines darkened an already dismal picture. The union organizations had been dismantled, and those known as workers' leaders deported or imprisoned. A great many miners were dismissed following the closing of certain mines, or the repressive activities of the military. Wages were indirectly reduced. Finally, relations between the different 'classes' who went to make up this chilly world of mining firms deteriorated: in some districts, especially Catavi and Siglo Veinte, actual segregation was established. Traditionally, workers and foremen had certain clubs and meeting places; the military, whose job it was to keep order in areas where the authorities, not without cause, lived in fear of outbreaks of violence, became a superior caste; and the miner, though often earning more than those who worked in the offices, was at the bottom of the social ladder, and held in contempt by everyone else. In churches and cinemas great

Kunde: 19/11

Best. vom 11. 12. 72 Best. Nr.

	ARROW
	AVON
	BALLANTINE
	BANTAM
	BERKLEY
	CORGI
	DELL
	FAWCETT
	FONTANA
	FOUR SQUARE
	GROVE
	HODDER
	LANCER
	MAYFLOWER
	PAN
	PANTHER
1	PENGUIN 02 1348
	POCKET
	POPULAR LIBR.
	SIGNET
	SPHERE

FRIEDR. DAENIKER + CO. — PAPERBACKS — 8027 ZÜRICH

chains divided the rows of seats where he might sit from those alloted to office workers, foremen and soldiers. At the co-operative his wife would pay the same price for inferior goods rejected by the maids who shopped for engineers or officers. Social services became more and more rudimentary: in Catavi, in 1967, only three people were employed in social service.

The military repression of September 1965 was even harsher than the repression of the previous May, when the arrest and deportation to Argentina or Paraguay of some hundred union leaders, among them Escobar and Pimentel, had not been enough to bring 'order' into the mines. In September, army units attacked the Catavi area at dawn: this was nothing short of a massacre, with the workers' militia, despite their courage and their skill with dynamite, being mown down by the better-armed soldiers. Officially it was reckoned that 30 were killed and 100 wounded, but no miners were in a position to make their own estimate. Five thousand workmen lost their jobs. In October a group of priests, led by the Archbishop of La Paz, Abel Antezana, besought Generals Barrientos and Ovando to 'change their policy towards the miners of the Altiplano', and in November the government took certain steps 'to prevent further disorders'.

Instability and unrest have been continuous from 1965 up to the present, despite ever-increased surveillance, and the government's return to administering Comibol. Further serious troubles broke out in June 1967 in Oruro, Catavi and Huanuni, all of which the miners proclaimed 'free zones'. On 24 June the armed forces occupied the rebel mining areas and killed a large number of people. On the next day General Barrientos appealed to the population at large, explaining why the troops had gone into the mines, and urging them to 'remain calm'. Despite sporadic attempts at negotiation and conciliation the military regime was virtually unable to have any dealings with the mining proletariat; they thus tried from

1965 onwards, not without some success, to win over the peasant community who were most anxious to preserve what they had gained in the agrarian reform of 1953.

Whether they were aware of it or not, this was good policy. The workers in the tin mines had a long tradition of fighting and a revolutionary experience based on a tactic of 'self-defence' – criticized by Castroist intellectuals (particulary Régis Debray in *Revolution in the Revolution*) as 'negative' and Trotskyist-inspired. This is certainly true, for the POR, one of whose leaders was Guillermo Lora, was largely based on Trotskyism, and its influence in the trade unions up to 1964 was considerable. That influence is quite possibly strong still, even though a young Christian Democrat leader, René Chacón, was elected in January 1966 as secretary general of the first miners' union 'reorganized' by the authorities. It is quite true also that 'self-defence' was found to be ineffective in 1965 and 1967 in resisting the armed forces; but the use of this tactic by the miners was the result of having to cope with the situation then facing them, and not of setting out to define revolutionary tactics and strategy in terms of carefully analysed ideological options. The best comparison we may perhaps find with the self-defence used by the miners of the Altiplano was the tactic used in Colombia by the peasants who grouped themselves into zones in the hope (up to 1962) of avoiding 'violence' on the one hand and too much attention from the authorities on the other.

In both cases – Colombia since 1964 and Bolivia since May 1965 – the use by governments of large forces of well-trained and equipped troops to break down the more or less passive resistance of miners and peasants showed what such self-defence really amounted to: a local and limited display of a defensive rather than an offensive revolutionary nature. But this obstinate and courageous group of Bolivian workers were, despite their determination both to work and to rebel, a minority. Though they played a decisive role in the battles which brought the MNR to power in 1952, according to Barrientos' 'electoral' outlook of 1965, when he offered himself for the presidency 'because it was the people's wish', it was the masses of the peasants whose support mattered most. Once the regime had begun yet again to compromise with foreign business interests in 1960 the pressure of the workers' militia became something to be feared, and Paz Estenssoro founded the peasant militia to counterbalance them; Barrientos, a native of Cochabamba, speaking *quechua* perfectly and familiar with the peasant communities of some of the valleys in that relatively temperate and prosperous area, naturally sought his first support from them.

Despite the acceleration of the industrialization process (food and textile industries, wool and leather industries) – a modest enough acceleration, it is true, if one reckons how vast the possibilities were, especially as regards power – agriculture still employed almost 30 per cent of the population according to the CEPAL estimates of 1965. This mass of farm workers, chiefly concentrated on the Altiplano, and averse to migrating further inland, was largely uneducated. The rate of illiteracy hovered around 60 per cent, thus making the Bolivian countryside one of the worst areas in all of Latin America. In 1961 there were still only 5,295 country schools and 7,190 teachers, all newly recruited and often qualified for the work by goodwill alone. At the same date there was an average of one doctor to every 4,000 people. (In 1968 these figures were barely any different, and in some cases in fact even worse because of the increase in population.) Underfed, under-educated, living in a cultural backwater, the mass of the country people – even less dominated by a skeleton body of clergy than in Colombia or Peru – live haunted by fear of repression and an often almost superstitious fear of authority.

The POR activists had, since 1952, been encouraging the takeover of large estates by force, believing that to consolidate 'peasant power' would provide the best guarantee for surviving the April uprising. They blamed Paz Estenssoro for sabotaging agrarian reform by proclaiming a prudent and gradual system of expropriation, allowing for indemnifying the previous owners and dividing the land into family holdings. But the traditions of a subsistence economy, together with the paucity of technical and financial means at the disposal of those who stood to gain by the agrarian reform, were two factors quite adequate to explain why production fell so sharply in the early days. Before the reform the poor small farmer, whether or not he was bound by the *pongueaje* system, was still the prisoner of his 'boss' because of his debts in the estate shop where he had to buy his food.

His serfdom is comparable to that of most other peasants living on the Andean plateau, or of the *caboclos* of north-east Brazil. The 1953 law did not ensure him a living standard much higher than that enjoyed by the poorest peasants in medieval Europe, but it did give him the beginnings of human dignity and a prospect of freedom. These poor peasant families who had gained by the reform were the best support the MNR had up to 1964. *Hasta la muerte con Estenssoro*, proclaimed their primitive banners in the central square in Cochabamba in October 1964. The peasant militia, armed with whatever came to hand, were certainly quite incapable of defending the Estenssoro regime 'to the death' if faced with a modern army, but it is hardly surprising that a large proportion of those peasants, especially in the more advanced region of Cochabamba, should associate the preservation of the reform with the success of the apparently populist action of Barrientos.

Throughout 1965, while the new regime hardened its attitude to the miners, delegations of peasants from Cochabamba continued to demonstrate in favour of Barrientos, and to support his candidacy for the presidency. They were riotous, simple demonstrations, which could hardly have made any serious impression on the other military leaders, and though they were not all 'spontaneous', they were an indication of the anxiety of the whole peasant class. In October, armed peasant militia invaded Cochabamba, where the (right wing) socialist Falange was holding its Congress, with the object of offering to collaborate with General Barrientos.

Barrientos opted for the militia and the innumerable crises which have followed one another from 1965 to the present have never been without the accompaniment of 'peasant demonstrations in favour of Barrientos'. It would certainly be an exaggeration to generalize from a phenomenon peculiar to Cochabamba: on various occasions from 1965 to 1968 Barrientos or his supporters have been stoned in the poor areas of La Paz, or in the villages of the Altiplano. But the psychological results of the agrarian reform and the existence of a strongly pro-Barrientos bloc of peasants were elements that were certainly underestimated by the men who decided to start a movement of large-scale armed insurrection in the eastern provinces of Bolivia in 1967.

The presidential election that was to legitimize the coup of November 1964, delayed several times, took place on 3 July 1966. In December 1965 the 'Popular Christian Movement', established by Barrientos to give him a political platform after the hoped-for alliance with the Phalange failed to materialize, joined up with other little political groups (Authentic Revolutionary Party. Social Democrat Party, Party of the Revolutionary Left, National Federation of Ex-Soldiers) to form the Bolivian Revolutionary Front (FRB). This Front – a collection of leaders without any followers – got 677,805 votes, or 61·6 per cent. The Christian-Democrat Community (CDC) won 138,000, and various recognized movements more or less connected with the fallen regime won some 10 per cent of the votes.

General Barrientos was elected president and Siles Salinas, the leader of the small Social Democrat party, vice-president. The FRB alone won a hundred seats in the new Assembly. But it was evident that this redistribution of the various political 'families' left a more or less rumbling opposition, not just of the right-wing socialist Falange, but also, and more seriously, the big left and centre-left groups – the MNR of Paz Estenssoro who was watching closely from his asylum in Peru, Lechín's PRIN, the National Liberation Front secretly supported by the two communist parties (pro-Chinese and pro-Soviet), and the Trotskyists, Liberals and Christian Democrats, all moving slowly forwards.

However only the MNR, though divided into at least three streams since Paz Estenssoro's overthrow, could claim an organization worthy the name at any national level. A great many of its activities and cell organizers who had been forced into clandestine action since November 1964 were to represent potential danger for the Barrientos–Ovando regime. The generals' promptness in exploiting the appearance of the guerrilla *focos* of Ñancahuazú in the spring of 1967, so as to lessen the potential of the older parties still more, indicated their profound fear of seeing those overthrown in 1964 coming forward again if there should be an insurrection that did not go beyond the triangle of Santa Cruz–Camiri–Sucre. The 'Castroist danger' was ridiculously exaggerated by the military, up until they captured Che Guevara near La Higuera. But a more definite attitude on the part of the MNR and the other left-wing parties, starting with the pro-Soviet communist party of Mario Monje, would certainly have done a lot to alter the type of response generally given to the problem of guerrilla warfare. The hesitations of the MNR and less obviously, of the PRIN, whose leader Lechín had retreated to Chile, together with the claims of the orthodox communists to be in political control of the guerrilla movement, must have done a lot to contribute to the failure of the movement organized by Che Guevara. Guerrilla activity, or at least its repercussions, were to make clear the fragile and artificial nature of that Bolivian Revolutionary Front which had been created simply to fulfil a purpose. The internal 'crisis' produced in

July 1968 by the flight of the Minister of the Interior, Antonio Arguedas, broke the FRB apart: the Social Democrats of Siles Salinas left the government coalition, leaving Barrientos with no option but to return to his natural allies – the armed forces and Cochabamba peasants. But it is important to note that a good part of the army made no secret of its preference for General Ovando, and that the only group from which the president could expect unconditional loyalty was the peasant communities in the rich Cochabamba valley.

The regime in power in the Plaza Murillo after November 1964 declared itself strongly nationalist and 'anti-oligarchic' – in other words more generally concerned with the national interest than the MNR and determined to maintain the social gains of the April 1952 revolution. But here all their fine socializing intentions could not stand up to the harsh demands of politics, and the implacable hostility of the miners. Agrarian reform was not undone, but it would be hard to say that it advanced any further. And as for the 'national interest', the Barrientos regime did no more than carry on, and in a sense intensify the policy adopted by the Paz Estenssoro government in 1960. The ten-year plan that the government had begun depended on American aid for one third of its financial support, and such aid also made it possible to regulate the country's economy to some extent, and to carry out the monetary reform recommended – if not positively demanded – by the IMF.

Consequent upon this decision the Paz Estenssoro government signed agreements in 1961 to return to mining operations in cooperation with the U.S., Federal Germany and the BID. In virtue of these so-called 'triangular operation' agreements, Bolivia received 37 million dollars' credit, but was committed to changing the structure of Comibol. This 'reorganization', involving the dismissal of large numbers of men, was bound to increase the rift between the Paz Estenssoro government and the mining unions. Juan Lechín, the permanent maverick of Bolivian politics, resigned the Vice-Presidency, and returned to the Castroist and communist opposition. Paz Estenssoro's small army of 10,000, now promoted to being the government's most vital support, was not long in finding it necessary to take over ...

But it seemed hard for it to succeed in making any real change. Though it made energetic protests to Washington over the sale of 28,000 tons of surplus tin from United States strategic reserves (Comibol estimated Bolivia's loss by this at two million dollars), and the fixing of what was thought to be far too low a price for tin, the Barrientos government still went ahead with the plan for the 'triangular operation'. It may well be argued that no other economic policy would have been possible in Bolivia without a total change in political options – options themselves very narrowly circumscribed. Yet it is impossible not to recognize that the line taken by the military regime was in no fundamental sense any different from that of the Paz Estenssoro regime during the second half of its existence.

The First City Bank of New York planned, symbolically, to open a branch in La Paz with an initial capital of half a million dollars. In March 1966 the Director of Comibol announced that 'private capital from abroad would in future be authorized to play a part in the working of the nationalized mines'. On the same day the BID granted Comibol a credit of 2½ million dollars, and AID allowed them a further credit of 6,100,000 dollars. A fresh loan of 4,800,000 dollars was granted the following August by AID, and BID followed this in September with a credit of 2 million. In November there was a further loan from BID of 12 million, to underwrite 'industrial and mining projects', and in that same month the IMF gave 18 million 'to help the government maintain a stable currency'. Given Bolivia's immense need and the terrible losses suffered by her economy with its special vulnerability to the fluctuation of prices for her raw materials (tin, silver, lead), none of these loans amounted to a great deal. But even this 'generosity' was accompanied by the granting of new facilities by the La Paz government to foreign investment – mainly north American. The famous Mathilde mine, with its wealth of zinc and cadmium, was taken over by the U.S. Steel Corporation and Philipps brothers. The Solmin Company investigated the sulphur deposits in Potosí province, and Gulf Oil was encouraged to prospect and drill around Santa Cruz – and in particular to build a pipeline from Camiri to Arica by way of Cochabamba in exchange for certain tax exemptions. The Case Grace Company was granted concessions it had been seeking since 1955 for sugar and live-stock raising.

With the competition from Japan which began to be felt in 1952, the American companies returned to the attack they had begun in 1920, receiving concessions amounting to a million hectares in the south east for Standard Oil. Bolivia's modest 400,000 tons of oil is little when compared with the Venezuelan giant's production of over 170 million tons. But the oil deposits are to be found in an area upon whose development the whole future progress of the country depends. Since 1956 Gulf Oil had been authorized to prospect and drill inside the district specially reserved to YPFB, the national company founded in 1937. Fourteen private firms, attracted by the extremely liberal considerations offered by the government, were granted 5½ million hectares in concessions in 1948. In September 1967 the board of YBFP protested against the establishment of a gas and petro-chemical company 'militating against the nation's autarchy in regard to hydrocarbides', and with the help of a general strike among oil workers, achieved the setting up of a 'National Council for petroleum and petrochemicals': this nationalist upsurge was an indication of how enormously the penetration of foreign capital and interests had increased in three years.

In January 1967 several leaders of the former Bolivian

miners' federation were arrested, and the peasants' confederation decided to withdraw from the Bolivian Revolutionary Front. That same month Barrientos declared the existence of a conspiracy, got the Chamber to approve the setting up of several private universities over the protests of the student associations, and granted an American firm the right to work a major zinc mine. Finally some thirty leaders of the MNR, the PRIN, the POR and the Communist Party were put under house arrest – a euphemistic term to describe deportation into the unhealthy and totally isolated army camps in the eastern sector near the Brazilian border: camps with names like London, Peking or Nuevo Berlin.

The atmosphere – fairly normal in Bolivia – was one compounded of an unstable political situation, permanent secret agitation by more or less illegal parties, an economy permanently under threat of collapse despite repeated injections of dollars, a mining proletariat in rebellion, and rumours of conspiracy on all sides, when the first shots rang out in the wild Ñancahuazú gorge south of Santa Cruz, near to Camiri where almost 90 per cent of Bolivia's oil comes from. For some weeks beforehand, in fact, army intelligence had known of a certain unrest in the area, but the Criminal Investigation Department had attributed the increasing movement of unknown people in the Camiri–Legunillas–Monteagudo triangle to the renewed activity of narcotics-smugglers.

What it was in reality was a large guerrilla base being set up by the Ñancahuazú by Che Guevara with the help of a number of Cuban and Bolivian officers, among them the Peredo brothers, formerly dissident communist leaders. From the point of view both of security and of strategy the site was an ideal one: the Ñancahuazú, a jungle river with innumerable tributaries, was virtually inaccessible. By it – presuming of course the necessary means of liaison – one could create links between the low-lying, warm plains of the east bordering on Brazil, Paraguay and northern Argentina on the one hand with, on the other, via the moderately high valleys like Sucre and Cochabamba, the Altiplano and the mining areas. To establish a revolutionary *foco* near to a relatively heavily populated farming area with means of communication with the mining districts – an inexhaustible source of determined fighters – seems to have been Guevara's prime objective in Bolivia.

It also seems likely, and a perusal of his Diaries seems to confirm this idea, that his secondary objective was to link the Bolivian *foco* with other guerrilla bases in the southern provinces of Argentina, in Paraguay, possibly in Brazil and certainly in Peru, where the two failed attempts – Puerto Maldonado, and the spring of 1965 – had left their mark on the high valleys of the Andes.

By a strange irony the Bolivian government had declared the week beginning 16 March the 'week of the sea', during which there were to be several demonstrations by the Bolivian people expressing 'their claim to have access to the sea'. On 20 March two army patrols disappeared into the Lagunillas district; accompanied by a guide named Vargas, who had noted the appearance of numbers of armed men, the troops were seeking signs there. They were ambushed in the Ñancahauzú gorge, some of their number were killed and others captured by the guerrillas, who let them go after forty-eight hours.

The confrontation was only admitted three days later in La Paz, but Barrientos immediately accused the Cuban government of being involved, and let it be said that Guevara himself was leading the revolutionary movement. Since the beginning of March, through information received from guerrilla deserters (later discovered to have been CIA agents), the Bolivian government had known that Fidel Castro's erstwhile lieutenant had been in the eastern province since the end of 1966. The army was ambushed, again with some deaths, on 10 April at Iripiti, north of Lagunillas. General Ovando, commander in chief of the army, took over the running of operations in person, and set up his headquarters at Choreti, near Camiri.

On 20 April three young foreigners, one of them the Frenchman Régis Debray, were arrested in the district. Debray, a philosophy graduate staying for a time in Havana, had already travelled a good deal in South America, especially in Bolivia; he was on his way from the base camp of Ñancahuazú where he had been meeting Guevara. He said that he was a journalist. So the 'Debray affair' began. He was interrogated by CIA agents, put in solitary confinement, threatened, accused of taking part in the guerrilla fighting, and his trial finally opened in Camiri on 26 September. He was condemned on 17 November to thirty years' imprisonment. Bustos, an Argentinian arrested at the same time, was given the same sentence.

Despite protests from a number of important figures and lawyers, all of whom castigated the flagrant irregularities of the trial, the Camiri military court condemned both men to the maximum sentence 'to make an example of them'. Before being condemned, Debray, though he rejected the court's arguments, did admit his support of the revolutionary uprising.

The lengthy Debray trial and the emotions aroused all over the world by the affair, distracted attention from the guerrilla movement which had already been threatened even before the first ambushes by the behaviour of left-wing political groups. At the beginning of January a meeting between Guevara and Mario Monje, the secretary general of the Bolivian CP, ended in deadlock. Despite its spectacular successes against the Bolivian army, Guevara's guerrilla group had to cope with tremendous difficulties in organizing food supplies and transport. The weariness induced by incessant marching backwards and forwards in the jungle, the betrayals and defections, the impossibility of getting the peasants of the area really involved, the weakness in the urban networks established in La Paz, Cochabamba and Santa Cruz, the leadership of Bolivian troops by north American instructors from the Panama canal base, and the almost total isolation of the guerrillas together with their division into two separate groups by July – all these things combined to cause the gradual process of disintegration which reached its conclusion – symbolically perhaps – in another wild ravine on 8 October, near La Higuera, north of Valle Grande. Encircled by five thousand Bolivian troops, Guevara and his comrades fought a brief battle. The wounded Che was captured and after being interrogated by various superior officers, among them General Ovando himself, as summarily executed the next day by order of the La Paz government. 'The guerrilla war in Bolivia is now over,' declared Ovando.

Since April 1965 rumours of all kinds had been flying around about Guevara, who vanished on his return to Cuba after a three-month trip around Africa and Asia. In Washington it had often been stated that Che had been physically 'liquidated' by the Cuban leaders for 'left-wing deviationism'; he was reported to have been seen in Vietnam, in the Congo, and in several South American countries; in Havana it was announced that he 'was carrying on the fight against imperialism somewhere in the world'. In fact that fight was brought to an end in a small town in eastern Bolivia which Guevara had first visited as a young Argentinian doctor, fifteen years earlier.

But the legend surrounding the man who had called for the creation of 'two, three, several Vietnams', and who, after reaching the pinnacle of power in Cuba, had abandoned it to devote his life to his convictions, that legend was only just beginning. Guevara, the Marxist revolutionary, prophet of 'new socialist man', combined with Camilo Torres, the guerrilla priest killed fighting in Colombia in

February 1966, to disturb the indifference of the people and the apathy of those in power.

Though the guerrilla war was 'finished', Barrientos's troubles were by no means over. The complicated negotiations with various American publishing houses over the sale and distribution of Guevara's notebooks were still continuing in June 1968 when the Cubans, having got hold of a copy, took the spectacular step of publishing the work themselves, with all its restless recording of the hopes and problems of an unfinished campaign. The man responsible for this 'lead' was Barrientos' own Minister of the Interior, Antonio Arguedas, who had fled to Chile; returning to La Paz in August, Arguedas began questioning the activities of the CIA. This new piece of melodrama led to a further weakening of the FRB, and resulted in Barrientos forming a government entirely composed of officers. Though civilians had never played a very convincing part in the FRB, now, nearly four years after the fall of Paz Estenssoro, the regime seemed to have fallen back more and more on the armed forces as its sole support, and it was clear that the Chief of Staff coveted the presidency for himself.

Students were restless, the influx of foreign capital was arousing more and more lively protests in nationalist bourgeois circles, the Church spoke out against the desperate living conditions of the miners and their families, the vital struggle against under-development appeared less and less convincing, and discontented officers like General Sempertegui – one of those who had led the anti-guerrilla operation – were ready to become involved in quite unrealistic conspiracies : the general picture in Bolivia was one of a country facing insurmountable problems where anything – from a complete military dictatorship onwards – might happen.

CHAPTER 3

Peru

STATISTICS

Area: 496,224 square miles
Estimated population in 1967: 12,012,000
Population density: 24 per square mile
Annual rate of population increase: 3 per cent
Annual increase in average per capita *income from 1960 to 1966:* 3·7 per cent.

PRINCIPAL PRODUCTS

Fishmeal (largest world producer), cotton, cereals, sugar, *guano* (animal fertilizer).
Iron (fifth largest world producer), copper, lead, zinc, silver, petroleum.

By day the dizzy flights of steps linking the lower to the upper town stand out sharply in the blinding sunlight. At the top of the Intihuatana, a round, tower-shaped biulding made for observing the sun during the Equinox, with its curious table of carved stone, poisonous bushmasters lie sleeping in the grass at the foot of the topless temple. At nightfall which, as always in the tropics, is rapid, the palaces, towers and hanging gardens of Machu-Picchu seem to vanish completely. All that stands out in the shadow is the triangular peak of the Huayna-Picchu. Eight hundred metres below, at the foot of cliff-faces as steep as the Aiguille de Dru, the río

Urubamba rushes down against the granite mountain and creates a canyon around this natural citadel where man has built this most mysterious and fascinating of cities. Beyond the gulf are more steep cliffs, more peaks covered in thick, deep green vegetation, and then the splendid circles of the Andes, with snowy peaks rising to over 6,000 metres. Right down below the Urubamba follows its winding course to the Ucayali, and further still, beyond the *yungas*, those warm valleys in the Andean foothills, it flows on to the Amazon.

The fortress of Machu-Picchu was discovered quite by chance. From above the 300 once-cultivated terraces one can still trace the road rising out of the gorges found in 1911 by Hiram Bingham, the young Yale archaeology professor. Today, though the stones of Machu-Picchu have probably been measured and studied more often than those of any of the other archaeological high places in the continent, some nagging questions about them still remain unanswered. The most generally held theory is that Machu-Picchu was an advance bastion for the Incas, protecting them against the incursions of tribes from the Amazonian plains – for this lofty, wild plateau provides a marvellous vantage point. But in fact the whole area north of Cuzco is full of fortresses, the most romantic being Ollantaytambo, and the most astounding Sacsahuamán, which overlooks Cuzco itself. Hugh blocks, some weighing several tons, cunningly fitted together to the last millimetre (how, we do not know) and polished with tools – of iron, bronze and gold – which we have not yet found; it is a gigantic complex forming a triple rampart of walls. The Indians of the upper Andean valleys had not discovered the wheel; and one can only wonder how many thousands of slaves gave their lives in the fantastic building of these – America's pyramids. Machu-Picchu has a quite special fascination of its own, there is more here than just a method of strategic defence, or even man's desire to challenge the impossible: when the mists rise from the gorges and roll round the Huayna-Picchu and snake along the slopes up to the summit of the next peak, all one can think of is Delphos, where other magnificent ruins of stone stand by a misty ravine. But here there was no oracle receiving answers from the gods. Here a civilization died – and no one has yet discovered the real reason for its death.

*

Inca rule lasted for four centuries – from the twelfth until the sixteenth when the Spaniards came. The legendary children of the Sun came from Lake Titicaca. They conquered the Aymará tribes and established themselves in Cuzco, which was to become the capital of their empire with its four provinces, the 'Tahuantinsuyu'. At its apogee that empire had some 25 million inhabitants and extended roughly over the area that now forms Bolivia, Peru, Ecuador, northern Chile, and part of Argentina. Historians are faced with one absolutely amazing fact about the Incas: they had no written language! Their story has had to be pieced together through the colourful and at times contradictory stories of the great chroniclers of the Spanish conquest, chief among whom was Garcilaso de la Vega. The Inca civilization, however perfect it may have been, was itself the successor of other pre-Columbian civilizations whose degree of perfection remains yet to be discovered. The history of the peoples then living on the Peruvian coast remains in almost total obscurity; on the hill of Ancón alone, near Lima, and in the north of the mid-Andean plateau near Quitox, there are still something like 35,000 tombs to examine. It seems probable that a vast Aymará empire extended over the whole of those highlands at some period we cannot yet ascertain, but pre-dating the coming of the Incas. Less than a hundred kilometres from Tiahuanaco in Bolivia, the sacred city of that now forgotten empire, is the island of the Sun, the cradle of Inca civilization, lying just off Copacabana in Lake Titicaca. The island is hidden by a rocky promontory and legend has it that the Inca treasure is sunk somewhere in those green depths.

For four centuries, then, the Incas painstakingly organized their empire. They were not as cultured as the Mayas of central America and Yucatán, but were primarily administrators and builders – the Romans, if you like, of America. While Europe was barely emerging from the Middle Ages this high region of South America already had an economic and social system so well-ordered that it is sometimes spoken of as a communist civilization. It was certainly a totalitarian state, with the functionaries of the Inca, who was both emperor and god, passing on orders by means of coloured strings, the *quipus*, which replaced written words. It was a rigid state where nothing was left to chance, where everyone received just what he needed to support life, and every smallest act was supervised. They may have been happy but their happiness was strictly controlled: an Indian had to live and die where he was born; on the other hand, whole tribes could be moved if reasons of state made it desirable. Even today in Ecuador one finds descendants of Lake Titicaca Indians – 'displaced persons' before the phrase was coined. Everything, even love, was regulated to the last detail: to men of twenty-four and women of eighteen marriage was obligatory. Each couple was given a piece of land considered necessary to subsistence, and for every child the state granted an additional piece of ground – twice as large in the case of a boy as of a girl. The sick, the handicapped and the old were looked after by the community. Healthy men worked on the state's land, and were also expected to cultivate the land of citizens who could not work before starting on their own family holding.

It was also the Inca who provided his subjects with the wool for their ponchos. Vast flocks of llamas and vicuña, belonging to no one and everyone, were tended by official shepherds. Families were divided into groups of ten with a responsible leader at their head: this clear-cut organization led to the existence of bodies made up of heads of 100, of 500, of 1,000, of 10,000 and of 20,000 families, with, at the top of the pyramid, the Inca himself assisted by his Council, and four major officials in charge of the detailed workings of this fantastic social machine in the four provinces of the Empire. Yet what is perhaps most remarkable is that the victorious Incas, though they subjected a number of other peoples in their centuries of power, never yielded to the temptation of forming a closed caste. The Inca elite was, in fact, open to newcomers – local chiefs they had conquered, notable fighters, scholars, lawgivers or judges – all these could become 'honorary Incas'.

*

Storehouses of food were established outside the towns or along the roads; from them officials took what was needed for the Court, the army and the priests. The magnificence of that Court has been conveyed by chroniclers in terms so lyrical as to cast some doubt on their objectivity. The obligatory marriage of the Inca-Emperor to his sister, the victories, the festivals celebrated at certain dates in honour of the Sun-god – all such occasions signalled the arrival in the capital of all the most important figures in the empire, with convoys of llamas weighed down with gifts. The Inca himself never travelled without the same rigorously observed ceremonial as ruled the lives of his subjects. He would use a massive gold litter studded with emeralds and the walls of his many palaces scattered round the empire vied with one another in splendour. When an Inca died or, in other words, 'returned to the home of his father the Sun', his funeral was the occasion for ceremonies of mournful magnificence. His servants and concubines would be killed, and indeed these Pharaoh-like ceremonies might cost the lives of over a thousand people. Legend even has it that the victims of these sacrifices presented themselves joyfully to the high priest's knife – but the masks of the mummies, still frozen with fear, in the ghostly museum in Cuzco give the lie to that particular tradition.

The network of roads in the Inca empire was its greatest pride – they were longer and stronger than the Roman roads and the obstacles they had to surmount were incredible. If one travels by air from Lima to Cuzco one gets some notion of the vastness of the undertaking. One also gets some notion of the unparalleled achievement of Pizarro and his companions in conquering the Peruvian highlands. For two hours one looks down on a chaos of rock and ice, a tortured landscape, hollowed out into vast funnels, marked by sharp ridges and frosty peaks. A fine sinewy stream glides briefly along the base of a ravine, hesitates at the edge in a foamy haze, and then rushes on beyond another ridge. Cuzco in the Quechua language means 'navel'; those who built the largest Indian empire in the Americas believed they were establishing their capital in the very centre of the world. When Pizarro first landed in Tumbes, near Guayaquil (in Ecuador), the Inca Atahualpa was in such total control of this universe that he saw no need to do anything about the arrival of these men, white and bearded like the god Viracocha. In a matter of months, this first Indian community civilization had collapsed under the thrust of this handful of fighters from Spain. If we are to believe Garcilaso de la Vega, the newcomers asked the Indians what their land was called, and they, believing the conquerors only wanted to know the name of the river at whose mouth they had stopped, replied simply 'Piru', which was the Indian word for river in that part of the country. 'Piru' became 'Peru', and so it remained.

Manco Capac (the mythical founder of Cuzco) himself or his children ruled for almost fifty years until the dawn of the twelfth century. But the deep obscurity in which the real origins of the Incas is hidden also conceals the various vicissitudes of the early Indian pharaohs. Light begins with the coming of the fourth Inca, Mayta Capac, of whom we can say with some certainty that he conquered the Aymarás and waged war as far as the borders of Chile.

He built roads through swamps, caring nothing for the sacrifice in human lives that this entailed. He had a suspension bridge built across the Apurimac, constructed out of lianas and a wood that would not rot. He planned massive migrations to consolidate his power over those he had conquered. His grandson Pachacutec returned to fight against the Araucanos of southern Chile, but never managed to get beyond the wild barrier of the Bío-Bío, by which Pedro de Valdivia was also later to find himself blocked. Pachacutec, 'the Reformer', began building that line of fortresses which many experts consider more advanced than the Great Wall of China.

The golden age of the empire of the four provinces came at the end of the fifteenth century, and Huayna Capac was its Louis XIV. At that date the 'Tahuantinsuyu' must have extended from the north of Ecuador to what is the central south of present-day Chile – over 4,000 kilometres – and from the Amazonian plains to the shores of the Pacific. Huayna Capac, as much a builder as a warrior, administrator and lawgiver, set about finally defeating the still restless tribes around Quito. He tried to get the Quechua language accepted all over his kingdom. According to Prescott, the Inca civilization under Huayna Capac was so advanced that it could be compared to the most developed civilizations of Asia; yet it was then, in the hour of its triumph, that this society was to be destroyed. The stormy love of the Inca Huayna Capac for the daughter of a tribal chief from Quito was certainly one of the causes for that unexpected downfall. For the ageing and besotted despot left Cuzco to go to Quito and decided to divide a kingdom whose entire strength lay in its unity between his elder son and legitimate heir, Huascar, and his younger son, Atahualpa, born of his love for that Duchicela whom historians seem determined to believe to have been very beautiful. The rivalry between the half-brothers, which began as a civilized one, turned into open war as the first rumours of the Spanish landings began coming in from breathless messengers.

It is generally accepted today that the Aztecs in Mexico and the Incas in Peru knew nothing of each other, and yet there is a lot of similarity in their mythologies and legends. The Aztec plumed serpent set out to sea towards the East; Viracocha, the white god of the Peruvians who controlled the thunder, also disappeared on the dark waters of Lake Titicaca, ordering everyone to expect his rapid return. It was natural, then, that Cortés in Mexico and Pizarro in Peru should have used similar skills in exploiting these analogous Indian beliefs. But it is also accepted by the best scholars that this was not the dominant factor: had it not been for the rivalries and bitternesses among neighbouring tribes, Montezuma would certainly never have been conquered. And the fight between the two brothers, Atahualpa and Huascar, made it far easier for Pizarro to advance to the centre of the Andean highlands.

*

Atahualpa, though imprisoned by Huascar, managed to escape from Quito and capture his rival. He at once proclaimed himself sole reigning emperor of the 'Tahuantinsuyu' and hastened to return to the centre of the world – the Cuzco valley. Meanwhile Pizarro's cannon were thundering from Tumbes on the coast. Atahualpa decided to meet the Spaniard on the plain of Cajamarca – a disastrous decision, as it turned out. But the Inca did not have any serious fears of this conqueror who took two months to reach the fateful meeting place, dragging along exhausted horses, men laden with glittering armour, and Indian mercenaries. Along the road

Pizarro heard contradictory accounts of the two rival Inca sons. (Similarly Cortés received messengers from the different tribes governed by Montezuma.) More seriously concerned with what still looked like the possible revenge of Huascar, Atahualpa reorganized his troops and waited for Pizarro. On one side was a young king with a hawk-like profile, barely secure on his still new throne, full of self-doubt, and aware of the forebodings of the elders. On the other a former swineherd from Estremadura, illiterate, yearning to repeat the achievement of Cortés whom he imitated in detail, a mercenary mad with longing for gold, but also the leader of a superhumanly brave group of men. For it took no common courage to cross the Andes, tramping through swampland and forest, getting ever deeper into this *terra incognita* with its endless vastness and its continual surprises. The Cajamarca tragedy had all the dramatic unity and fatality of a classical drama: the whole thing was over almost before it began, between dawn and dusk. The proud Inca who entered in the first scene, surrounded with the majesty of his Court, was by the end of the play no more than a bemused, weak, pitiful prisoner, probably only too ready to die. His death was determined in a single gesture: Pizarro's chaplain, Fr Vicente de Valverde, solemnly offered him a Bible, demanding that he embrace the Christian faith and accept the sovereignty of Charles V: the magnificent Inca hurled the Bible to the ground. To the Spanish soldiers who had been ambushed with weapons in their hands – like Cortés' knights in Mexico – this was the signal for slaughter. Their harquebuses decimated the Indians and struck them with total panic. With Atahualpa a prisoner, dragged along by the hair, the Inca empire was finished. The 'Tahuantinsuyu' collapsed, though the rearguard of the Indian army, led by Ruminagui, left the Cajamarca valley to return to Quito by forced marches.

The subjects of the Inca were unmoved; they had been living under an absolute tyranny for too long, and all this meant was a change of master. Their god who was now a prisoner seemed anxious only to buy his freedom, and to get rid once for all of Huascar, who was in a dungeon in Cuzco. Pizarro suggested a bargain: if Atahualpa would fill the room where he was being kept in Cajamarca with gold and precious stones, he would be set free. Messengers from Quito to Cuzco ransacked the provinces to collect the ransom; Huascar learnt what was happening in his dungeon and offered even more gold than his brother in exchange for his lost throne. Atahualpa, mad with rage at the thought that the Spaniards might give his brother the advantage, at once ordered that Huascar be strangled. But even the fabulous ransom finally amassed after two months spent searching the four corners of the empire did not save Atahualpa. The ultimate humiliation was reserved for him: he was forced to be baptized a Catholic and renounce his gods, and on 29 August 1533 the grotesque Juan Atahualpa, made a Christian against his will in the last moments of his life, was garrotted before Pizarro, under the eyes of an apparently uncaring crowd.

No doubt the Inca empire was too perfect; by striking a blow at its head the whole thing was destroyed. Buried with great pomp, Atahualpa's body was stolen during the night by Indians who carried it secretly to Quito. For the second time the Inca was buried while all his wives stabbed themselves on his tomb. Four centuries after that apocalyptic Indian *götterdämmerung*, mourning is still worn for Atahualpa in certain remote villages by the short dark, silent men who walk hunched up against the icy winds of the Altiplano. But Cuzco is now only an uninteresting, little-known provincial town; it has been destroyed several times by earthquakes, and its ancient walls are poorly concealed under the weight of the cathedrals and monasteries built by the conquerors.

When Pizarro entered it for the first time, in company with

the son of Huascar, a pale shadow of a legality no longer recognized, it was sparkling gold under the Andean sky. His victory was comparatively easy but it profited him little. For all this gold that seemed ready for the taking turned the heads of his own best lieutenants. Almagro, who had gone to fight against the Araucanos in the Chilean deserts, barely got back to Peru before claiming his share of Atahualpa's treasure. The desperate fight between Pizarro and Almagro covered in a veil of blood the early years of what should have been a model conquest. And even the defeat and execution of Almagro failed to save Pizarro, for his despotism and increasing power had begun to disturb the Court in Madrid. At the height of his glory, obsessed with building palaces and churches in his beloved Lima, Pizarro already stood condemned by Spain. An unknown magistrate from Valladolid, Vaca de Castro, was ordered to achieve a reconciliation between the 'Almagrists' and the 'Pizarrists'. But it took so long to travel from Spain to America that the messenger got there too late: Pizarro was already dead, murdered in his turn by Almagro's supporters, his body full of dagger-marks, and his blood marking one last cross on the ground.

*

One of the highest railway trains in the world stops at Sicuani to catch its breath, so to speak, and have a mechanical check made of its, by now, smoking axles. It is a small town at the southernmost point of the Cuzco valley. Though it is 3,500 metres high, a few clumps of frail eucalyptus on the banks of a bubbling stream give it a soft and pleasant look in its frame of icy rock walls. After Sicuani the railway moves sharply upwards, winding to the foot of glaciers which seem, in the rarefied air, so close that one could lean out and touch them. At Aguascalientes, this little Andean train makes another regulation stop; a few passengers jump down and make a dash to the sulphur springs, where they have a quick wash, and run back breathless to the train as it sets off again with all its weary bones shaking. The line crosses the pass at almost 5,000 metres, and then moves down again through the yellow aridity of the high plateau to Puno on the banks of Lake Titicaca, by way of Ayaviri and Juliaca. All the way from Sicuani to Puno it is the same: the sky is an unchanging blue; rotten smells come from the Indian markets with their tents crowded together; on each side of the rails, behind the windowless, dust-coloured earth huts, groups of children chase balls without any shouting or noise; and there is the same silence in the stations, where Indians lie in the shadow of the platforms, dreaming of who can say what, wrapped in their ponchos full of holes and stiff with dirt. They have the same high cheekbones – blue because of the permanent cold which has burst the blood-vessels just under the skin – and the narrow eyes of the distant ancestors who may well have come from Mongolia; they move little, smile little, speak little. Their entire attention seems to be given to the slow chewing of coca leaves.

Four hundred years after the execution of Atahualpa and the murder of Pizarro nothing has really changed in Peru as regards the relationship between the mass of Indians and the Spaniards or their descendants. Around Lake Titicaca the Aymará peasants still make furrows in their desperately hard ground with long wooden ploughshares that have barely developed from those used in the Incas' collective labours. In the yard behind a Cuzco stall thickset Quechuas, with short bare legs, tread out primitive straw and mud adobe. And all over the desolate Peruvian Altiplano young shepherds with profiles that look like something carved out of mahogany play the same three notes on their melancholy flutes. Indians and Spaniards have sometimes interbred but have not yet managed to form one people, let alone one nation. Spanish civilization has been superimposed on that of the Incas, but there have been few interchanges between the two. Peru is

European but it is Indian too: one may look upon it as a modern state, with police, with industry, with some 4 million inhabitants; or one may see it as a primitive, unknown, under-developed, magnificent but desperately poor land of 8 million Indians. Both pictures are completely true – and there is no connection between them. The Europeans, whether more or less white, or more or less mixed in blood, live along the coast, from which they have hardly moved inland at all. The Indians have remained perched on their inaccessible mountain terraces. For years the colonial aristocracy of Lima considered journeys to the interior of the country dangerous, and in any case, quite pointless. Even today Peruvian students, though nationalistic and fighting hard to conquer illiteracy, feel themselves to have more in common with the foreign visitors they meet in Cuzco hotels than with those disturbing and inscrutable Indians who watch unsmiling as the tiny train runs along its way from Cuzco to Machu-Picchu. What the Mexicans have begun to do, and partially succeeded in doing, the Peruvians are only just beginning, on a modest scale and with the greatest circumspection. On the hills around the Cuzco valley, however, the order to integrate the mass of Indians into the national life has been issued. Opposite one of those fierce escarpments which dominate what used to be the Incas' centre of the world, Peruvian soldiers have put up the vast slogan: *Viva el Peru*. It is a battle cry, a declaration of faith, perhaps a demand – in any case the beginnings of a faint hope. But much has yet to be done. Even more than in Mexico or Ecuador, the Indian masses are the vast majority of the population. Though at present an inert body, if they were to come alive tomorrow, they could be an overwhelming force.

*

Wedded to the customs of their ancestors, fierce, taciturn, partially stupefied by the combined effects of *soroche* and coca, these millions of people provide an indispensable labour force for both farms and towns. They are the only people who can bear working in the mines, more than 5,000 metres above sea level. Whereas the Mexican Indian, though possibly still illiterate and extremely poor, does form part of the Mexican nation and receive a certain consideration from the government, the Indian of the Andean highlands remains resolutely apart from the world of Lima – a world he does not understand, does not know and does not want to know. Today it takes less than two hours to go from Lima to Cuzco by air, but the Quechuas of the Ayacucho, Cuzco or Apurimac provinces, farming their poor fields of onions, barley or maize, living in the enclosed circle of their subsistence economy, have neither the means nor the wish to come down towards the coast. If they do, it is only because they are forced by hunger, and they come like thin, brown wolves, wearing their boleros and knee-length trousers, to swell the human flotsam of the shanty-towns of Lima – that lush, refined, pleasure-loving city. For the ownership of the land has not changed for four hundred years either. Under the rule of Manuel Prado, elected President of the Republic in June 1956, the peasants of the highlands won the right to form into unions; given the economic and social climate then prevailing, this amounted to a minor revolution. But the actual organization of land ownership was not affected. The Indian communities still know which fields belonged to them in the fifteenth century before the Spaniards came. If the status of the Indian peasants (almost a tautology, that phrase, in Peru) is ever to improve, there must be a settlement of accounts. One of the first things the Spaniards did, in effect, was to declare an *encomienda*: the conquered country must pay tribute to its conquerors. The Spanish crown gave Pizarro's officers the right to levy taxes, to crush and exploit the Indian masses, and to seize their land. The ownership of land naturally developed into the formation of huge estates, and with them came serfdom.

To cultivate their thousands of hectares the large landowners called on the local working people; and when *haciendas* were sold the Indians working on them were sold with them. It is reckoned that at least half the Indian population of the high plateaux had vanished by 1580 – no more than fifty years after Pizarro's landing at Tumbes. Hunger, exhaustion, illness – mainly smallpox and measles brought over from Europe – had combined to achieve this. The appearance of a new *mestizo* class made no real difference to this desperate picture where the contrast between two civilizations, two ways of life, was probably more marked than anywhere in the world. Nowadays those of purely white blood are reckoned to be 10 per cent of the total population, and those of mixed blood about 30 per cent; along the coast there has been immigration from Japan, amounting to 1 per cent, and there are also a few Negroes. Undoubtedly the mestizos are the most active group in Peru: artisans, shopkeepers, occasionally manual workers, these intelligent people have, for the past fifty years, been in the forefront of every movement that has tried to shake the dust off the old trappings of the Peruvian aristocracy. All one can say is that all their efforts, though often well-intentioned, (but not always well-managed) have not yet succeeded in overthrowing what is still basically a colonial society.

*

From June to October Lima is permanently covered with a thick ceiling of grey cloud. Out to sea, both north and south of the city, the sky is usually bright and clear. To the east the sparkling peaks of the Andes rise out of a carpet of cotton wool into which aeroplanes must descend in order to find the runway of the largest and one of the most modern airports in the whole of South America. The fine rain which comes from both sky and sea is called by the Peruvians *garúa*: it brings with it a humidity to both crops and pasturelands in the valley of Lima. But it also gives a certain air of sadness to this former city of kings. Pizarro loved Lima; he could not establish his capital in a place as far from the sea as Cuzco so he chose the vast terraces along the bank of the river Rimac, with fifteen kilometres of limestone cliffs running precipitously down to the ocean. On 18 January 1535, the day Lima was founded, Pizarro laid the foundation stone of the cathedral, and also of the vice-regal palace. He ornamented his town, lovingly watching as squares and churches were built. His mummy is still in the cathedral there; the pathetic skeleton of the most cruel and merciless conquistador of the sixteenth century, assassinated at sixty-six, rests in a glass coffin, and all around his monument the steeples of all the other churches built by this bloodthirsty fighter who was also such a fanatical Catholic are still standing: San Francisco, Santo Domingo, the Merced with its monastic silence, the cloisters of San Pedro. Some were destroyed in the 1940 earthquake, but they have been rebuilt.

Until independence came to the South American republics, Lima was the real capital of all Spain's colonies in South America. It has the oldest university, San Marcos, and the Torre Tagle palace which now houses the Ministry of Foreign Affairs is a jewel of colonial architecture. The place has the air of a timeless paradise: a murmuring fountain barely disturbs the silence of the Sevillian patio; the magnificent wooden lion's head, where the scales used to hang for weighing gold and silver, now welcomes the diplomats who have their offices behind its bronze-studded doors. The splendid home of the Marquis Torre Tagle has found a worthy use as has the home of the Perichole (the *perra chola*, literally mongrel bitch, was the nickname of a favourite of the viceroy's). But the centre of Lima is a maze of streets and passages, of narrow arches, old houses with barred windows, Arab-style balconies from which elegant society women can see without being seen, and huge studded doors.

Near the coast and at the feet of the Andes, set between the sea and the mountains, Lima is the natural clearing-house for all the products of the country, both the fertile areas on the coast and the mining centres of the interior; and, though only 12 degrees below the Equator, it is cooled by the famous Humboldt current. This coolness makes it possible for tropical flowers and plants to grow well and abundantly. With 1,800,000 people Lima is the sixth largest town in Latin America, and its port, Callao, is the finest harbour on the Peruvian coast. Enormous work has been done to increase its capacity and now 75 per cent of all Peruvian imports come via Callao. A new industry has also been developed there – the manufacture of fishmeal.

Rio has its *favelas*, Caracas its *ranchitos*, and Bogotá its *barrios*. The shanty-towns of Lima are called *barriadas*, and they are clustered against the side of San Cristóbal hill, right next to the elegant, sweet-scented residential districts of San Isidro and Miraflores. Up above the skyscrapers of the city centre, the towers, squares and palaces hidden in the mist, the hovels of the *barriadas* rot in the accumulated filth of years. Bands of ragged and scurvy children run, barefoot and laughing in the airless alleys. 400,000 human beings are huddled together in these *barriadas* – either mestizos or Indian families who have come from the far-off sierra with their children and little bundles of possessions. With no means of livelihood, no friends, no skill or trade, they live by doing odd jobs or begging, and it is they who form the major part of the Peruvian sub-proletariat. It is no longer possible to ignore this festering abscess which is gradually growing amid the magnificence of Lima. Since 1960 steps have been taken to help these unfortunates, but it is evident that only the most powerful measures can possibly achieve anything in the battle against infant mortality (70 per cent of these children die before the age of two) and illiteracy.

*

A crash programme has been undertaken: this natural centre for revolutionary ferment can only be controlled by immense and speedy reforms. It is perfectly clear that the Peruvian government has the capacity for doing this, and that Peru could be one of the most stable and well-balanced of all South American countries. There are none of the basic problems of survival here: the country is enormous and only half inhabited. There are vast stretches of land still waiting to be conquered, cultivated or made use of. The abundance and variety of its mineral wealth still make Peru that Eldorado of which the Castillian noblemen dreamed in the twelfth and thirteenth centuries. Its economy has the good fortune to be one of the healthiest in all Latin America, not suffering from the scourge of being a single-product or single-export economy. On the contrary, five or six products cheerfully compete to keep the volume of exports evenly spread. Peru is a mining country and also an agricultural one: it sells lead, copper, oil, silver, zinc – and also cotton and sugar. It does not depend on its neighbours and is far less aware of American pressure than they, even though 60 per cent of its imports (machinery, vehicles, manufactured objects and cereals) come from the U.S. The only genuine problem in Peru today is the redistribution of the national income. As long as only 2 per cent of the 12 million people in the country exercise almost total control over the nation's wealth, anything could happen.

As in the far-off days of the conquest, the real obstacle is still the difficulty of speedy and certain communication among the three natural divisions of the country: the coastal area, the *sierra*, and the *montaña* (including the eastern side of the Andes, and the tropical zone). These three centres of population have hardly anything in common. The coastal strip is hardly ever more than 150 kilometres wide, but it goes down the coast for 2,600 kilometres; it represents only 7 per cent of the total area of the country, and on these golden sands which give Peru something of the air of an African beach it almost never rains: at three- or four-yearly intervals only. But irrigation, which was well advanced even before the Spaniards came, makes it possible to cultivate this land intensively and wisely. Towns, so many oases rising up in the aridity of the plain, succeed one another from the swampy borders of Ecuador to the edges of Chile. Remains have been found of several irrigation systems in areas outside those oases, drawn from the streams flowing down from the Andes; one can therefore easily conceive of new parts of this narrow strip, where 27 per cent of the population live, being fairly easily turned into cultivable land. Vast numbers of islands, incredibly rich in guano, are dotted along this coast, whose cold waters are alive with a great variety of fish; on those empty islands thousands of birds have made their homes, and each year their excrement provides almost 300,000 tons of guano which can be used as fertilizer in the irrigated land. There is tragedy whenever a stream of warm air from the Equator unexpectedly sweeps along the shore: the fish suddenly leave water in which they can no longer live, and birds die by the hundred. Torrential rains sometimes flood the irrigation canals, and then the huts of the fishermen and guano workers in the villages collapse. In such apocalyptic disasters, people flee along ruined roads, chased by hordes of vast insects which have appeared from nowhere.

*

The three great northern oases, between Tumbes and the río Santa, produce an abundance of rice, sugar cane and cotton, and a certain amount of cereals. Their names sound like Indian war cries: Piura, Chiclayo, Trujillo. Piura and Chiclayo between them provide 75 per cent of the country's total rice production, and Trujillo 56 per cent of its sugar. But – a symbol of Peru's economic balance – this northern region is also industrial, with petroleum around Talara and steelworks at the mouth of the río Santa. Talara looks like one of the

Chilean nitrate settlements: built for oil, living by oil, its bungalows, its derricks, its little houses and its tiny lawns are all laid out beside an empty ocean, under a deadly blue sky. Chimbote, at the mouth of the Santa, is more like Colombia's Paz del Río: the steelworks, established in 1956, two years after the one in Paz del Río, but with the same help from French firms, uses the iron ore from the deposits at Ica, 400 kilometres south of Lima. It gets its power from barrages in the Santa valley – built despite the incredible difficulties created by constant landslides. On 20 October 1950 what is known in Peru as an *aluvión*, which is a kind of avalanche of mixed mud, stones and snow, came down from the Andean wall above, and swept over the main structure of the hydro-electric plant: within seconds five million cubic metres of rushing water, with waves 30 metres high, swept away the camp and the supports of the bridge. So violent was the torrent that one of those supports, 1,500 tons of concrete, was found 25 kilometres downstream in the middle of the river Santa. 500 people were killed, and it was thought that the Huallanca plant could never be rebuilt. However, the work was undertaken again in 1954. Fresh from the triumph of their successful work in Colombia, some French engineers got the order offered by the *Corporación peruana del Santa* and things went ahead very quickly. The railway from Chimbote up the gorges of the Santa to Huallanca carried all the necessary materials and equipment. The electric pylons which today carry current from Huallanca to the Chimbote steel works are the highest in the world: they cross a line of peaks of up to 4,600 metres, and the cables are 90 kilometres long all told. The Indian villages in this difficult country between the Andes and the coast are continually threatened by *aluviones*. Huaráz, for instance, was ravaged in 1951 by one of those fearful landslides which killed 5,000 and carried off a newly-opened hotel as though it were a wisp of straw. On 10 January 1962 another *aluvión* came down the sides of

Mount Huascaran and poured into the valley: by the time the rescuers reached the edge of this river of mud, 200 metres wide, 4,000 people had died. Those who inhabit these high valleys live in continual awareness of this permanent threat of death. Yet it is in Huaráz that the Indian women wear the most carefully chosen and graceful clothes: this land of women in mourning is also a land of layers of skirts in bright and varied colours.

In the southern coastal district, beyond Lima, Chincha Alta and Pisco, the country becomes even drier. In the oases there are vineyards and orchards, rather than the vast cotton and sugar fields of the north. Arequipa, the second city of Peru, lies on a warm plain at the base of the almost perfectly cone-shaped volcano Misti, which is 5,851 metres high. A railway from the port of Mollendo serves Arequipa and then goes up across the Andes and the *puna brava* as far as Juliaca by Lake Titicaca. The white city of Arequipa, 75 kilometres from the Pacific, stands in the desert, amid its *campiña*, like Damascus in the centre of the eastern *ghutta*. This *campiña* is an island of prosperity in a sea of grey earth and petrified lava. Harvests of wheat, maize and onions are gathered several times a year, and its fruit rivals the best from Chile. 'Arequipa', its townsfolk say, 'is a donkey wallowing in a field of lucerne'. Legend tells us that this most turbulent city in Peru was founded by the Incas. In Aymará, the word Arequipa means 'behind the peaks', but in Quechua it means 'Yes, stay here': it is hard to choose between them! But what is quite certain is that the people of Arequipa, dynamic, excitable, obstinate, have a volcanic temperament. For a century this city has beaten all records for revolution and uprising, and mutinies in the Arequipa garrison have been the signal for most of the *pronunciamientos* of recent years. Where Lima is colonial, languid, warm and wealthy, Arequipa is combative, aggressive and violent. As the crow flies, there are 1,063 kilometres between the two towns, and that might appear quite enough;

but it is not, for Arequipa represents precisely the two active elements in Peruvian society – the mestizos and the military.

*

The Peruvian Altiplano is a kind of twin to the Bolivian, of which it is really the continuation. This desolate steppe-land is framed by some ten or so frozen peaks, all around the 6,000 metre level, among them the Nevado de Pisco, the Nevado Alpamayo and the Huascaran, the highest point in Peru. Copper is mined there, around the Cerro de Pasco, vanadium at Mina Ragra (a quarter of the world's total production), lead, zinc and other ores – either of less value or in small amounts. Peru's mining production is thus far more diversified than Bolivia's – not from any geological difference, but because of a more advanced and intelligent system of exploitation. The Cerro de Pasco, at 4,000 metres and with 30,000 inhabitants, is the oldest mining centre; silver was found there in 1630 and up until 1680 Peru was the world's largest source of silver. Over the centuries foundries were established alongside the mines, and bars of silver were sent across the Andes in convoys which had to be defended against attacks from highwaymen. The laying of the central railway line linking Lima with Cerro de Pasco by way of the río Rimac, which began at the start of this century, opened new vistas for this area where they had now found veins of copper, lead and gold. The Cerro de Pasco line was opened in 1907 and still causes technicians to marvel, with its 68 tunnels, 55 bridges and 22 hairpin bends to enable it to get up to a height of 4,780 metres and then down to Oroya at 3,700. There is a branch line from Oroya to Cerro de Pasco. Further south the Huancayo valley produces 40 per cent of Peru's wheat; the land, belonging to whites or mestizos, is worked by Indians. But the closeness of the mining areas and the relatively easy communications with the capital and the coast have combined to make marketing easier – which is not the case from Huancayo and Cuzco, between which the road descends below 2,000 metres four times and rises four times to 4,800. In these isolated valleys each little community lives totally closed in on itself and has no dealings of any kind with its neighbours.

The Peruvian *montaña* is actually the most tropical area of all. It is vast, 60 per cent of the entire country, yet with only 13 per cent of its total population. North of the *montaña* the huge forest is divided by tributaries of the Amazon, and to the south there is an infinity of rivers never yet navigated, flowing into the Madre de Dios, that largest of all the huge river's tributaries. Rivers are the natural means of communication in the *montaña* since the extreme density of the jungle makes it virtually impenetrable by other means. The trade in rare woods (fifty-eight different species, so far, from iron wood to balsa wood) is barely beginning: loads of hewn tree-trunks go down the river to the saw-mills of Tingo María and Pucallpa, to be exported by way of Iquitos on the upper Amazon – a town of 50,000 people and major market for medicinal plants and rubber. Near Pucallpa one firm has set about developing 400,000 hectares of very good land, where the rainfall is high. Iquitos, founded in 1863, has had a history not dissimilar from that of Manaus in Brazil: the rubber boom gave it an importance quite disproportionate to its size and position; it was then for a long time the most isolated town in the continent but it became important once again when promoted to the position of a main stopping place on the long road from the Pacific to the Atlantic. In 1940 it still took a good month to get from Lima to Iquitos; in 1943 a road was opened through Oroya and Huanaco to Pucallpa, but the last part of the trip to Iquitos still had to be made by boat. The journey time has today been considerably shortened by the advent of hydroplanes and it now takes only three hours to get from Lima to Iquitos. Fairly soon now the area south of the Peruvian *montaña* will no longer be the land in the 'centre of the world'. A road now under construction through the forest will link Cuzco with Puerto Maldonado, the last Peruvian outpost on the Madre de Dios before you enter Brazil. When that is complete there will be no part of this huge country (more than twice the size of France) left in awe-inspiring emptiness.

*

The conquest of Peru began from the coast and moved inland. But after the adventures of the early years settlers tended to stick to the shoreline, daunted by the hostile barrier of the Andes. Since the Spanish regime had virtually worked out all the gold mines the young republic lived at first by marketing the valuable fertilizer from the guano islands – though its possession of them was disputed by Spain from 1863 to 1879, and by Great Britain and the United States even up to the middle of the last century. With the reserves of guano falling came the discovery of the great fertilizing value of the nitrates in Atacama province: however in 1883 these were almost totally taken over by Chile. Peru then began to irrigate the narrow but fertile land of the valleys, cultivating sugar cane in the north and cotton and wheat elsewhere – but never abandoning the national cereal, maize, which gave Peruvians their food and also their drink, *chicha*. To their diminishing gold and still abundant silver were added other metal ores, and then soon came oil.

In fact Peru today has many new possibilities open to it, in the depths of the Amazonian forest whose true wealth is still, as in Brazil, relatively undiscovered. One of the absolutely vital needs of the Peruvian economy is to exploit more of its unused land; the two others are to modernize its mining methods and to develop its steel industry. The volume of imports has expanded considerably in proportion to that of exports, in recent years, which means an increasing imbalance in the economy and a chronic balance-of-payments deficit in foreign trade. Yet alongside this weakness Peru has a number of advantages: the *per capita* income has continued to increase, though obviously one must remember that statistics about living standards apply primarily to that minority (whites and mestizos) who take an active part in the life of the country.

But it is clear in any case that Peru has already got beyond the classic stage of the under-developed Latin American country – that of exporting all its raw materials and importing all its manufactured products. Unlike Chile or Bolivia, its tragedy is not an economic, but a human one.

*

One wonders in fact how much longer Peru can continue to progress while its 5½ million people along the coastal strip live in the twentieth century and its 6 or 7 million Indians in the *sierra* remain in the sixteenth. It is a question of interest not only to Peru, but to all Latin America: more than any other Andean country, Peru is a test case.

It would seem that the conservatives who put the army in power in 1948 and were still in control of Peruvian politics from 1956 to 1962, despite tactical support from the large popular party, the APRA, are not particularly concerned with the problem. The '40 families' who own most of the *haciendas* along the coast and the industrial establishments in the capital do not seem to feel any immediate threat. However, the increasing unrest produced by the appearance of Castroist movements and communist agitation are beginning to modify their determinedly optimistic outlook.

Communism had a certain initial success in Peru, enrolling supporters from quarters as varied as workers, peasants, the middle class, the military and intellectuals. The reason for this is simple. The deliberately laid stress on the struggle against imperialism (and for imperialism read 'American imperialism') favoured – and often actually achieved – the adoption of the popular front tactics laid down by Moscow in 1935. What is perhaps most surprising is the success communism had in sections of the armed forces, but in fact it is not hard to explain. High-ranking officers normally come from the upper class (which also stood to gain most by the achievement of national independence) and the wealthy sections of society. Other officers generally come from a middle class which has been increasing in political importance over the past forty years. This latter class – the industrial bourgeoisie, businessmen, technologists, professional people – is precisely the one most humiliated by seeing foreign capital and technology (and 'foreign' nine times out of ten means American) controlling the country's economy. However, the fact that this rising bourgeoisie has managed to gain new social and economic status is due to the industrialization largely made possible by that same foreign capital. Another of its essential characteristics is that it is composed for the most part of mestizos, who are specially sensitive to the idea of national independence; and up to now their resentment has outweighed what would be objectively to their advantage.

Though more and more Peruvian students are going to the United States for their higher studies, the University of Lima is a focus of anti-American feeling almost as virulent as those of Caracas, Mexico City or Santiago, in all of which there has traditionally been a strong attraction to Marxism.

But the Communist Party as such has never been very powerful in Peru – at least in any absolute sense, for relatively it has always been more important here than in other South American countries. After the Second World War – perhaps the moment of communism's finest chance – the party had 35,000 card-carrying members and the votes of all its supporters brought the number up to 100,000; whereas in Argentina, though twice the size of Peru, the number was barely any larger. Proportionately there were even fewer in Venezuela or Colombia. The problems peculiar to the Peruvian CP were primarily the lack of effective cadres, and the existence of incredibly poor – and therefore apathetic – masses living under the close control of landowners and clergy. It is still common for large landowners to 'bring' their labourers to the polls on election day. Consequently Peruvian communism has made its chief impact more by its, at times indirect, influence on nationalist and anti-imperialist (i.e. anti-Yankee) movements. The alliance between communism and nationalism has already produced some surprising results in Latin America. The leaders of the Komintern, and later the Kominform, have understood this. The Peruvian, Eudosio Ravines, a former secretary general of the communist party in Peru (who broke with the party in 1948) was in Moscow together with the Brazilian Luis Carlos Prestes for political talks with Manilski and Dimitrov, and in his book *The Road to Yenan* clearly explained the soviet justification for the tactic of collaborating with 'bourgeois nationalist movements struggling against imperialism'. It was important to 'carry on that struggle', even if it *was* being waged by 'anti-socialist' elements as well.

From 1948 to 1958 the Peruvian communist party was therefore forced into this tactic of 'critical support', but with the eruption of Castroism they had to reconsider their policy. For the movements inspired by Castro's example, in Peru as well as in Colombia, Venezuela, Brazil or Central America, were far more concerned with getting results – with improving the situation as quickly as possible. Such a reassessment was all the more necessary in that for far too long, whether from ignorance or incompetence, the Peruvian communists had neglected the problem of the Indians.

Mariátegui and Haya de la Torre were the first people in Peru to see that problem clearly. They were attracted at first, like so many other Latin American intellectuals, by Marxism. Mariátegui, a journalist and poet who worked in a printers' firm, tried to find solutions which would apply perfectly to local problems. 'It is not enough,' he declared, 'to claim that Indians have a right to education, culture, progress, love, and heaven; we must begin by categorically claiming their right to the land.' Mariátegui's agrarian theory was rejected by the communist conference in Montevideo in 1929 on the grounds that it made 'the future of Latin America depend on what happened to assist integration' (and this was described as Trotskyist). Shortly afterwards, Mariátegui died, a broken man, at the age of thirty-nine.

*

Haya de la Torre spent at least half his life either in exile or in prison. Even his party, the APRA (American Popular Revolutionary Alliance), was founded outside the country, in Mexico. 'Aprism' is an odd doctrine: it combines anti-American nationalism, a certain Marxist influence, involvement with the Indian past, definite elements of fascism, and even an application to history of Einstein's theory of relativity. APRA was and still is the most powerful political party in Peru though it did not become so without great struggles, for opposition from the armed forces for many years forced the Aprists to work in secret. The major role played by the armed forces in Peru began from the earliest days of independence; the fight to win that independence was harder in Lima than anywhere since it was the capital city of Spain's empire. Independence dislocated the old system of the viceroys and Peru, having been the lynch pin of that system, had, for over a century, extremely difficult relations with its former provinces as they gradually became independent. There were indeed a few tentative approaches towards some kind of limited unification, such as the Bolivia–Peru confederation of 1836, fiercely combated by Chile. More commonly there were wars over the ownership of areas of either strategic importance or mineral wealth, such as the war between Peru and Chile in 1881 for control of the Atacama desert. Lima had another major dispute with Brazil and Bolivia over the territory of Acre. This long series of battles, often settled to Peru's disadvantage, largely explains the permanent and disproportionate part played by the military in the life of the country. From the foundation of the republic until 1870 there was a series of authoritarian regimes imposed by the army, but it must be noted that they were not all reactionary. Marshal Castillo, twice president of the republic, in 1845 and in 1856, for instance, decreed the abolition of slavery. He fostered immigration by groups of Europeans, chiefly German and Irish, and it was during his presidency that the railway was laid from Lima to the port of Callao. In 1870 civilians at last managed to achieve a foothold on the political scene, as a result of support from the navy who were jealous of the privileged position of the army. Then came Leguía.

Leguía, a brilliant financier, ruled with a firm hand. Elected for the first time in 1908, he retired in the normal way in 1912, but came back in 1919 as the result of a *coup d'état* he had himself inspired. His first term had been relatively liberal. The second, having begun without any legal basis, continued as an exercise of personal power. Until 1930 he dealt with all opposition and subjected the press to strict censorship. Yet it was during his presidency that the first Peruvian dared to break the silence which the great property-owning families had enforced for four centuries. This was González Prada: though he had no money himself he belonged by birth to the conservative landowning oligarchy which had accepted dictatorship since 1821 for fear of being forced to face the facts. He founded people's universities for workers and peasants. A poet, a writer and an orator, he was a pure product of late nineteenth-century Peru: a radical and an anti-clerical. He was the foreshadowing of the reality of the vast reforming movement of the APRA. For Haya de la Torre, who founded it, also belonged to one of the oldest aristocratic families of Peru – not the least curious thing about him. He was a man no one could ignore for he was a kind of natural force, with his vast torso and huge hands, his quivering nose, dark face, and violent gestures. 'Imperialism,' he said, 'is the last stage of capitalism for industrial peoples, but for our people it represents the first stage. Our capitalism is born of the arrival of modern imperialism.' González Prada was a fine orator; Haya de la Torre was an angry pleader who raised the temperature in Lima by several degrees the moment he appeared at a meeting. Imprisoned in San Lorenzo by Leguía, Haya went on hunger strike. He looked like dying, when the government decided to deport him, and he had barely arrived in Mexico, at death's door, when he organized a student meeting and announced the creation of the APRA to defend 'the common ideals of all of America': the fight against dollar diplomacy and imperialists of all kinds, the nationalization of land and industry, the americanization of the Panama canal, solidarity with the exploited classes. From Mexico, Haya made a tour of the United States, Russia, Germany, Switzerland, England and France. He spent two years in Oxford. His movements were watched with close attention by students and working people in Peru. At first the APRA gave the impression of being a radical party of the left whose revolutionary programme was based on an impassioned defence of freedom and justice. 'Not Rome, nor Berlin, nor even Moscow – only Aprism can save Peru!'

*

Haya's first exile lasted for eight years, after which he returned to Lima. In 1930 Leguía had been overthrown by a *coup d'état* – the signal for which had, as usual, been given by the Arequipa garrison. General Sánchez Cerro established himself as president, had Leguía put in prison, and declared: 'I would like to see bayonets red with the blood of Aprists.' Haya, a candidate for the presidency, was imprisoned for the second time, but received a respite when Sánchez Cerro was murdered, and Marshal Benavides took his place. His party, however, was condemned as 'an international sect' and outlawed. In 1939 the election of Manuel Prado, a member of one of the '40 families', did nothing to alter the precarious situation of the APRA, whose leaders, like Haya, had to go on living in hiding at home or in exile abroad. But the aura of legend surrounding the powerful and agonized face of Haya also contributed to consolidating the popularity of his party, and the movement was so strong in 1945 that, though unable to offer its own candidate, it succeeded in getting Bustamante elected president. Bustamante, a clever lawyer but an undistinguished politician, had promised that, if elected, he would govern with the support of the APRA, which had just been authorized to present itself legally as a recognized party; and from then on the APRA formed the most homogeneous group in the Lima parliament.

After the additional elections of 1946 it held 21 out of 50 seats in the senate and 65 out of 147 in the chamber of deputies. Though disturbed by this meteoric progress, Bustamante nevertheless hesitated yet again over declaring Haya de la Torre's movement illegal, despite insistent demands to do so from General Odría, his Minister of the Interior. The first steps towards socialization recommended by the Aprists (there were three APRA ministers in the government) aroused violent hostility from the conservatives, especially those relating to price and currency controls. The daily, *La Prensa*, representing the big cotton interests, launched a campaign against the Aprist ministers, and Bustamante publicly disavowed Haya de la Torre. There then followed several bloody incidents; the director of *La Prensa* was assassinated and Bustamante appealed to Odría, who was also the Army chief of staff, to 're-establish order'. The APRA decided to make it an all-out battle but its attempt at a *coup d'état*, planned with the help of the navy, was crushed at Callao. And on 28 October 1948 the Arequipa garrison mutinied. The putsch had Odría's blessing and he himself took the leadership of a provisional junta and was constitutionally elected president two years later. The APRA was banned and its leader sought asylum in the Colombian embassy; it was a curious move, and marked the beginning of a long juridicial dispute between Colombia and the Odría government, which declared Haya de la Torre 'unworthy to be a Peruvian'. The right of asylum is a sacred one in Latin America – but it is an unwritten rather than a written law. Faced with the opposing demands of Peru and Colombia the international court in the Hague had to admit itself baffled. And Haya, that dynamic, violent, excitable man who could hardly keep still for a minute, was obliged to cool his heels in the Colombian embassy until the spring of 1954.

At last he was given a safe-conduct which allowed him to leave Lima and once again go into exile abroad. He had spent his time reading, studying, writing and thinking, he had put on weight; he was hardly the same man as the Haya who had eluded Odría's police five years before. He, the champion of anti-Americanism, chose the 'third way' of the Colombian, Santos, the Venezuelan, Betancourt, and the Costa Rican, Figueres: in other words the way of determining to trust the liberals, the trade unions, and the Democratic Party of America. In fact Haya was remaining true to himself, for from the beginning of his career he had been more of an 'anti-communist' than an 'anti-imperialist'. He was an idealist who had once organized a 'tree crusade' in the *sierra*:

You who pass by, who have raised your arm to cut me down, look at me carefully before you do. I make your house warm in winter, and give you shade against the sun in summer. My fruit feeds you and quenches your thirst. I provide the foundations for your house, the legs for your table, the bed you sleep in, your cradle and your coffin. I am the handle of your spade and your plane, the yoke for your oxen, the grille for your irrigation canals, the door of your hut. I am the substance, the goodness and the flower of beauty. I am the landscape. I am the material from which your forefathers made their aqueducts. If you love me as you should, then save me from those who do not know all this...

This treatise composed by Haya the poet for the illiterate Indian peasants had no effect upon them at all. On another occasion Haya decided to go with his supporters to visit the poorest areas of Lima, handing out toys, sweets and cakes on behalf of the Aprist movement. It is clear from his 'tree crusade' and such charitable journeys that Haya was not the dogmatic and opinionated revolutionary he appeared to be in 1930, but a reformer with a dream.

*

Later events proved that this second image of Haya de la Torre was in fact the true one: he proclaimed himself *Jefe Máximo* of the APRA. His anti-communism fed on his memories of October 1948 when the Peruvian CP gave its support to Odría's *pronunciamiento* – probably because it could not forgive the APRA for having, in 1935, refused the offer to unite in a *Frente popular*. The lasting bitterness between Aprists and communists which began during those difficult days of 1948, still persists, and helps to explain Haya's change of attitude from 1954 onwards. On arrival in Mexico the 'most famous political refugee in Latin America' got in touch with the leaders of the ORIT (the Inter-American Regional Organization), a body related to the American trade unions. In the past Haya had thought that the solidarity of the American proletariat was not to be depended on 'because in the United States the golden age of capitalism makes most workers able to achieve a certain degree of comfort'. 'That comfort,' he added in 1945, 'would not exist without the labour of those who are slaves to north American imperialism all over the world, and the constantly increasing investment of yankee money abroad, especially in Latin America. Given the American workers' almost total ignorance of living conditions for the workers in the other half of the new world, it is thus difficult to hope for any genuine solidarity ...'

In 1954, however, Haya went back on what he had said

then, and accepted the viewpoint of the leaders of the Democratic Party then in power (like Figueres in Costa Rica) or recently overthrown by military coups (like Betancourt in Venezuela): 'American policy, which consists in supporting military dictatorships in Latin America, themselves supported by the communists, or at least playing their long-term game, is absurd. It is far better to trust in the liberal forces and the workers of America ...' Such a thesis obviously precludes any exaggerated stress on the 'misdeeds of American imperialism'. It led to a certain ill-feeling between the Aprist leaders exiled between 1948 and 1955 (such as Haya in Mexico and Seoane in Chile), and the still instinctively anti-*gringo* masses, who could not really see much to choose between American capitalists and trade unionists. Haya de la Torre, under surveillance by the police, imprisoned in the Colombian embassy in Lima, had a certain aura of martyrdom. But Haya set free, the protégé of the yankee trade unions, became less popular.

*

There can be little doubt, however, that the success of Aprism in Peru and other Andean countries was largely due to its concern with improving the lot of the mass of the Indians. Despite its excesses and its failures it probably even contributed to getting Peruvians to understand something of the social realities of the country. This is especially true of the middle class. Haya de la Torre had had victory within his grasp in 1945; in planning his campaign for the elections of July 1956 he took account of the mistakes made from 1946 to 1948. The allotted term of Odría, 'the soldier from Arequipa', was coming to its end, and it seemed logical to everyone in Peru to hope for a return to civilian government. As is usual before general elections there was a lot of behind-the-scenes manoeuvring well before voting day. The belief of Odría's own supporters could be summed up roughly as:

'Peru is not yet ready for party rule', and in that light the Arequipa putsch which had brought Odría to power on 28 October 1948 appeared simply as a move in the public interest. The conservatives as a whole had supported the *coup* since it seemed to prevent what they saw as the greatest of all dangers, the coming to power of the APRA, but they had not abandoned all hope of having a civilian president, a man of good social standing who would foster economic liberalism and American capital investment in mining and oil. They seemed to forget that, unless it got active support from the army, such a policy could not be achieved. Odría, who had defeated the 'demagogues' in 1948, had since 1949 criticized 'the selfishness of the conservatives and the rich bourgeoisie'. But Odría was not another Perón. He favoured foreign investment and in 1950 his government established an effective system of free exchange. The object of this was as far as possible to prevent rich Peruvian exporters from amassing reserves of dollars for themselves in foreign banks. From 1950 to 1956 Odría's economic policy was successful – they were prosperous years, though of course their prosperity only affected two Peruvians in ten; however, all that mattered to the wealthy business class was the maintenance of order, and to everything else they closed their eyes. A year before his term ended Odría was hesitating between three possible courses: to abandon power and save his strength for the future; to try to find a successor who would carry on his policies; or to get himself re-elected by proving that ordinary elections were not possible. The determined hostility of a large section of the conservative group prevented his adopting the third of these.

The Odría group finally chose as its candidate a businessman, the legal adviser to some large foreign companies: Don Hernando de Lavalle. He was a most reassuring choice, being sufficiently independent to stand some chance of getting in, yet flexible enough to consider the interests of the great families if he did so. The second man to stand for the presidency was Manuel Prado, who had been president from 1939 to 1945. Prado, a man of culture and letters, a subtle politician, with firm friendships in the business world, and also a certain popular success because of his well-known ability to get on with everybody, thus appeared as the 'civilian' candidate, as opposed to Lavalle, the 'military' one.

*

The last-minute entry into the lists of a third man rather complicated the machinations of both politicians and military: this was Fernando Belaúnde Terry, an architect who, though like the others a member of one of the great families, was more seriously concerned with the real problems of the country. Belaúnde came from Arequipa; one of his uncles was ambassador to the United Nations, and his father was President of the Council. Himself a deputy from 1945 to 1948, Belaúnde had carefully stayed out of politics during Odría's military regime. He was a bourgeois liberal and he began an American-style electoral campaign by touring the country from north to south and east to west. Fifteen days before the election the result was totally unpredictable and the three candidates seemed to be running neck and neck. Never had presidential elections appeared so close, and in effect Lavalle, Prado and Belaúnde differed little one from another. Their differences could only be understood in the relatively narrow context of the policies of the great families: their rivalries were family rivalries and, in the last resort, the result of the 1956 elections hung upon the attitude of the APRA. Logically the Aprists should have voted for Belaúnde, the youngest, most dynamic, least compromised, and most sincere of the three. But this was 1956: Haya de la Torre, Seoane and Priale were not the leaders they had been in 1930. They had grown older, and to find in Belaúnde's programme items which they had approved fifteen years earlier disturbed them more than it attracted them. They had approached the 1956 campaign with the wish to reassure people: 'Let us return. Let us put out our papers. We ask no more than that ...' Haya re-affirmed his 'friendship for the United States' and the APRA even promised to support Odría's policy of free exchange. Their sole wish was to be allowed to come home, to patch up their differences and be restored to 'the big democratic family'.

Haya and his friends opted for Prado, who offered them the best pledges of future participation in public life. Since 1948 Manuel Prado, living in exile in Paris, had been in touch with the Aprist leaders. Though a Catholic and a conservative, a large landowner and member of a number of administrative councils, he was ready to sponsor the return of those who had formerly stood for the class struggle and the emancipation of the Indian masses. This meant a lot, for in 1956 the Aprist vote was particularly important since women were voting for the first time – which would mean half a million votes for whichever candidate the APRA approved. Prado thus won easily. But Belaúnde's personal success showed that the Aprist bloc had not simply followed the advice of their leaders like so many sheep, and their failure to do so prefigured the conflicts of interest and splintering that was to take place within the party. In Lima itself most Aprists voted for Belaúnde; indeed in the week before the elections he actually looked like winning, but Prado moved forward and gained 540,000 votes as against Belaúnde's 433,000. Odría's candidate, Lavalle, only got 73,000.

*

The APRA's tactical support for President Prado from 1956 to 1962 certainly ensured the passing of certain social legislation to help the people living in the *barriadas*, and a better organization for the workers' and peasants' trade unions. But the APRA, the only Peruvian party with a really modern structure and organization, became tame: it lost all its passion; it dreamt of merging together all the Andean countries; it became a narrowly nationalist and reformist party whose support came from officials, white-collar workers and the lower echelons of business management. The great revolutionary impetus of the years in prison and exile came bit by bit to be replaced by the prudent muttering of leaders who hoped to keep their painfully won tranquillity; it was no longer a party of permanent revolution. Prado's conservative regime pleased the APRA by increasing the salaries of certain professional jobs and giving social benefits to bank workers; but the great dream of liberating the mass of Indians was virtually abandoned.

It was certainly no easy matter to stir up those self-enclosed communities of Indians. The Aprists followed the communists in discovering that. But so obvious was the need to 'integrate' them that all the candidates in the 1962 elections, including the orthodox Aprists, made that part of their platform. The government between 1956 and 1962 followed a policy of austerity and defence of the country's currency; but for the ten million people who lived without ever seeing a coin the safeguarding of the Peruvian *sol* could have absolutely no meaning at all. The peasants of the sierra, indifferent to the fluctuations of the economy, were equally indifferent to the vicissitudes of politics. The Prado period, though relatively calm, did go through a few storms. *Pronciamientos*, re-shuffles, dismissals, arrests, suspension of constitutional rights: the political life of the country from 1958 to 1962 was punctuated by all these things, just as it always had been in the past.

As might have been expected the Arequipa garrison displayed its traditional displeasure on several occasions, but did not seriously shake the institutions of the country. Belaúnde Terry, who had momentarily caused a quaking in the edifice so patiently built up by the partners of the politico-military club, developed a taste for public controversy. He was arrested in Arequipa in May 1959 but released soon afterwards – a proof that he was at last accepted by his peers, since the road to the presidency always seemed to go via prison! Pedro Beltrán, the powerful editor of *La Prensa*, who had also been arrested by Odría in February 1956 after the mutinies in the Iquitos barracks, was the first to take up his pen after the elections the following June to criticize the Prado government's economic policy. Apparently extremely proud of being the most hated man in Peru, he was a cultivated aristocrat with an American wife; he represented the sugar-growers and oil men, and was endlessly pulling wires behind the scenes from 1956 to 1962 just as he had before 1945. Beltrán had supported Odría against the APRA; having quarrelled with the General for reasons that remain obscure he had nevertheless helped to persuade him of the need to hold free elections. He became resigned to Prado's victory, since in his eyes it represented the lesser of two evils; but he attacked it when it seemed to him that Prado, a man of order and commercial knowledge, was departing from a healthy financial orthodoxy. To the ever sharper criticisms of Beltrán, Prado reacted (to no one's surprise) by saying: 'Prove your own ability then. Take over the government yourself.' Beltrán agreed, but said, prophetically: 'Like missionaries who go out to savage tribes, I must be ready for them to eat me.'

He was not eaten, but he was very nearly lynched. Having taken power in 1959 he was certainly able, by the end of the year, to show a good balance sheet and repay 14 million dollars owed to the IMF. Two years before the programme of Kennedy's Alliance for Progress, Beltrán tried to do what Washington wanted by endeavouring to force a real fiscal reform – the U.S.'s number one demand of almost every South American country. On the other hand the very modest project for agrarian reform was not even discussed in the legislature. The pressure of the landowners was once again too strong and Beltrán, with his links with large business firms and big industrial interests, was ill-placed to fight it. He abandoned the attempt with few regrets. However, his ability to run the government made him one of the most important candidates for the presidential election of June 1962. He resigned in November 1961 to qualify for an attempt to win the presidency.

Before leaving the Palacio Pizarro, in the declared hope of coming back there for a further six years, Beltrán also wanted to turn to the people for support; that in fact was how he began his electoral campaign: he decided to go to Cuzco, where he was met with volleys of stones from a crowd of angry peasants. A delegation of union leaders demanded 'in the name of the people' that he leave Cuzco as soon as possible, and the Workers' Federation of the town called a general strike. It took the intervention of troops and the police to restore order. This was a thoroughly revealing incident, for it showed that the skilful young politicians in Lima, though they stood against the old families and interventions by the military, were of no concern to this mass of peasants whom they wrongly felt to be a homogeneous body. The events of Cuzco may perhaps have pointed to a certain success of Communist and Castroist propaganda among the destitute Indians of the *sierra*; but they also brought sharply to light the glaring contrast between the two halves of the country: the lower altitudes, taken up with European-style parliamentary rivalries, and the highlands where elementary problems of survival supplant all other considerations. In 1962, as in 1956, the basic questions had barely changed: the land was still not being properly cultivated, and at least 72 per cent of Peruvians were suffering from malnutrition.

*

Despite this warning signal preparations for the presidential elections of June 1962 were in no way different from those for June 1956. Two of the same candidates were standing: General Odría and Belaúnde Terry the architect; and there were two others: Haya de la Torre and Beltrán. Yet no one could really describe these as new men: Odría had been president from 1948 until 1956; Belaúnde, the outsider, had been brought in in June 1956; Haya de la Torre had had thirty-five years in the APRA and six of 'peaceful coexistence' with the conservative leaders and the army. One a soldier, one a liberal member of the rich bourgeoisie; one an idealistic reformer. Beltrán's name adds to the list a representative of Peruvian capitalism. It was something of a circle. Odría, a hesitant dictator but a convinced democrat, had undoubtedly moved somewhat to the left; he abused the 'plutocrats', which seemed almost to guarantee him success. He declared himself the candidate of the people and in a sense perhaps this was true. It was equally clear that Belaúnde, on the other hand, had become less progressive and more opportunist than in 1956 and had definitely moved to the right. This was evident in his choice of running mate: Edgar Seoane, the brother of Manuel Seoane, Haya's lieutenant. But Belaúnde, the leader of the 'Popular Action' party, also loudly proclaimed his concern over the situation of the Indian masses. Haya remained still Haya – huge, truculent, arrogant, an ageing prophet convinced that he was still the Peruvian revolution incarnate.

It was obvious, however, that some kind of split had occurred in this movement which was supposed to be a popular and revolutionary alliance. In June 1962 three tendencies of apparently equal importance within the APRA were in distinct conflict: Odría, leader of the Popular Front, Belaúnde, head of Popular Action, and Haya de la Torre, president of the Popular Alliance – which was on the left, which on the right? By a curious paradox 8 million Indians who, being illiterate, had no vote, were once again the turning point of the election: yet who really cared about them, in 1962, in 1956, in 1948, in 1945, or even before? Who will care about them in the future? What after all did it really matter whether the election was won by Odría, Belaúnde, Haya de la Torre or Pedro Beltrán? The answer to that question could not be found in Lima, but up above, on the wild *sierra*, where the endless wind raging on the *puna* carried away the voices of all speakers on its furious breath.

However, once again the army sent all the disputants packing. As in 1956 the results of the presidential elections took a long time to be scrutinized; the candidates would each in turn be in the lead for a time, and no one seemed definitely the winner. But at the end of June a minute scrutiny of the ballot boxes in the northern provinces seemed to give Haya de la Torre a clear advantage; in Arequipa and Lima the army grew restless, for the one man they could not bear to see president was this one, which only went to show how far behind the times the officers were in their analysis of the Peruvian political situation. For it was long since Haya had been that excitable Marxist who raged against American imperialism: 'It is not I who have changed,' he said 'but the imperialists ...' He may perhaps have been giving a pledge of his good will in stepping down in favour of General Odría, but even this astonishing decision did not succeed in preventing the putsch planned by the army. On 18 July they deposed president Prado and held him in a gunboat off Callao. General Ricardo Pérez Godoy, leading spirit of the putsch, declared void the elections of 19 June on the grounds that cheating had taken place. He established a provisional military government and promised another general election in June 1963, thus following the well-known tendency of all Latin American officers to think that any political problem can be solved if enough time is allowed. It was obvious that to annul the election solved nothing whatsoever; it was equally obvious that the vast majority of the Peruvian people still had dangerously little interest in the disputes among their 'princes'. Forty-eight hours after the illegal deposition of President Prado, Lima did not look particularly disturbed, there was only a little hostile shouting by the students of San Marcos University and a symbolic strike by the miners. But what was new and important was the formal condemnation of the putsch by the United States: the Kennedy government had been shocked and appalled in March 1962 to see President Frondizi of Argentina deposed and arrested by the army, but had done nothing. It was not possible for Washington to let a repetition in Lima of the Buenos Aires *coup* pass without comment. For the overthrow of democratic institutions in Peru, following so closely on the fall of Frondizi in Argentina, seemed to herald the approach of yet another blow to the United States in Latin America – the fall of the bastion of Venezuela.

In the June 1963 elections the architect Belaúnde Terry won, with 39 per cent of the votes as against 34 per cent for Haya de la Torre and 26 per cent for Odría. The new president's personality was not slow to make itself felt, both by his supporters and his opponents. He depended on his own party in association with the Christian Democrats, but this was not enough to give him control in a Parliament where the combined opposition of 'Aprists' and 'Odriists' was a major obstacle. The obvious wish of the 'old political men' and the business community to get rid of Belaúnde Terry was held in check only by the certainty that his Vice-President Edgar Seoane, more conscious of social questions than Belaúnde, would be even harder to handle.

An inter-Ministry Commission of 'popular cooperation' began to try in 1963 to catch up on the time lost by earlier governments over the problems of the highlands. Two pilot regions with mainly Indian populations, Cuzco and Puno, were chosen for the first attempts in the work of persuading the wretched masses of the high plateaux towards moderation.

Belaúnde put before Congress a carefully worked-out development plan under the headings: agrarian reform, fiscal reform, educational reform, literacy campaign among the peasants, housing programmes. He was wise enough to propose that the armed forces take part in the national economic development programme. But, paradoxically, this rational and objectively progressive plan was immediately and fiercely opposed by the combined supporters of Haya de la Torre and the former dictator, Odría. It may seem odd that the Aprists of the extreme revolutionary left should have been willing to collaborate with those who represented the old families and the oligarchy just because Belaúnde Terry was the political opponent of both groups. But the APRA of the heroic past had long given way to a bourgeoisified group hamstrung by its own internal contradictions. There were far too many APRA activists for whom the cult of personality had replaced political vision. It was quite true that Belaúnde's programme could be faulted on a number of points and was somewhat over-timid. But no one could seriously claim that had the APRA been in power it could have produced anything better. The basic contradiction of the APRA had not altered: the claim to be inspired by Marxism at home while seeking a compromise with a supposedly liberal U.S. abroad. Haya's party, obsessed by anti-communism, continued in a blissful refusal to recognize the deep contradiction between the interests of the workers of north America and those of the toiling masses of south America. His ideology may have been more rudimentary, but Belaúnde was trying with more effective means and considerable good sense to make Peru into a less terrible place than it had been when he was growing up. In a sense Belaúnde Terry was saying the same thing as Frei of Chile: 'We have little time to lose. Our social credit is running out. We have little time to lose unless we are prepared to be submerged in the tidal wave that threatens us ...'

It was the first indication of just such a 'tidal wave' that began to appear in the air of the formidable Peruvian *sierra* in the middle of 1965. Three armed revolutionary *focos* were formed at that time, and were so active that echoes of them were heard in lazy, far away Lima. Belaúnde Terry certainly had little time to lose if he wanted to avert the threat of a popular tidal wave pouring down from the icy heights of the Andes onto the comparatively gentle coasts of the Pacific.

The generous and idealistic intellectuals who decided to launch an armed revolutionary movement in the *sierra* of Peru belonged to the MIR (Movement of the Revolutionary Left): Luis de la Puente, Uceda, Guillermo Lobatón, Escobar, and their friends could therefore reckon on the determined hostility of all the traditional political groups in Peru. Never would the APRA – stagnant, bourgeoisified and anti-communist – admit that the 'solution' to the Indian problem was in any way beyond them. And in this Haya's party were at one with the military and the supporters of Odría. As for the communists, divided as they were into rival factions, pro-Soviet or pro-Chinese, they were bound to be hostile to the armed struggle, either because they supported the Soviet line of peaceful coexistence, or because they rejected the Cuban theories considered 'incorrect' by the Maoists. The latter, however, specially influential in San Marcos University, were gradually forced to change their attitude: just as they finally decided to give their support to the guerrilla *focos*, those *focos* were destroyed by a fierce attack by the Peruvian special forces. Ideological analysis became largely submerged in counter-revolutionary praxis. The leaders of the MIR, whose political links with the MIR of Venezuela and the MOEC of Colombia were very evident, had to cope with tremendous difficulties, not the least of which was the campaign of vilification launched against them in Lima. For the most part they were people with university backgrounds who had studied in France during the previous years; yet they were likened to common bandits and cattle thieves. After some initial successes in the La Convención valley, the guerrilla movement was speedily regrouped around the Mesa Pelada and in the eastern foothills of the Andes. Silently but effectively the Peruvian mounted police, with every modern means available, reduced the guerrillas, either capturing or killing them. But the real reason for the failure of the MIR leaders, imprisoned or summarily executed within six months of the beginning of their operations, was not the specially resolute nature of the army's counter-offensive: coming themselves too from the coastal area, belonging to an intelligentsia sickened by the poverty of the peasants, but having hardly any contact with them, they had overestimated the capacity of the *sierra* Indians for revolt; the MIR members made the mistake – far from being a new one, and often to be repeated, especially in Bolivia in 1967 – of believing that by simply establishing a guerrilla *foco* the 'objective and subjective conditions for revolution' would automatically have been created. They were not necessarily wrong to condemn the wait-and-see policy of the communists: the communists, by applying European patterns to the Peruvian situation, and endlessly waiting for all the 'political conditions' to be ripe, were certainly placing too much emphasis on the urban workers. It is thus easy to see why they mistrusted the peasants. The failure of the MIR does not mean that their theoretical analysis was wholly wrong: the *sierra* certainly *did* provide a genuinely pre-revolutionary situation. This fact became increasingly understood in Lima, among liberals, and even in some conservative circles. Such men as Belaúnde Terry and his allies in Popular Action and the young Christian Democrats, were ultimately just as convinced as the unfortunate MIR leaders of the need to 'do something', if that terrifying human tidal wave were to be prevented.

What happened in the *sierra* from 1961 to 1963 was proof enough that the peasants could be stirred to action if they were offered a reasonable and clear objective. A young doctor, Hugo Blanco, whose activity was to be pejoratively described as 'Trotskyist', managed to organize peasant trade unions in the Convención valley around Cuzco. Under the banner *Tierra o Muerte** whole villages set out to march to get back the land that had belonged to their people before the Spanish conquest, land which had, for the most part, been quite inadequately cultivated by the large landowners or capitalist companies. Behind a widely unfurled Peruvian flag, men, women and children simply established themselves on the land and demanded possession of the rapidly overwhelmed authorities. There was certainly some violence when the landowners called on the forces of law and order, or gave their *gamonales* (foremen, usually mestizos, who exploited the Indian day-labourers unmercifully) the command to fire. But Blanco's movement, which managed to win the confidence of the peasant leaders, set out to be peaceful and non-violent. Blanco, an outlaw and a wanted man, did once, when caught in a tight spot, fire on the police; he was arrested in May 1963 and sentenced to twenty-five years in prison, to be spent in the prison-ship Frontón, off Callao. His arrest put a stop to the movement to get back the land, though the government tried in a lot of cases not to give judgement in favour of the large landowners. The mistake of the MIR leaders was undoubtedly their belief that the peasants of La Convención could move directly from the phase of 'occupying the land' to that of 'guerrilla warfare'. Though revolutionary intellectuals can make that step easily it would be an almost insurmountable obstacle for men accustomed for centuries to living in slavery. The events and local risings which increased after 1963 did, however, indicate a growing restlessness in the wild highlands of the Peruvian Altiplano.

Politically one of the results of the guerrilla movement was to strengthen the hand of an army whose impact on the life

* Land or Death.

of the nation had always been considerable. Another similar and equally important result was to weaken still further Belaúnde Terry's already fragile parliamentary support. He was an intelligent and courageous planner who approached his task as president in 1963 in a spirit similar to that of Dr Eduardo Frei in Chile. They were of course very different men, but both stood for a style of government which marked a radical break with the style of the caudillos, military dictators or popularist demagogues still in power in so many other Latin American republics. From 1962 to 1963 Belaúnde Terry took advantage of military help in setting off on a voyage of discovery of the *sierra* and Peruvian Amazonia. He could be seen rolled in a poncho and riding on mule-back or in a jeep on the steep roads winding up the Andes. This short journey gave him the conviction that there must be found 'a genuinely Peruvian solution to Peruvian problems'; that modern technology must work in with the traditions of Old Peru. It was no easy matter. As soon as he became president he came up against the hostility, and indeed fury, of both APRA men and supporters of Odría. Every government plan was bitterly disputed and everything was done to prevent its being put into effect. Here again Peru and Chile were in a smilar case. But Belaúnde had even fewer advantages than Frei. He did however manage to get his programme of popular co-operation started: the new body created for this purpose sent architects, agronomists, social workers and doctors into the *sierra* to help the Indians discover that 'The Lord helps those who help themselves'. And the State did indeed provide technical aid and equipment. But this programme aroused the suspicion of both the *gamonales*, and the left-wing critics, and was greeted with reservations by local authorities, minor officials and heads of the *ayllus* (Indian communities). It is hard to say a great deal about the Belaúnde government's agrarian reform: the settlement projects were small in scale (San Lorenzo, Apurimac, Convención, and the area round the

Amazon), and in any case did not envisage any major change in agrarian structures. The combined hostility of the landowners and Congress (which considerably cut down the credits alloted to the reform and the programme of popular co-operation) made a nonsense of any real effort, desperately needed though it was.

One of the very few spheres in which Belaúnde received fairly strong support from Congress was the bitter struggle he undertook against the oil companies, obliged by law to pay 60 per cent of their profits to the Treasury. Negotiations between the government and the International Petroleum Company, a subsidiary of Standard Oil, went on for several years. Peru's total oil production is no more than two million tons every year, but the control exercised by foreign capital over this basic sector of the country's economy was significant. Some hundred American businesses were established in Peru (total investment being reckoned at 500 million dollars), and one company alone had some three million hectares of mining concessions. So the Belaúnde government's announcement in August 1968 that agreement had been reached with IPC on the disputed problem of La Brea–Pariñas is worthy of note. Belaúnde chose the fifth anniversary of his inauguration as president to make the announcement to Congress. The doubts expressed by the Aprists, the deputies of the Odría camp, and even the Christian Democrats – who had left the government coalition at the end of 1967 – proved that 'Belaúndism' was certainly on the decline. To make matters worse the economic and financial situation was not good: the austerity plan in force until 1969 cut down heavily on imports; the currency which had been strong was under threat of continual revaluations and the balance of payments was affected. The drought of the early months of 1968 brought on a crisis in cotton, and fishmeal – the country's major export – was not selling well, though Peru was still the world's largest exporter of this product. From 1953 to 1963 the country's rate of expansion had been on average 7·7 per cent per year. That rate was now falling badly and one may well wonder whether, in these circumstances, the purchase of ultra-modern fighter planes from France was really advisable. It certainly was a useful pointer to Peru's intention of being less dependent on the United States and also satisfied the wishes of the armed forces, but a great many Peruvians felt in consequence that the threat of another military regime was growing fast.

CHAPTER 4

Ecuador

STATISTICS

Area: 106,178 square miles
Estimated population in 1967: 5,508,000
Population density: 32 per square mile
Annual rate of population increase: 3·2 per cent
Annual increase in average per capita *income from 1960 to 1966:* 0·8 per cent.

PRINCIPAL PRODUCTS

Bananas, cocoa, coffee, cotton, rice.
Copper, lead, sulphur, gold, silver.

The Equator, after which the country is called, passes only a few kilometres north of Quito, at the foot of the frozen majesty of the 5,840-metre high Cayambe volcano. At a turning in the road a rudimentary *mappa mundi* set up on a stand by a French geological mission reminds the traveller of the point at which the northern hemisphere becomes the southern. The air has an unreal lightness about it. The white glaciers are reflected in masses of tiny lakes, almost like something in a Japanese print. Indian women, their long hair hanging loose and wearing turquoise shawls, wash brilliant red ponchos in the pure, cold water, beating them with wooden paddles. Bare, brown-skinned children run silently alongside a stream. The cool breeze from the mountains rustles through dark forests of pines and eucalyptus. This *sierra* landscape of Ecuador has little in common with what we would expect to find on the equator.

Quito itself, 2,800 metres up, is specially valued as a place for rest and relaxation. This may seem hard to believe. The city, founded in 1534 by Sebastián de Benalcázar, displays its rose-coloured roofs and the blazing gold of its baroque churches in a narrow Andean pass. Its ten rich families, patricians of the *gente decente*, live grandly in their pastel-coloured colonial mansions. The sun rises regularly at six in the morning throughout the year and sets equally regularly at six in the evening. This is the signal for the innumerable church and monastery bells all over the town to ring out their characteristically rapid notes. In the dark the vast mass of poor, inscrutable and proud Indians look as though they were standing guard over the doors of the cathedral of San Francisco, described with good reason by art historians as the Escorial of the Andes. The golds and the sheen of rare woods glimmer in the glow of the lanterns that light up the façade, while other tiny, flickering lights pierce the darkness here and there, as Indian women crouch to cook maize and bananas on whatever little fires they can manage to keep alight. As the flames glimmer in every corner of the square they show up faces lined by the hunger of centuries; there are beggars, porters now lying down to rest but with their ropes still wound round their bodies, gangs of young *olvidados* * with glittering eyes and girls of doubtful character moving round in the darkness; such is the night life of this once magnificent city now drowsing beneath its fifty-seven churches, jewels of seventeenth and eighteenth century Jesuit baroque art. The permanent destitution of the Indians stands as a reproach to all that useless, unattainable wealth, the splendid doors, the chancels with their rococo decorations of gold in La Merced, Santo Domingo or La Compañía. The order

* Forgotten people.

of things seems fixed forever. And inexorably, during the rainy season, the weather dictates a different rhythm of life in Quito: then the mists disperse, moving back to the slopes of the district where the rich and the diplomats live. The night then is disturbed only by the wailing of masses of stray and flea-bitten dogs.

*

Quito presents the short-term visitor with two surprises: the sale of shrunken heads as made by the Jivaros, and of Panama hats. The heads are usually imitations, made wholesale in factories some of which are not even in Ecuador. The hats are genuine: here they are known as *montecristi*, because the best and most expensive of them are finished by artisans from the mountain village of that name in Manabi province. The so-called 'Panama' hat is thus really Ecuadorian. The unusually fine and flexible fibres needed for Panama hats come from the leaves of a palm which only grows in the humid forests of the coasts of Ecuador, southern Colombia and the upper reaches of the Amazon. The Panama hat industry has recently developed to some extent in northern Peru, at Cajamarca, and also in Colombia, around Medellín. But Ecuador is still far ahead of them in producing and importing *montecristis*. Competition from Japan, which produced imitation panamas made of paper fibre before the war, has not yet seriously affected Ecuador's industry. Almost 100,000 people, most of them small village artisans, work at patiently plaiting the *toquilla* straw with their fingers, which must be continually moistened. However, no one has ever succeeded in correcting a mistake that dates back to 1849: the prospectors in the great California gold rush were in those days the best customers for *montecristis* and they bought them from stalls on their way through Panama. That accounts for the name, and it has stuck.

The road from Riobamba, near the foot of the Chimborazo

volcano, to Otavalo, near the Colombian border, passes through one of the most astonishing unspoilt landscapes in the world. There are canyons over 1,000 metres deep, and necklaces of lakes like glass; and everywhere – in the fields of the huge *haciendas*, or in the villages with their white-washed houses jostling up against one another – are Indians with the slow movements and absent gaze common to all those taciturn Andean dwellers. Humboldt, the German geographer, gave a name to this area, unique in South America: Volcano Avenue. There are fifty-one in Ecuador alone; their conical silhouettes, forever covered in snow, stand out like a long primitive backbone, whose highest and best-known point is Chimborazo, at 6,310 metres. Cotopaxi, 5,900 metres, holds second place in the sagas of Indian mythology – for the man of the *sierra* still continues to fear this collection of gods, immutable, frozen, rumbling, and terrifying. This south American Olympus is regularly shaken by murderous earthquakes: on 5 August 1949 one specially violent quake killed 5,000 people. In the old houses in Quito the descendants of the Spanish conquerors make novenas before shrines in which Christ the King stands surrounded by wooden saints of many colours, masterpieces by unknown artists. But the Indians of the *sierra* still confuse the Virgin Mary with their own ancient goddesses as they utter their incantations to the supernatural powers. In Otavalo, market days see endless processions into town of ponchos, crimson, scarlet and blue, coming along the trails in the hard light of the high plateau, travelling for hours, perhaps even for days. The richer ride on horses, their saddles studded with silver; the women carry their *muchachos** folded in their shawls, and as they go one catches a glimpse of embroidered blouses and glass beads. Both men and women in the Otavalo district wear their hair long and plaited. They spend the whole day in silence and dignity in the main square of the town: when

* Children.

they sell a piece of cloth or a chicken, they do it without raising their voices, but husband and wife agreeing in low tones. The Ecuadorian government are very proud of the Indian communities of Otavalo, whom they present as an example of a native paradise – and they seem to be right in doing so. Otavalo is in fact an almost unique case, not just in Ecuador, but throughout the Andes. Yet, even there, the people are as fervent when they kiss their hands to ward off ill-luck in the old Indian manner as they are when they bow to their bishop.

*

Out of 5,508,000 people, Ecuador has at least 2 million pure-blooded Indians who still have their centuries-old customs and live in an almost closed economy. According to CEPAL, the remaining 60 per cent of the population is made up of 50 per cent mestizos and only 10 per cent whites. Ecuador's prime problem is thus to try to integrate this mass of Indians into the national life. One way is the economic one: to raise the living standard of the peasants and farm labourers; this is a reasonable solution which has, up to now, met with the fixed and omnipotent hostility of the wealthy landowners. In this the situation in Ecuador is not basically different from that prevailing in the great majority of Latin American countries. The republic of Ecuador is roughly three-fifths the size of France; some geographers, taking into account the successive losses of land following conflicts with Brazil and Peru (losses, incidentally not recognized by Quito) estimate the area as being even smaller. In any case, after Uruguay, Ecuador is the smallest country in South America; 50 per cent of its people live by agriculture, but the system still has many features of what can only be described as feudal exploitation: 240 large landowners alone possess 1,600,000 hectares – the same amount of land as is owned by 350,000 peasants. Most peasants are employed on pieces of ground let to them by a landlord to whom they are obliged to hand over half of all they produce. The situation is made still worse by the fact that the land is woefully under-used. It is generally reckoned that though the country has 30 million hectares of cultivable land, only 4 per cent of that is actually being cultivated. There is a similar imbalance with pasture land, with only 7 per cent of what could be used actually being used. It is true that the value of land varies according to whether it is in a coastal area, in the inter-Andean corridors, or in the foothills of the Andes. But there are haciendas of over 20,000 hectares (with Church estates being among the largest), whereas for most peasants the norm is the tiny unproductive holding. The average wage of farm workers is derisory. Finally, what is known as the *huasipungo* system is an almost impassable barrier to any rational development of agriculture. The word *huasipungo* comes from the Quechua, *puncu*, the door. The *huasipungo* is literally the Indian who has to sleep behind his master's door and by this system he is literally a serf, bound to the land which he must work in exchange for a minute holding on which in theory he may do what he wants.

The desperate poverty of the vast mass of the *peones*, and their almost total absence of awareness of how bad their situation is, follow naturally from this feudal and paternalist form of exploitation. To the Indian, his *patrón* is not merely the owner of the land, but ultimately anyone who seems to him to live better than he does. One governor was making a tour of southern Ecuador. Noticing a group of peasants in a field, he asked them, 'What is the name of the president of the Republic?' The Indians, smilingly doffing their hats, replied in chorus: *'Quien será, patrón?'* (Who is that, *patrón*?)

The great Ecuadorian native writer Jorge Icaza records that it is almost impossible to get a peasant to locate his village. If you ask: 'What village do you come from?', he invariably replies: 'I come from the hacienda of *Patrón* Gómez...' To him the boundaries of the world stop at the boundaries of the estate where he works. He has no *pueblo*, no village, no country. His birth, his life and his death all take place within that limited and unchanging universe in which God and the *patrón* are omnipotent. Those who have studied the natives of Ecuador are convinced that education is the necessary accompaniment to a rise in living standards: a poor man cannot be freed from his condition of slavery without a minimum of cooperation on his part. Icaza further says – and Ecuadorian liberals agree – that the human solution must be what is known as *acholamiento*: the gradual integration of the mass of Indians into the community in two stages: first by forging links between the Indians (40 per cent of the population) and the *cholos* or mestizos (about 50 per cent), and then by as harmonious a fusion as possible of the two races and cultures: Spanish and Indian. Obviously *acholamiento* demands a more or less total transformation in the economic structures to enable the Indians of the *sierra* and the *cholos* from the coast or the high plateaux to work together. But the Indian is loath to leave his mountains and come down to the more fertile land of the coastal areas. Consequently *acholamiento* calls for both agrarian reform and a speeding up of industrialization.

*

The as yet impossible dream of the intellectuals of Ecuador would in sum consist of a society consisting almost wholly of *cholos* – of active, industrious, intelligent and ambitious mestizos of the kind who already occupy all the most important administrative jobs. They have still to rid themselves of a sense that as mestizos they are inferior, even though it is four hundred years since Charles V proclaimed that conquistadors and Indians were equal in the eyes of the law. As things are, and will no doubt continue to be for a long time yet, Ecuador is a country in which the gulf between the illiterate and destitute mass of Indian *peones* and the *cholos* is growing ever deeper, despite the praiseworthy and often generous work being done in the Andes, which is particularly progressive in Ecuador. The increase in industrialization (in particular of textiles, cement and oil from the Santa Elena peninsula) is helping to create an industrial proletariat. But the mass of Indians in the countryside have hardly been touched – indeed in a sense they are regressing, for a number of Creole families have handed over their land to foreign firms, mainly north American, who are driving the *peones* from their *huasipungo* wooden huts.

Yet sometimes the peasant does revolt. Since the arrival of the conquistadors the history of the Indian race in America has been punctuated by desperate and bloody uprisings, which have always failed because of their total lack of organization. Such movements have been most frequent in the areas once ruled by the Incas, and in every case have been led by men claiming descent from them. Indeed it is astonishing how much effect such a claim can still have on the people. The most famous of all the risings was that of Tupac Amarú in 1781; he declared himself to be a descendant of Manco Capac, whose tomb is probably in the lofty necropolis of Machu-Picchu. Whether he was or not matters little. He won the support of Indians weary of Spanish oppression and raised an army of 40,000 men which got as far as the gates of Cuzco and La Paz. He was betrayed, arrested, tried and finally quartered in the Plaza de Armas in Cuzco. He remains alive only in the memories of the *indiecitos*, the little Indians, who smile and are resigned.

Ecuador is fifty years behind Mexico, where agrarian reform began to be carried out in 1910. Guatemala, another predominantly Indian country, made a similar attempt in 1951, and since 1958 Cuba has more than made up for the time lost since the end of the nineteenth century.

In Guatemala agrarian reform did not achieve any profound transformations. The State itself – with the utmost prudence – let out the land it had expropriated from certain large landlords and from the United Fruit Company. When the Arbenz government was overthrown in July 1954 the reform had hardly touched the highlands where most of the Indians lived; essentially it had helped only the mestizos on the Pacific coast in the district of Escuintla.

*

In point of fact it is impossible for any government now to shut its eyes to the fact that the background of almost all the political struggles in Latin America is the problem of the land. It is basically a continent of peasants – poor peasants. There is no point in industrializing an under-developed country if doing so is only going to deepen the gulf between a developing working class with new advantages, and the still destitute masses of the *peones*. Industrialization, though necessary, can only result in enriching a new industrial middle class, unless it is accompanied by a breaking down of the old feudal structures in the countryside. For the great gaping sore in Latin America is the latifundism inherited from colonial times. It is merely that a Creole feudalism has replaced colonial feudalism. Argentine *estancias*, Brazilian *fazendas*, Colombian *fincas* may be of vast size. At the end of the nineteenth century 80 per cent of all land in Latin America still belonged to 10 per cent of the population: 600 families in Chile, 2,000 in Argentina, vast *fazendas* in Brazil – everywhere the situation is the same, but now it has been aggravated by the advent of foreign companies which need enormous areas of land to grow tropical fruit or to raise vast herds, in either case contributing to the depopulation and impoverishment of the countryside. The consequence of latifundism is that land is cultivated inadequately and badly. Single-product economies (coffee in Central America, Colombia and Brazil, oil in Venezuela, gold and tin in Bolivia) result in the paradox of countries with enormous agricultural possibilities having to import food.

As long as Latin America was relatively sparsely populated there were no catastrophic famines; but Latin America is the continent with the largest population explosion in the world. There is bound to come a time, therefore, and it may not be very far off, when the governments are forced to face facts. This is especially evident in Ecuador and its Andean neighbours, Peru and Bolivia.

Ecuador's trump card, however, lies in the presence of a group of intellectuals who are really trying to solve the problem of illiteracy. In March 1945 a congress of Ecuadorian journalists meeting in Quito decided to launch a national campaign 'to save people from their own ignorance', drawing their inspiration from the Russian populists of 1876. They recruited willing teachers and had over 5,000 picture- and alphabet-books printed. Their campaign was taken up and carried on by all kinds of bodies, public and private, national and international: from the Office for Ecuadorian Culture directed by Benjamín Carrión to UNESCO. As a result of this enterprise, illiteracy was considerably reduced, falling from 70 per cent to 50 per cent. The best writers in Ecuador, Jorge Carrera Andrade (author of *La Tierra siempre verde*), Gonzalo Zaldumbide, Fernando Chaves, Guilbert, Augusto Arias, Joaquin Gallegos Lara, etc., continued to demand social justice, and point out the urgency of raising the standard of living among Indians. Thanks to such men the *Casa de la Cultura* in Quito became a centre radiating intellectual activity, and making tiny Ecuador equal in this area to Mexico, Colombia or Chile.

*

Guayaquil, on the Pacific coast, is no more than 465 kilometres from Quito as the crow flies. But with the western

Andes lying between, it is another world, a low-lying swampy plain, palpitating with heat. Guayaquil, with 600,000 inhabitants, is larger than Quito (500,000), and brings to mind the humid, noisy and colourful ports of the tropics or the Caribbean coast. Like Panama, Vera Cruz or Cartagena in Colombia, Guayaquil never seems to go to bed. Long into the night, while loudspeakers continue to thunder out wild mambos, alternating with sonorous poems, young black couples stay in the shadowy corners of the squares beside the quays, clinging together, gazing at the foreign cargo-boats. The whole of this coastline, with its deserts in the south and tropical forestland in the north, its population of blacks, mestizos, mulattoes, *zambos*, those of mixed Negro and Indian blood – to say nothing of Chinese and Japanese immigrants – presents a complete contrast with the *sierra*.

The economic development of the coastal region is of recent date. It began first just in Guayaquil and the valley of the Guayas river but eventually tropical farms and plantations extended right along the coast. It was cocoa at first which made Ecuador the world's major producer of chocolate at the beginning of this century. In 1920 there were estimated to be no fewer than 6,000 cocoa plantations. From 1916 to 1920 the country exported an average of 43,000 tons of cocoa a year. But from 1923 onwards *monilia*, a parasitical plant disease, attacked the trees and spread like lightning, which made it necessary to destroy some enormous plantations in the hope of saving the rest. The decline in world cocoa prices added to the misfortunes of an industry which, though it had regained some of its vitality by the end of the Second World War, has never returned to its original level.

Banana plantations replaced cocoa. Exports of bananas rose from 45,000 tons in 1939 to over 2,000,000 tons in 1967, thus making Ecuador the world's largest exporter of the fruit. But plant disease and over-use of the land have combined to threaten this fragile monopoly.

The dynamism of the coast stands in sharp contrast to the proud immobility of the *sierra*. A new industrial and business bourgeoisie around Guayaquil is becoming more and more powerful and urgently demanding a place in the political arena – up to now ruled by the landowning aristocracy of the interior. This human and economic dualism between the coast and the *sierra* is now beginning to replace the traditional, anachronistic opposition between conservatives and liberals. The middle class of Guayaquil are attempting to stir the landowners out of their age-old apathy; and this, together with the parallel advance of a demanding proletariat (dockers in the port of Guayaquil, workers in the banana plantations of the American United Fruit Company) is gradually making this seething city the leading political force in Ecuador.

*

Between 1925 and 1962 Ecuador had no fewer than 30 presidents, 7 constituent assemblies, half a dozen Constitutions, and an indeterminate number of revolutions. The gigantic volcano Chimborazo depicted on the tiny country's coat of arms seems also to provide the inspiration for its political life.

Alfredo Diez Canseco has compared the fate of his country to that of Poland – torn apart by her neighbours. In effect Ecuador had half her territory cut away during the course of the nineteenth century. The publication of geographical maps has not always coincided with the signing of the treaties between Ecuador and its neighbours, Peru and Colombia; it took almost a century to resolve the Ecuador–Peru border conflict, and twenty years after it had been signed in Rio de Janeiro, it was still not accepted entirely without reservations. A number of arrangements were worked out during the second half of the nineteenth century whose only result was to exacerbate antagonisms and bitterness. The dispute concerned an area of some 300,000 square kilometres, and even today the maps of this part of Amazonia differ according to whether you buy them in Lima or Quito. Ecuadorian and Peruvian experts are both trying to produce geography texts for schools, but the arguments still rage.

In theory the history of Ecuador since 1830 (the date of its achieving full independence) is quite straightforward: it is characterized by the alternating power of two parties under the leadership of two generals – Juan José Flores, the conservative, and Vicente Rocafuerte, the liberal. But the list of upheavals is so long and the number of omnipotent *caudillos* who ruled for months or even only weeks so large, that there is some excuse for Ecuadorians' having forgotten some of them.

One name does however stand out from the tormented darkness of those earliest years: Gabriel García Morena. He was an absolute despot who established in Quito one of the most strange and cruel dictatorships in all of South American history: a man at once enlightened, tortured and violent, García Moreno placed Ecuador under the aegis of the Jesuits. In fact he dedicated the country to the Sacred Heart in 1873, levied taxes for the Holy See, set up ecclesiastical courts, and put all teaching into the hands of the clergy. Rigid censorship rejected any publication that might be thought to be tendentious or to smack of modernism, and the prisons were far too small for the numbers sent there to meditate on the virtuous life by this Grand Inquisitor. In 1875 a bullet put an end to a career which, though brief, left ineradicable memories. García Moreno's body was torn to bits by rioters on the steps of the presidential palace in Quito; and the great liberal writer, Juan Montalvo, who had been living in safety in Paris for eight years, cried with satisfaction: 'It was my pen that killed him ...' García Moreno's theocratic dictatorship was followed by a wave of liberalism. But further *caudillos* of a less unusual kind soon brought such democratic outbursts to a close. And Montalvo returned into exile, taking up his pen once more to castigate the cruel, stupid or corrupt little tyrants ruling in Quito.

The 'waltz of the presidencies' began again after the world crisis of 1929–31. Between August 1931 and the end of 1935 Ecuador had four different presidents; after that the volcanic excitements seemed to some extent to subside. In 1944 a military junta put José María Velasco Ibarra in power, a man whose personality has dominated the Ecuadorian political scene uncontested for the past thirty years. Elected for a further term as president from 1952 to 1956, Velasco Ibarra was still there in 1960. Tall, thin-faced, a man of culture and generosity, he represented those great Creole families of Ecuador who ran the country. His reputation as a liberal regularly won him the trust of the electorate, but with equal regularity his authoritarian temperament led him to demand the fullest possible powers, and constant accusations of dictatorship were made against him in Quito or Guayaquil during the last months of each successive presidential term. Since he had studied in Paris, Velasco Ibarra was one of the most truly Francophile presidents of America; he made the 14th of July a national holiday in Ecuador, and was one of the first (in company with the Collegial Council of Uruguay) to grant recognition to General de Gaulle's provisional French government in Algiers in 1944. In 1945 he went so far as to give special instructions to Ecuador's UN representative 'to consider it an express order always to align his delegation with the position held by the French on all matters concerning French interests in the world'.

In 1948 Velasco Ibarra failed for the first time to be re-elected, which he accepted with ill grace. General elections, described by Ecuadorians as the freest and most democratic ever held in their country, brought Galo Plaza to the presidency, a man who holds a special place in the gallery of Ecuadorian political leaders. He was the son of a well-to-do family, running on a liberal ticket: brought up in the U.S., he was determined to follow the example of so many American students who 'work their way through college', and sold potatoes and oranges in the streets of New York. An athlete and footballer, he was quite prepared during his vacations to take part in bull-fights, and indeed there was a time when his fame as a matador exceeded his fame as a politician. Appointed ambassador to Washington, he returned to Quito in 1948 to organize his electoral campaign rather on the lines of a sports coach. Galo Plaza, the only matador to become president in America (or anywhere else in the world), soon found the arena of politics to be far more dangerous than that of bull-fighting.

He had barely settled into the presidential palace when he had to put down a putsch led by Colonel Mancheno, who had been Minister of War in the Velasco Ibarra government. Ten months later he had to deal with the rising led by Guevara Moreno, former Minister of the Interior. 'We must give our people the means to work and to improve their standard of living', was Galo Plaza's response to the military, 'and we must do it at once. Freedom is a meaningless word to people with bare feet and empty stomachs ...' He restored the freedom of the press.

*

In 1952 Velasco Ibarra returned to office with just as detailed and generous a programme as he had had in 1944, but once again liberal journalists were in trouble. His third success in 1960 once again aroused just the same hopes – this time Velasco having a comfortable majority, with 400,000 votes to a mere 180,000 for Galo Plaza, the liberal candidate. Velasco had the support of a Popular National Front, including both communists and the rightest of the right wing. Such a coalition of opposites was ambiguous to say the least, and Velasco's first year after re-election was the same. To cope with domestic problems and make it possible to devalue the currency, Velasco adopted an independent attitude in the ever-delicate sphere of inter-American relations. In particular he refused to take part in the U.S.A.'s intervention in Cuba, or even to give it his approval; he spoke bravely and without mincing his words: 'The Cuban revolution', he declared to Congress, 'will end by discovering its own limits just as did the Mexican revolution of 1910 – which also caused much anxiety ...' Despite thus daring to displease Washington, the money-lender of the Alliance for Progress, it was actually Velasco's conflict with his own vice-president, Carlos Julio Arosemena, that produced the crisis of November 1961 and Velasco's third fall from power. Arosemena, a banker's son and a liberal, had led a transitional government in 1948. Though sympathetic to Castro and the Cuban revolution he did not go so far as to want to see a really left-wing regime in Ecuador. And it was undoubtedly more from a wish to defy president Velasco – one of whose most faithful friends he had been until 1960 – than from any personal conviction that in 1961, he made a tour of Moscow and various iron-curtain countries. To show his disapproval, Velasco refused to allow him any role as vice-president, and himself set off on a tour of Ecuador early in November. He went to Tulcan, then Cuenca, and was in Guayaquil on 5 November; disturbances broke out there and after a week of total confusion, with rivalries between different factions of the army (Velasco and Arosemena were each in turn arrested and then released), Congress officially appointed Arosemena president of the republic. The Americans were disturbed to hear that he had won with the help of the officers of the Ecuadorian Air Force, known for their progressive views, and the delight of the students in Cuenca, the citadel of Castroism in Ecuador, over the success of this liberal reinforced their anxieties. However the formation of the new government did much to reassure them: there was no representative of the extreme left in it and the first actions and statements of the new president made it clear that his victory must be seen in terms of the voice of the Ecuadorian business world, determined to owe obedience to no one, at home or abroad. Velasco Ibarra settled on Buenos Aires as his home in exile – which at least proved his consistency in departing in his own characteristic way, and his hope of one day being able to return yet again to the scene.

On 11 July 1963 President Arosemena was in turn overthrown. Surrounded in his palace by armed troops he offered only a token resistance, and a *junta de gobierno* composed of four officers took up the reins of power in the old colonial palace in Quito which had resounded to so many gunshots and cries from the crowd. Arosemena was put with some ceremony onto a plane to take him to exile in Panama. The official justification for the *coup* was a surprising one: the junta made the expected complaint 'that he had favoured communism in Ecuador', but added too, that 'he had been too addicted to drink'!

This note of austerity set the tone for the new regime which outlawed the communist party and promised general elections 'when the time was ripe'. This was a promise as vague as it was sincere. The first two years of the junta's power were in fact marked by the continually repeated promise of general elections, each time differing in nature. The people must have got used to this curious four-headed government: as a collegial group, the junta was most careful never to give the impression that any one of the four had precedence over any other. Newspapers in Quito or Guayaquil would give accounts of the openings of barrages or schools in remote villages with photographs showing Rear Admiral Castro Jijón, General Gándara Enríquez, General Cabrera Sevilla and Air Colonel Freile Posso all walking in step in the forefront. One significant example of this frantic concern for equality appeared when General de Gaulle passed through Quito: the French head of state was naturally presented with Ecuador's highest decoration, the Grand Ribbon of the Order of Merit; the four members of the junta expected in return to be given the Grand Cross of the Legion of Honour, but all they got was the insignia of Grand Officer of the Legion of Honour. After a few weeks of consideration (and some rather unseemly bargaining between the Quai d'Orsay and Quito) the four sent their decorations back to Paris. An official communiqué described it as a question 'of national dignity'.

In March 1965 these officers, who had outlawed the communist party at home, opened talks to negotiate an increase of trade between Ecuador and the countries of the communist bloc. In agriculture the military government published in July 1964 an agrarian law which was to put an end to an archaic system of landholdings: private property was safeguarded to the extent that it 'fulfilled an economic and social function'; fertile land 'left uncultivated for three years would be considered unoccupied and open to expropriation'; limits were fixed to the amount of land any individual might own, though such limits would vary in different parts of the country; an Institute for Agrarian Reform was created, and given the task of making an inventory of all available land. There was certainly nothing very revolutionary about all this and it is easy to see ways in which the law could be sidestepped, but it did reveal the state of mind of these men who, though they had come to power by means of a nineteenth-century type of *coup*, really wanted to adapt themselves to the winds of change of the twentieth century.

This collegial military government, which preserved Ecuador's long tradition of political originality, was overthrown in 1966 without any major disturbance. The people of the country were tired – for reasons differing from one class to another – of this formal, and in the end not very effective, regime. Facing a rising and generalized discontent the junta, when asked to withdraw, did so gracefully. Congress was asked to elect a provisional president, and the choice fell on Dr Arosemena Gómez, leader of the Democratic Institutional Coalition (CID). He was elected with the support of the conservative party, who hoped that in exchange for this they would win the presidential election in June 1968, and have Dr Ponce Enríquez installed in power. Conservatives, liberals and socialists (very few in number, these last) prepared for yet another struggle in which all the different candidates would loudly declare their determination to integrate the mass of the peasants into the national life.

The only noteworthy incident during the campaign took place abroad: at the Punta del Este conference in April 1967 President Arosemena Gómez refused to sign the declaration produced at the end by the 'American presidents' in protest against 'the inadequate aid given by the U.S.A. to Latin America where the fate of democracy hangs in the balance'.

Velasco Ibarra, defeated in 1961, once again won the election, but with a slight margin which was hotly disputed by his closest competitor (a result of certain irregularities in the Guayas province). Velasco used to say, 'Give me a balcony, that's all, and I can be elected president anywhere ...' Then 75 years old and still amazingly vigorous, Velasco Ibarra was to need all his self-assurance to cope with the formidable political problems, and an economic crisis far worse than had faced him at the end of his previous term as president. 'What the country needs,' he said over and over again, 'is a government that will act ...' Velasco had never been tempted to give too detailed a political programme and he did not do so in 1968 – whereas the outgoing president Arosemena Gómez was hastening to put out a statement on the need to reduce officialdom, warmly disputed by his successor who would not assume his position for another two months. Arosemena Gómez gave him a kindly warning: 'Never have Ecuador's problems been so acute. The population is growing at a rate of 3·4 per cent per year. The living standards of the masses have gone down. Exports of raw materials are in danger, bananas, coffee and cocoa – and the financial situation is terrible. We lack capital and political passions have been tearing the country apart for the past thirty years ...' Velasco Ibarra's supporters in Congress held only 35 of the 132 seats, which seemed rather few in so explosive a situation. But Velasco's great hope lay in the fact that the 20,000 men in the army seemed disposed to give him another chance.

CHAPTER 5

Colombia

STATISTICS

Area: 439,734 square miles
Estimated population in 1967: 19,215,000
Population density: Nearly 44 per square mile
Annual rate of population increase: 3·1 per cent
Annual increase in average per capita *income from 1960 to 1966:* 1·3 per cent.

PRINCIPAL PRODUCTS

Coffee (world's second exporter), cotton, rice, sugar cane, bananas. Oil, iron, emeralds (one of the world's largest producers).

Bogotá, 2,600 metres above sea level, is cold, grey and depressing beneath a sky more often gloomy than bright. Cali, whose very name is endearing, stretches languidly out under its palm trees in the hollow of the warm Cauca valley. Medellín, hard-working, dutiful, quiet and austere, displays its textile factories by hillsides where coffee grows, 1,500 metres up, in the invigorating light of a perpetual southern spring. Cartagena, on the Caribbean coast, has sails spread out to dry all the year round under a blazing sun which makes even the filthy water of the marshes glitter. Barranquilla, still further to the east, smells of tar, of oil, of the fish market, of timber, and of the vast insipid fruits stored in the warehouses there. The *llanos*, those wide plains of the east, have a scent of dry and dead grass, and one can travel hundreds of miles without meeting another living creature. Private planes land there for safaris, laden with ammunition pouches and bearing an excess of rich food for over-organized expeditions. Torrential rains pour down regularly in the warm valleys between the three branches of the Andes, as they come to an end where the Atlantic and Pacific meet. But overlooking Guajira peninsula the isolated piece of *sierra* by Santa Marta raises its snow-capped peak to a height of 6,000 metres. The savannas, the Colombian plateaux between 1,500 and 2,000 metres up, are reminiscent of the Jura or the Vosges. The Atlantic coast is low-lying, horribly hot, studded with walls and fortresses which have been captured, rebuilt, burnt down and dismantled innumerable times in a relatively short period. The Pacific coast, on the other hand, is not easy of access; it is uninhabited, inhospitable and dangerous, and in most places so thick with tropical forest that one has to go down as far as Buenaventura before coming to a relatively safe harbour. Only a few kilometres from Bogotá, at the end of the motorway that threads the length of the savanna up against the third level of the Andes, larches and pines stand beside fast-running streams. But after the slope up to the Tequendama cataracts and the slope down, almost every twist of which is marked by a cross to the memory of some victim of this acrobatic cliff-road, Girardot, beside the río Magdalene, is stifling in the tropical humidity. The lorries, carrying their heavy loads from Buenaventura to Bogotá by way of Cali, have to climb to over 2,000 metres three times, while twice coming down to less than 1,000. The río Magdalena will sometimes vanish into its own sand, and then suddenly overflow its banks to a distance of several kilometres. Colombia has indeed some of the most marked contrasts to be found anywhere in South America.

*

This country in the extreme north west of the continent is twice the size of France, and thus the fourth largest country in South America. It is also the only country with coasts on both the Atlantic and the Pacific, which makes it a crossroads for all sea and air routes, and should therefore in theory make it open to every kind of influence; yet the truth is the reverse: Colombia is a very isolated country. The ridged spine of the Andes opens out into a kind of fan here, and, unlike Peru and Ecuador, the *sierra* has not divided the country in two, creating a barrier between the men of the coast and the men of the mountains. The complexity of the contours has made the east the most uninhabited area. There are at least three climatic zones, *tierras calientes, tierras templadas,* and *tierras frias,* each with its own special style of life and its own customs, making Colombia a land of the most varied temperaments and possibilities. Each separate branch of the Andean chain has its own peculiar character: the eastern one, 1,250 kilometres long, has the widest and most fertile savannas; coffee grows well there, as also do sugar, wheat and maize. The savanna of Bogotá has become the political centre, but the size of the capital is not out of proportion with other cities here as it is in some places. In 1967 Bogotá had 1,690,000 inhabitants; but Medellín was approaching a million, Cali had 800,000, and there were over 600,000 people in Barranquilla, while there were at least eighteen other towns of over 100,000. The central branch of the Andes, the spinal column of this spreading system of mountains, looks down on the valleys of the Cauca and Magdalena. It descends somewhat in the north, forming the plateau of Antioquía, the main centre of Colombia's economy. Finally, the western branch itself divides into three lesser branches which move down by successive steps to the northern plain near the jungles on the Gulf of Darien. The network of waterways gives an assistance that man could hardly have hoped for:

the Atrato, 700 kilometres long, rising in the western Andes and flowing into the Caribbean, is navigable for some 200 kilometres; the Magdalena can carry ships up to 1,200 kilometres inland, despite the (well-named!) Honda rapids. Ships with combustion engines have replaced the old wood-burning steamships and made it far easier to move goods, and there is a whole series of river-ports – Puerto Wilches, Girardot where the route to Bogotá begins, Barranca Bermeja, the petroleum centre, and Puerto Agudelo, where heavy loads embark for the Paz del Rio steel works between Tunja and Bucaramanga – all along the Magdalena, which forms the major means of water transport and communication in the country. There are some 81 boats and around 200 barges involved in this river navigation. The Cauca, the main tributary of the Magdalena, also presents a navigable stream some 500 kilometres long: an ambitious American hydro-electric project was to make the Cauca valley a kind of 'Tennessee Valley Authority' for Colombia, producing energy and an increase in agricultural wealth, but though the possibilities for energy are enormous, production has not yet reached anything like a high enough level.

Skyscrapers, huge blocks of glass and steel, barrages, *ranchos*, straw huts, little houses on stilts. ... The human variety matches the geographical: the cool and calculating businessmen of Bogotá and Medellín do their best to look like English gentlemen, with bowler hats and umbrellas; in Cali or Cartagena, mestizos and blacks live rather as people do in New Orleans, in the streets, on wooden balconies, alongside their hammocks; in the *sierra*, the mestizos wear *ruanas* –a kind of miniature poncho that is no more than a square of wool protecting chest and back, grey, drab, not very noticeable. Out of a population reckoned in 1967 to be 19,215,158, 26 per cent are thought to be of purely white blood, 68 per cent mestizos, 2 per cent *zambos* (Indian/black mestizos) and Indians: Colombia is no longer a place of clear-cut differences among the various races which have combined to form its population.

*

There are at least fourteen centres of population all totally distinct from one another, geographically, racially and economically. In some the people are mestizos not unlike those living in the highlands of Venezuela; elsewhere they may be pure Indians; in other places the black element is obviously dominant, while in yet others the whites have totally refused to interbreed with Indians or Negroes, as in the Antioquía valley. Apart from Costa Rica, the only Central American country with a 90 per cent white population, Medellín, the capital of Antioquía province, is unique in Latin America. The people there are tremendous workers, thrifty and fiercely sectarian; they are descendants of Basques and *cristianos nuevos* (converted Spanish Jews), and have preserved the pioneer outlook. Enterprising and energetic, their customs austere and patriarchal, they normally tend their own coffee plantations, and have always stood out firmly against the temptation to mix with black or yellow races. Costa Rica remained white because it was almost an empty land, and the Spaniards, Scandinavians and Germans who settled there did not even have to consider the advantages or otherwise of inter-breeding. But the Antioqueños fought determinedly to preserve their racial purity. The white buildings and offices and the long windowless walls of the textile factories in Medellín are enough to indicate how far in advance it is of the rest of the country in economic development. But despite the recent diversification of production, despite the recent coming of the steel industry, coffee still remains the major export, and the essential earner of foreign currency: 328 million dollars in 1966.

Coffee-growing only became widespread in the Antioquía valley during the second half of the nineteenth century: today more than 10,000 plantations, small and not so small, produce nearly all that special kind of coffee known as '*café suave*'. A federation of producers, formed in 1927, watches over the scientific improvement of methods of cultivation, the selection of grades, and the stability of prices in the world market, in which Colombia holds the second place (with 20 per cent of the world's production: eight million 60 k.g. sacks in 1965). Even in the nineteenth century the Antioqueños began to settle the southern regions going down the sides of the central branch of the Andes towards the valleys of the Cauca and the Magdalena. The towns of Sonsón (50,000), Pereira (230,000) and Manizales (150,000) are all under a hundred years old, and were the result of the determination of the first pioneers of Antioquía. Manizales, perched on a mountainside, is now the major business centre for the whole southern part of Antioquía and the northern part of Cauca provinces. Its bold situation on a balcony of rock makes it a strategic centre of prime importance. But Pereira and Armenia, in the province of Caldas, true 'wild west' towns, have also had their own remarkable expansion quite unconnected with that of Medellín.

The Antioqueños, clinging so lovingly to their coffee fields, find comfort in their faith with all the enthusiasm of recent converts. Medellín is a citadel of Catholicism in a country where the priest is still the most important figure in society. Medellín, the Manchester or Detroit of Colombia, stands in somewhat the same relation to Bogotá as São Paulo does to Rio de Janeiro.

Antioquía is a land of a thousand and one mountains: it was lust for gold that brought it its first pioneers, and they made a settlement on the banks of the Cauca. The arrival of a wave of white immigrants, a century later, marked the beginning of the fantastic development of this lower valley. The red roofs of the mushrooming town spread out around parks where the orchid, Colombia's national flower, grows wild. To the coffee which is its wealth, and the orchid which is its glory, Medellín adds, for good measure, cotton and gold.

*

Bogotá, founded on the site of an important Chibcha village, is not very close to the big river. The thorny problem of linking the capital with the coast has its own peculiar difficulties; the building of roads or railways must be done in the face of the most enormous natural obstacles, for the peaks surrounding the town reach a height of over 3,000 metres. The high plateau and the savannas of Colombia were settled with great rapidity – there were only five years between the founding of Cartagena de Indias by Pedro de Heredia, and that of Santa Fé de Bogotá. During the next two years, three towns appeared at more or less the same altitude: Pasto and Tunja in 1539, Socorro in 1540. But for years communications remained difficult in the extreme. The coming of the commercial aeroplane however changed all that: the change to air transport was at once a natural development and an absolute necessity. There was barely any transition between the mule and the aeroplane, since only mules could cope efficiently with the stony trails between the savanna and the tropical plains. The airports of Botogá, Barranquilla, Medellín and Cali look to us more like railway stations, with the constant coming and going of passengers carrying suitcases.

*

Jiménez de Quesada and his companions were searching for Eldorado. Their first encounter was with the Chibchas – hardworking and peaceful people who had certainly not reached the development achieved by the great Indian empires of Peru and Mexico at the time. Theirs was a theocratic society. Having undoubtedly come, like other South American Indian tribes, from far in the north, the Chibchas had travelled up the Magdalena and scaled the cliffs of the Andes. But Colombia, a real turning-point in the Indian migrations in South America, later became the starting point for the return journey north. Archaeologists have found traces of incessant movements, some cautions, some hurried, some spread over centuries. The Institute of Anthropology established by Professor Paul Rivet in Bogotá is only now beginning to make a systematic exploration of the remains of this civilization, of which we still know so little, and whose own special characteristics remain to be disentangled from later foreign accretions. The Chibchas had undoubtedly passed the tribal stage in their society; equally surely, their community numbered at least a million, and their chief god was, as with the Incas, the sun. The Caribbean Indians of the Atlantic coast, who had invaded their territory for a short time, had taught them the techniques of melting gold for use, and making it into an alloy with copper. The Chibchas perfected these methods, cutting gold into plaques upon which they drew designs. The Gold Museum in Bogotá has a few of these treasures of Chibcha and Quimbaya art.

It was in 1939 that the Bank of the Republic of Bogotá began, with the government's approval, to buy from private owners whole collections of the gold objects produced by Indians in pre-conquest days. Quimbaya vases, bowls, figurines and brooches, masks for purposes unknown to us, diadems which once crowned those whose names we have not as yet discovered, curious ornaments for noses and ears – all exist today as witness to the degree of culture achieved by the Chibchas and those who preceded them.

Botogá has remained as Spanish as Lima, though in a very different way. There the north American tempo is more evident – and also the Indian languor. The skycrapers on the Avenida Jiménez, the banks and the offices on Carrera Séptima, overshadow the historic church of San Francisco. New centres of activity have come into being as the town gradually spread northward, beyond the Hotel Tequendama and the residential districts. At night the multi-coloured lights of the advertisements shine back in response to the friendly winking of the Monserrate light, perched on its hill, which from a distance stands out like a beacon above the city's glittering dust of smaller lights, all flanked by the black mass of the Andes.

Since 1964 the capial has developed considerably. It covers over 20 kilometres from north to south, all along Andean hillsides, which are often shrouded in mist. A network of up-to-date roads was built in preparation for Pope Paul's visit in August 1968, and Virgilio Barco, the major appointed by President Lleras Restrepo, launched a plan for public services geared to a city expected to have 3,600,000 inhabitants by 1978. Streets, like Calle 26 were widened and new buildings thirty stories high were planned; alongside this, it must be said that the development of the poorer districts was also carried out, though in a most disorganized way, despite the real efforts of such groups as the Esmeralda and the Kennedy Centre to stem the human tide coming in from the countryside in search of jobs. Bogotá still has the great advantage that it is not the over-large head of a weakened body, for the other large urban centres are absorbing a good part of the exodus from country districts.

Another very Spanish element in Bogotá is provided by those delightful old buildings at the very foot of Monserrate, with the grille-work, the narrow alleys, the mozarabic balconies, the gardens rustling with fountains. Spanish too is the crowd of women in black mantillas waiting in long lines for their turn in the confessional after the offices and factories have closed for the day. And very Spanish indeed is that closed world of high society, clinging to its privileges, austere, giving few but splendid parties, and visiting the Country Club or the covered swimming pool which reproduces at a height of almost 3,000 metres the atmosphere of a Caribbean beach, with palm-trees, bamboos, lianas and banana-trees.

But English, or at least Anglo-Saxon, is that great institution the Jockey Club; as in Buenos Aires, no women may join, and political leaders whether conservative or liberal, the coffee-baron businessmen of Medellín, the large landowners, all take refuge there behind the heavy curtains and disappear into the enormous leather armchairs. Conversation is quiet: the Jockey Club is a combination of the Café de Flore, the corridors of Parliament, and the lounges of a men's club. 'Bogota,' say Colombians, 'is the Athens of South America,' and it is quite true that the purest Castilian is spoken there, and the intellectual tradition is very strong. But that Latin American Athens also has its eyes on New York; almost all the streets and avenues are numbered, not named, and though there is no Broadway, there is a very similar diagonal road that makes it possible to avoid the worst traffic jams of Carreras Sexta and Séptima.

On the Avenida Jiménez de Quesada, almost opposite the church of San Francisco, stand the offices of *El Tiempo*, one of the finest papers in all of Latin America. It is the organ of the Liberal party and was burnt and looted by a conservative party raid in 1952, but rebuilt. Eduardo Santos, president of the republic from 1938 to 1942, was the owner of the paper, a family concern; Lleras Camargo, president in 1945 after the departure of the liberal López, and again from 1958 to 1962, also had close connections with *El Tiempo*, as also has Lleras Restrepo, president since 1966.

*

Colombian school books are categorical: 'Bogotá has a climate of permanent spring....' Those who actually live there are less dogmatic, for in fact argument has always raged about the climate of Bogotá. Jean-Baptiste Leblond, a French naturalist, a commissioner of the French King in Guyana, ventured into Colombia around 1780. He described the savanna to the Paris Academy of Sciences in these terms:

A plain twelve leagues wide and far greater in length which looks all the year round like the prettiest countryside in Europe, surrounded by verdant hills where herds of animals roam at will, covered with pasture land for the many cattle there are, and with well cultivated fields, scattered here and there with villages and hamlets, farms and rustic cottages. Vegetable and flower gardens attract your eye with all the flowers of spring and all the fruits of autumn; but this same endless bounty of nature, far from attracting the attention and stirring the love of novelty which makes our seasons so delightful, creates an indifference to this unvarying beauty, these pleasures that never fade...

Leblond never got used to the climate of Bogotá, despite its claims to be all that was healthy and delightful: 'This climate is, furthermore, so curious that, if you are exposed to the sun the heat is too much for you and makes you exhausted, while if you seek the shade, you feel a cold that penetrates to your very bones.'

His comments produced heated replies from the Colombians, especially from a certain José María Salazar. This was nothing new under the rare Bogotá sun. That hide-and-seek Andean sun – either too pale or too bright – shines for at least three months every year, from January to March, for the season. For the final Castilian characteristic of this most Spanish of all South American capitals is the *afición*, love of bull-fighting. Bogotá has connoisseurs of bulls as knowledgeable as any in Madrid or Seville, and only bicycle races and football matches (the 'millionaires' club' of Bogotá is still alive in everyone's memory) can compete with bull-fighting in popularity.

*

The plain of Cali has close links with the plateau of Antioquía, and complements its economy. The Spanish found little gold there, so they introduced sugar cane. The Indian work force soon became inadequate, and Negroes came to assist or replace them. Situated at the foot of a pass linking the Cauca valley with the port of Buenaventura across the Andes, Cali's importance dates from the opening of the Panama canal and the building of a railway line from it to the Pacific coast, and it long ago outstripped the southern cities of Popayán and Pasto. Pasto sleeps around its Baroque churches at the foot of the Galeras volcano, and aristocratic Popayán, once the favoured residential town of the rich planters of Antioquía, missed its vocation as the nation's capital. However, the boom of the bell of its cathedral of San Francisco, cast out of fifty pounds of silver, still declares its old splendour to the valley.

Cali is indeed magnificently endowed. There are two sugar crops every year; nearby there are coal and precious stones, and rice grows with fantastic ease in its plains. Yet it has to struggle also against the over-exuberant invasions of nature. Only a hundred kilometres from the town, in the middle of the forest, the building of the barrage of Anchicayá faced the French technicians employed with the same problems as the Huallanca barrage in Peru; continuous rain, humidity seeping into everything, disastrous rises in the water level, and landslides, all combined to temper the initial enthusiasm of the technicians and give them some notion of the natural obstacles they would have to cope with. Lastly, the specially large exodus from the surrounding countryside has swollen the population of Cali to an excessive degree over the past five years. In 1930 this charming city in the Cauca valley, famed for the beauty of its women, had no more than 30 thousand inhabitants; it will shortly have passed a million, and the shanty-towns that have grown up around it pose a formidable problem – similar to that faced by so many of the Latin American cities with their fringes of slums.

*

The *cumbia* sounds all along the Caribbean coastline; in Santa Marta, in the banana plantations and in the harbour whence a disillusioned Simón Bolívar never again set sail; in Barranquilla and the primitive gambling houses on stilts of Puerto Colombia; in Cartagena, the Saint-Malo of the tropics. Here all festivals take on a collective note: it is a whole new life, joyful and noisy, a different décor with its great motionless palm trees. The shrill *cumbia*, with its monotonous syncopation, is a Colombian adaptation of rhythms that are African; accordions, tambourines and *raspas* are all played madly on feast days, market days, and to accompany processions. Cartagena de Indias, between its two bays, Boca Grande and Boca Chica, is a museum town and presents the sensual facet of a country more often sombre and melancholy. It really is African: the road along the shore passes between low houses with wooden verandahs. Young Negresses in white dresses lie in deck-chairs reading, with their lively dark eyes ready to take in any sign of life in the street. In La Boquilla, at the furthest point of the Boca Grande, the fishermen pull their boats up onto the shore to dry out – flat boats with two triangular sails. Gentle singing can be heard from among the bamboo huts which stand in rows under the sleek trunks of the cocoa-trees.

*

In Cartagena, beyond the thick walls against which the sea beats, the hill of La Popa stands out of the mists and sea-spray. The fortress of San Felipe de Barajas held its own in turn against the fleets of Drake, Morgan and Vernon. The surrounding parapet from which the sea seems only a hand's breadth away, the heavy gates of the palace of the Inquisition and the cross of Saint Peter Claver, the old powder magazines, the outworks, the underground passages – everything is still intact, or almost so. Every stone used in building the fort had to be brought by boat, and the store-roms are larger than those on Gibraltar. It seems hard to imagine that this same sky which at night seems to be brewing up a storm that never actually comes, that this sky once looked over manned fortifications here; or that there was the same dazzling merging of sea and sky, with great red and black bands veined with pale green, in the days when the watch would give notice of pirate flags in sight.

Cartagena de Indias, the first bastion of the conquistadors on the South American continent, often had to fight for its life. It was burnt, pillaged, devastated, rebuilt, abandoned, sacked. In the chilly nave of San Pedro the women of Cartagena came to beg the Lord for a respite, for less of bloodshed and violence. Then the church-fortress was dedicated to Peter Claver, the apostle of the slaves, and its vaults reinforced against cannon-fire. One can well see why the site attracted Pedro de Heredia: this lieutenant of Cortés, scion of a noble Madrid family, fresh from his conquests of Santa Marta, could not fail to appreciate the overhanging cliffs and easily-protected sea channels of Cartagena. As the necessary stopping point for the heavy Spanish galleons carrying gold from Peru and emeralds from Colombia, the town still bears the mark of colonial times: narrow little streets with old houses bleached by the sea-winds. It has also preserved traces of the many attacks made on it over the centuries: after the English came the French – after Drake and Hawkins, Morgan and Ducasse. Then after the pirates of the Elizabethan age came the slavers, the buccaneers and many more. One can picture the Spanish soldiers running to their look-out posts, and watching anxiously as large and powerful ships advanced on their stronghold. After Drake's attacks this town, whose defences were considerably reinforced by Antonelli, seemed impregnable. It was stronger than the most famous fortresses in the new world: Porto Bello in Panama, El Morro in Havana and San Juan de Ulloa in Mexico. The arrival of the ships of Louis XIV destroyed the illusion: with the help of Ducasse, the 'pirate king', Pointis took Cartagena, after systematically destroying all its defences.

Between Cartagena and the mouth of the Magdalena lie vast areas which are flooded regularly in the rainy season – April to October. El Dique, a natural canal flowing out of the Magdalena, is further to the south; its silting up gradually cut off the town and Cartagena slowly lost its pre-eminence over its neighbours, Barranquilla and Santa Marta; however, the laying of a railway line to Calamar made it once again a centre of some importance and tourists have done the rest. The fashionable Caribbean beaches, memories of pirates and bandits, the charm of the old streets, the golden light that shines on its canals and lakes – all these combine to make Cartagena one of Colombia's most visited towns. From Bogotá, from Manizales, and above all from Medellín, people come to relax in the hotels and guest-houses that stand all along the smooth sandy beaches, from Marbella to Canapote. On the island of Manga the rich of Antioquía have built themselves homes out of view among the bougainvilleas; at night sounds of guitars and tambourines can be heard from the stuffy streets of the Getsemaní district; under the awnings in the fish market children lie asleep, their arms crossed, their bodies bare, in the empty barrows. Lights flicker here and there in the darkness; they come from the fires lit by Negro women, in their colourful scarves, to cook tiny cakes of maize meal. Men in ragged clothes, their hair matted, their faces like polished wood, wander by the harbour with its rich scent of rum from the open cafés, with its stray dogs, and the pedlars who will sell you drugs, or women, or illusion.

*

The day the furnaces began to work, the engineer gazed with astonishment at the workers who came calmly towards the raging fire – wearing espadrilles!

The establishment of a big foundry in 1954 at Paz de Río

– now called Paz *del* Río – was a decisive and symbolic point in the development of a whole national industry. Workers came from the factories of Bogotá, of Cali, of Medellín, or of Bucarananga, to be joined by metallurgists from Boyacá. The espadrille-shod foundry-workers of 1954 were the first of many. At that date most of the engineers in Paz del Río were foreigners, but today the vast majority of the staff in this steelworks in the Andes – from the sweepers to the leading technologists – is Colombian. Paz del Río produces more than just railway lines: it produces the experts needed by a country that wants to enter the steel age.

Though objections have been made against the steelworks of Belencito on the ground of the relatively high cost of production there, further large extensions were being considered in 1967. Belencito produces steel blocks, girders, rails, cables. The industrial zone that has grown up around the steelworks includes a number of secondary industries – in Sogamoso, Nobsa, Paipa and Duitama. The average production is something in the region of 200,000 tons per year (about 15 kilos of steel per head in 1965). This is not large, for Colombia, like most other Andean countries, has enormous problems to face in her advance along the road to industrialization – transport, capital, qualified workers, etc.

But the effort has proved itself worth while. For these countries making cast iron and steel is not just a spectacular way of showing that they too are modern nations: it is an absolute necessity if they are to achieve real economic independence, and avoid – especially in the case of Colombia – being shaken by every fluctuation in the price of coffee shares on the New York stock exchange. It is impossible to make long-term economic plans as long as the national economy lacks a healthy foundation and depends on growing a single crop or manufacturing a single product.

To the east and north-east of Cundinamarca province, of which the capital is Bogotá, is the province of Boyacá, almost entirely situated in the eastern Andes. Its landscape looks more desolate, its peaks wilder, its villages more primitive than those elsewhere, and there is certainly nothing to indicate how close the equator is. The melancholy and romantic shores of Lake Tota remind one of a Scottish loch, cold and mysterious. Still further east, mountain streams like the Ariporo, the Payero, the Upía, the Cusiana pour down into deep gorges to the vast *llanos* below where they go to widen one of the tributaries of the Orinoco. Yet it is in this vast and up to now neglected area that the discovery of rich deposits of iron and cokeable coal provided the impetus needed to establish a whole steel industry.

*

Back in 1823 a society was founded, the Colombian Company, to work the iron deposits in Cundinamarca. A few rudimentary blast-furnaces were put up at La Pradera; but the *ferrería** of La Pradera met with disaster – the first rails the firm produced there could not take the weight even of the little locomotives of those days, and not until 1942, with the discovery, during the course of a systematic geological survey, of the magnificent iron deposits of Paz del Río, did the steel industry in Colombia make a fresh start. The mountain of iron discovered by accident during the building of a road through Boyacá seemed extraordinarily rich: 48 to 50 per cent iron ore. The reserves were estimated to be 100 million tons; the ore was phosphorous, like the ores in Lorraine; and to crown it all, it could be mined from the surface. At the same time large deposits of cokeable coal were discovered nearby, of which the reserves were reckoned to be at least 10 thousand million tons (2 thousand million of which would also be cokeable).

To start with, the Instituto de Fomento Industrial planned just a foundry to treat 30 to 100 tons a day; but given the

*Iron foundry.

extraordinary wealth of the deposits they found, they decided to establish a complete plant of the classic pattern, with a coke-works, blast furnace, steelworks and rolling mills. The Instituto de Fomento Industrial consulted some American firms, and the American Rolling Mill Company advised the setting up of a plant for processing 25,000 tons, with an electric furnace. This was turned down, since it did not look as though it could possibly prove profitable, and it underestimated the national market. In 1948 the Koppers Company presented a project: a plant producing 700 tons a day, with investments amounting to 94 million dollars. American businessmen did not seem too confident of the chances of Colombia developing her own autonomous steel industry.

*

In the meantime, the Empresa Siderúrgica Nacional of Paz del Río had been founded, with a man of outstanding personality at its head – Dr Roberto Jaramillo Ferro. In 1950 he got Paris to agree to the participation of French banks and companies in setting up the steel industry in Colombia.

Obviously, in the nature of the case, private capital will not be attracted to Latin America for long-term investment in heavy industry. The Colombian government, which had in this case to stand in for the lack of private investors, did not really want to establish a state industry; the political traditions of the country are too strongly against it, for Colombia has earned its wealth by free enterprise. Liberals have never thought in terms of any form of nationalization, and conservatives have continually fought to increase the share allotted to private enterprise.

A special 2·5 per cent tax was levied on incomes over a certain level, a tax which could be payable either in a sum that would be sent straight on to finance Paz del Río, or by direct subscription to the work being done there. But foreign investors still had to be attracted. The IBRD refused financial support. General Eisenhower's Republican administration was not disposed to foster any project for industrial development in the Latin American countries, the U.S. motto being, 'Trade, not aid'. Washington considered it profitable to invest private American capital in American-owned or largely American-controlled firms working purely to realize the wealth of the sub-soil, but to finance local refining plants which would eventually compete with the American firms now having a virtual monopoly of trade south of the Rio Grande seemed in 1954 quite specially unwise to Wall Street. So Colombia turned to Europe.

*

Belencito, where the Paz del Río steelworks are, is 260 kilometres from Bogotá, to the north east, on a plateau 2,700 metres high. Within a radius of less than 50 kilometres of Belencito there are iron and coal mines, the vast natural reservoir of Lake Tota and quarries of very good quality limestone, with reserves estimated at 60 million tons. On the other hand, the problem of transport between Belencito and Bogotá, and on to the Atlantic ports, was enormous: from Bogotá to Sogamoso the road was dreadful. Barranquilla was not really equipped to cope with the 60,000 tons of machinery sent from France, and from Barranquilla it had to be sent about 800 kilometres up river in barges, be transferred from river to road at Puerto Agudelo, and take a mountain road of 350 kilometres to Belencito itself.

Paz del Río is a good illustration of Colombia's continual efforts to diversify her economy. Needless to say it has not been an unqualified success, for the money poured into it by the state gives a false picture of the balance sheet. It is obvious that Paz del Río is still making a loss after fifteen years; the rails, the iron wire, the sheet-iron it produces cost more than the same products imported from abroad. But the quality of the products is excellent, and the time is approaching when this steelworks in the Andes will be a real competitor in the international field. In the long term, then, the business will pay off. But even if it did not, Paz del Río would still be a symbol: in a small area, and in one place, it has shown magnificently what Colombia wants to do, and how far she has yet to go to do it.

In recent years, for instance, the drilling of oil has certainly assisted the development of light industry: in 1966 the production of petroleum reached 8,400,000 tons, earning 71·6 million dollars. But this was only made possible by massive investment from the large oil companies (750 million dollars altogether).

Since 1905 the State has given concessions to private firms in the Magdalena and Catatumbo valleys. Since 1921 the Tropical Oil Company has been drilling on a large scale, with the State keeping, up until 1951, only a 10 per cent share of the gross production. To secure its own interests the State founded Ecopetrol (Empresa Colombiana de Petróleos), and in 1957 opened a refinery at Mamonal on the Caribbean coast. At present there are more than twenty-two concessions being worked, some by the nationalized company, others by one or other of five private firms: Colombia Petroleum Co., International Petroleum, Shell–Condor, Texas, and Nueva Granaada. Most of them are situated in the Magdalena valley, and the oil is refined in five places, the most important of which is Barranca Bermeja, the country's chief petroleum centre.

This indirect control of one of Colombia's major sources of wealth is far from satisfactory, but in this Colombia, like Venezuela, Peru or Chile, has to struggle against interests and customs established for decades past.

However, the obstacles to industrialization seem minor when compared with the problems facing agriculture. The land is badly under-used. Above all it is badly distributed: according to the estimates of CEPAL and the FAO, fewer than 1 per cent of the population own over 40 per cent of the cultivable land. Apart from areas reserved for barley and cotton, all other crops are far too small, partly because of the failure to merchandize and partly because of the basic system of land ownership. Most holdings are too small, and the estates used for raising herds are too large. Once again the disadvantages of *minifundio* are combined with those of *latifundio* – the classic scourge of all the Andean countries. So it is hardly surprising that 4·6 per cent of the population earn 40 per cent of the income, while 95·4 per cent share the remaining 60 per cent, and the same statistics tell us that in 1966 the average *per capita* income was no more than 339 dollars. If one adds to this the fact that the rural population still represents 49·6 of the total, it becomes clear that the problems of improving the living standards of the lower class are especially acute in the countryside where things have barely changed since the days of the conquest. Again, according to CEPAL, the standard of living in Colombia was described as 'superior' for 5 per cent of the population, 'average' for 15 per cent, 'at survival level' for 55 per cent, and quite 'sub-human' for the remaining 25 per cent. In other words, in 1968 one Colombian in four still lacked the basic amenities of modern life, and the food he was getting condemned him to a slow death. We may add that the most recent UN statistics state that the life-expectancy is under 50, and 44 per cent of the population are illiterate – this being especially serious in the countryside, despite the campaign against illiteracy undertaken by Fr Salcedo on Radio Sutatenza (which was visited by Paul VI in August 1968).

Up to now every project for agrarian reform has come up against the determined opposition of the large landowning class. The immensely rapid increase in population is, however, forcing the Colombian government to fight to preserve life at any kind of tolerable standard. What Colombia lacks above all is an adequate number of trained leaders and technologists. It will need more and more of them, for it has one of the highest population growth rates in all of Latin America; its annual rate is well above the total average. In 1951 the birth rate was 4·59 per cent, the death rate 1·78 per cent, and the natural growth rate thus 2·81 per cent. In 1960, these figures has changed to 4·14 per cent, 1·41 per cent, and 2·72 per cent. It was expected that in 1970 the birth rate would be 4·93 per cent, the death rate 1·73 per cent, and the rate of increase 3·2 per cent.

Another important phenomenon I have already noted is the exodus from the countryside; peasants are leaving their fields to go to the towns. In 1951 the urban population was 4,416,000 as against a rural population of 7,043,000. In 1960 the figures were rather different: 7,066,000 in towns as against 7,705,000 in the country. By 1966 50·4 per cent of the population lived in towns, and 49·6 per cent in the country. Thus by 1970 there were expected to be some 12 million town-dwellers, and 8 million in the country. One need hardly spell out the enormously increased problems to which this leads in relation to the labour market, housing and public services. And, a further point: the Colombian population is 'young' – the proportion of children and young people is relatively high. The country needs technical schools and ordinary schools, it needs classrooms and it needs teachers.

*

The conquest of Boyacá opened the way to South America for the Libertadores; 2,500 soldiers under the command of Bolívar and Santander routed 3,000 Spanish troops, surprising and demoralizing them. On 10 August 1819 Bolívar, rising up from the distant plains of Venezuela, at last entered Sante Fé de Bogotá amid general rejoicing. The fate of Latin America was largely decided there, in the savannas of Colombia.

There is not a lot to say about the colonial period. Colombia at first was governed by 'presidents' appointed by the metropolitan power to administer 'New Granada'. The first such president took office in Bogotá on 21 February 1564; he was Andrés Díaz Venero de Leiva, and his authority extended to the provinces of Santa Fé, Cartagena, Tunja, Muzo, Popayán and Antioquía. There were a million Indians in the area and a few hundred Spaniards. In 1717 the King of Spain changed the president of Santa Fé into the Viceroy of New Granada, and this form of administration continued until 1810. There were signs of the approaching battle for independence, however, in the so-called rising of the *communeros* in 1781: Creole town- and country-dwellers both protested against the colonial taxes imposed on them by Spain. (It was at very nearly the same time that Boston rose against the East India Company's monopoly.) The Viceroy in Cartagena, informed of what had happened, had the leaders of the *comuneros'* revolt shot. Thus do all revolutions begin.

In July 1810 a government junta under the leadership of Camilo Torres, author of a pamphlet of eloquent condemnation of colonialism in Latin America, decreed the removal of all Spaniards from public office in New Granada. Nariño, one of the forerunners of the liberation movement, who had been under arrest by the authorities since 1794, was of course part of the conspiracy. Spain reacted with violence: 15,000 men captured Cartagena, and hundreds of the conspirators, among them Camilo Torres, were shot. But Simón Bolívar's liberation armies brought fresh hope to the freedom movement. All the *comuneros* of 1781 had asked for was a little justice; but on the battle field of Boyacá in 1810 what emerged was a new republic, independent of Spain.

*

There was a period when Colombia, Venezuela and Ecuador, all free, joined forces in a single Gran Colombia, but rivalries, bitterness and conflicting ambitions brought this to an end. In Colombia, from 1830 until the end of the century, political life was entirely dominated by battles between liberals and conservatives. It used to be said that there was little to choose between them: merely that the conservatives went to the 9 and the liberals to the 10 o'clock mass. Obviously this catch-phrase can have expressed only part of the truth, for there was real, bloody and merciless civil war between the two parties for a good part of the nineteenth and of this century. And even today, though a sixteen-year truce was declared in 1958, one cannot be quite sure that violence will never again break out.

Back in 1910 certain reforms were adopted in order to try to create an atmosphere of mutual tolerance. In 1930 the liberals came back to power and produced a series of talented and highly respected presidents: Alfonso López from 1934 to 1938, Eduardo Santos from 1938 to 1942, Alfonso López again from 1942 to 1945, Lleras Camargo from 1945 to 1946 (finishing Lopez' term after his resignation). Then came the turn of the conservatives to profit from the growing dissensions in the liberal ranks, and in 1946, Ospina Pérez was elected. A powerful but over-complacent party gave way to its regular competitor, strengthened by years in opposition. Optimists might conclude that Colombian political life was really hardly more interesting than English, where an alternation between Whigs and Tories had for so long governed the rhythm of one of the most democratic nations in the world.

But after 9 April 1948 this judgement could no longer stand. The liberal leader Jorge Gaitán was assassinated at 1.15 p.m. in the centre of Bogotá. Gaitán was more than merely a political leader; he was a very much loved man, generous, fiery, and a brilliant speaker. The inter-American conference was taking place in Bogotá, and Gaitán, the leader of the left wing of the liberal party – almost certain to win the presidential election in 1950 – had called a meeting of 100,000 people to attract the delegates' attention to the rapid deterioration taking place in the Colombian countryside, where armed bands were creating a reign of terror. It was an impressive, silent and dignified demonstration; in full view of all those taking part in the inter-American conference, there was then a week's rioting in the streets, with the centre of Bogotá set on fire, dozens of apartment blocks destroyed and stores pillaged. Common law criminals, freed by chance from the opened prisons, transformed what was a political rising into a sack of the city. When the police managed to restore order, as a result of the conservatives and liberals – equally horrified by the scale of the disturbances – coming to an agreement, there were 5,000 dead to be mourned in the streets of Bogotá. General George Marshall, the U.S. representative at the inter-American conference, saw responsibility for the rising as resting with the communists. But this was altogether too simple: the liberal president Eduardo Santos described the underlying causes of the trouble in a few eloquent phrases: 'In reality', he wrote in *El Tiempo*, 'the 9th of April has made us understand that there is a desperate situation of barbarism here, also a desperate state of poverty. The State and society must have the courage to face the fact that they cannot be absolved of responsibility for that barbarism and that poverty; they must feel genuine contrition, and a determination to improve matters in the future'.

*

Eduardo Santos was mistaken in thinking that what had happened in April 1948 would be recognized as an alarm signal. President Ospina Pérez, a moderate conservative, was replaced in December 1949 by an old conservative leader, intransigent and unscrupulous: Laureano Gómez, a kind of 'tyrant from the Andes' such as from time to time will come down from those cold and hostile mountains.

From 1949 to 1952 this man brought back all the conservative old guard, and the liberals were virtually excluded from public life. For several years the country was ravaged by a merciless guerrilla war between the army and the liberal *bandoleros*, with summary executions, farms burnt down, property pillaged and atrocities of all kinds. Several provinces lived in a state of utter insecurity. Laureano Gómez, an avowed admirer of Hitler and Mussolini, though their stars had long ago set, and a former pupil of the Jesuits, managed to produce a schism in the Catholic Church in Colombia, despite that Church's having been the conservatives' strongest support for over a century. He decided to give Fr Felix Restrepo the job of working out a new fascist-oriented constitution; for, to Gómez, communism began with the right wing of the liberal party. In a few months Congress, the Supreme Court, the Council of State and the Workers' Confederation had all been dissolved, or put under State control. But the worst things of all took place in the heart of the countryside: the *peones* were made to carry passes bearing the following statement: 'The undersigned president of the conservative authority certifies that the bearer has sworn that he does not belong to the liberal party. Therefore his life, his family and his goods are to be respected.' Unhappily there were many villages where these passes were countersigned by the parish priest.

Colombia is undoubtedly a profoundly Catholic country – probably the most Catholic in all South America. But, unlike Mexico, the lower clergy in Colombia, Spanish by birth, appeared, at least until 1964, more concerned with their stipends and privileges than with charity or understanding. All too many were mediocre men, embittered and unsuccessful; the lower clergy in Colombia as a whole gained a reputation for obscurantism, and their power over the people, especially the peasants, is still considerable. To some extent, the Church's image in Colombia has been saved by the hierarchy: in 1950 they strongly opposed priests' making compromises in secret political battles. On 9 November 1949 the president of the Senate and several members of Congress asked for police protection, and Gomez's response was to have Parliament occupied by the security forces. He put out various decrees about this state of siege, and all regular sessions of the national Congress ceased, as did those of the State legislature and the municipal councils. All gatherings, all meetings were banned. During the state of siege, governors were authorized not merely to carry out their functions as agents of the executive but also to take whatever steps they deemed necessary to preserve order. Censorship of press and radio was imposed all over the country; the ministries of War and Home Affairs, as well as the governors, were given authority to stop any publication they were unable to censor adequately. Gómez dismissed Vice-President Santos, elected by Congress for a year, and appointed as vice-president the Minister of War, Roberto Urdaneta Arbeláez, the organizer of the police special brigades. Urdaneta announced a plan for eliminating bandits: troops began a systematic search of the *llanos* where numbers of peasants had sought refuge from the white terror; whole villages were razed, and young boys who were captured had their right hands cut off.

Gómez made no distinction between communists and liberals – but it seems probable that this was a political stance: the police equally made no distinction between liberals and Protestants. American Protestant missions had made serious inroads into Colombia, and in the middle of the twentieth century there was a campaign of religious intolerance to try to tear up by the roots every plant sown by Protestant missionaries in this Catholic preserve. Schools were burnt down – in the name of Christ!

The cloud was lifted to some extent in 1951: an official government communiqué stated that 'the civil war is coming to an end'. Up to then no one, either abroad or even in the embassies in Bogotá, had heard any mention of a civil war. This war, now being acknowledged for the first time, had been going on for more than two years, on the door-step of the Panama canal, apparently without the U.S. having any notion of it. Indeed the real truth did not emerge until two years later, in 1953. The civilized world was thunderstruck to learn that this civil war – not admitted as such – had, in five years, cost 200,000 lives. Of course the press had spoken from time to time of 'an attack on a police station by a gang of *bandoleros*', or 'the army's setting fire to a group of villages', but no one had any notion of the thousands of corpses hurled into rivers or left for the vultures. The white terror met with the response of the red terror: there was little to choose between the two camps when it came to cruelty, as rival gangs of 'liberals' and 'conservatives' mercilessly exterminated one another at the foot of the *sierras* in Tolima province. When the unbridled violence finally came to light it sickened the majority of Colombians, and a splinter group of moderate conservatives led by Ospina Pérez decided to oppose Gómez's determination to stand again at the next election.

*

The man who put their decision into effect was General Rojas Pinilla, Commander in Chief of the army. He was a career soldier, and though he had been Minister of Communications in the first Ospina Pérez government, was apparently not ambitious politically; he was a fighter (he visited the Colombian battalion in Korea), and agreed to organize the quickest and quietest revolution in the country's history. Gómez, paralysed with fear, was arrested at his home on 13 June 1953; Urdaneta was offered a choice between exile or prison. Tanks were stationed at strategic points in the capital but the people as a whole welcomed the fall of Gómez and his clique with delight, though remaining wary. Just what did Rojas Pinilla want? He at once formed a cabinet entirely composed of conservatives, and it became clear that all that had happened was that the moderates in the conservative party had had their revenge on the extremists. Once again there was talk of a national union government, and of collaboration between liberals and conservatives, but in fact it soon became clear that any such hope was a chimera. For the first time the army was in power and soon showed that it almost certainly had no intention of giving it up.

It took General Rojas Pinilla a few months to achieve partial peace in the ravaged country; one after another the *bandoleros* handed over their weapons, and refugees who had left the country returned. This restoration of order certainly won popularity for the government. But the disappointment among liberal leaders, the unrest kept alive among the hard-line supporters of ex-president Gómez – particularly among the lower clergy – and the reservations of even some of the moderate conservatives, soon gave cause to think that the government was not as immovable as might at first have appeared. The maladroit appointment of an officer, Colonel Agudelo, as head of the University, aroused indignation among the liberals and astonishment among the moderate conservatives.

Then came 9 June 1954. The murder of Gaitán in 1948 had unleashed a general uprising; now the student demonstrations on 9 June were a sign of the gulf between Rojas Pinilla and public opinion. As in 1948 the American embassy spoke of 'communist activities directed against the Panama canal', but the truth was that Rojas Pinilla liked the taste of power, and the Catholic Church, which had applauded the fall of Gómez and recognized this regime with its talk of peace and harmony, began to reconsider its opinion once the General President of Colombia looked like trying to play Perón there. Rojas formed a 'Christian and Bolivarist' party, intended to be 'unique and a real third party'; this military-style Colombian justicalism, whose authors were strategists rather than skilled politicians, immediately had the leaders of both major parties aligned against it. This was certainly an achievement!

Before Rojas Pinilla no one had ever managed to be the enemy of conservatives and liberals at once. Marie Eugénia Rojas de Moreno Díaz, his daughter, took up less gracefully the torch that had fallen from the hands of Eva Perón; she was to be seen at charity fêtes caring for the poor and those in trouble, handing out gifts from the Christian Bolivarist party. The General did his best to win the Church's support for his ambitions, and barely a day passed without the national daily papers reporting official ceremonies sanctioned by the presence of religious dignitaries.

But behind this reassuring façade intended to discourage examination, the drama began again; however, the press was not allowed to make the slightest allusion to the 'burnt villages' and '*bandolero* attacks'. The history of Colombia had a few more bloodstained pages added to it. When he seized power Rojas Pinilla had declared that 'giving all the necessary guarantees to workers is one of the foundations of national progress', and that 'a trade unionism dedicated to serving the working class and improving the conditions of the people deserves all the support the State can give'. But this 'imported workerism' showed itself quite unable to deal with an increasingly explosive social situation.

The year 1957 opened in a state of uncertainty for Rojas Pinilla; his term was to end constitutionally on 7 August 1958. Wishing neither to stay where he was by force nor to hand over his power, he chose the dangerous third course of presenting himself for re-election. This called for an amendment to the constitution, since by law no president could remain in office for two successive terms. The Constituent Assembly summoned in May 1957 for this purpose re-elected him for the period of 1958–62 without any apparent reservations. Three days later, Rojas Pinilla was overthrown and he left the stage as he had entered it – quickly and quietly. The General with the sad smile left for exile, as Laureano Gómez had in 1953, and like Gómez he was expected to come back again one day and return to the same post or a different one. There was not even a coup d'état, the heads of the armed forces, having met in San Carlos palace, advised the General to go and he really had no alternative since both parties, the Catholic hierarchy with Cardinal Luque at its head, the University and the business community, were all of one mind. Abandoned by the Church, the conservatives and the coffee barons, and with no support from the armed forces, Rojas Pinilla had no cards left to play. Yet his fall had a special significance about it: the military junta which provisionally took his place were forced to agree to the formation of a national union government made up of ten men, all civilians, five conservatives and five liberals.

*

The overthrow of Rojas Pinilla had taken several weeks to prepare and only came about through a spectacular reconciliation between the two party leaders – Guillermo León Valencia of the conservatives, and Lleras Camargo of the liberals.

The strictly ideological differences between the two major parties were slight; in theory the conservative party was right wing and supported the established order, defending and, if need arose, protecting the Church; it comprised most of the clergy, the landowners, and the majority of the peasants. Its power lay in the country. The towns, on the other hand, tended to be liberal; and, again in theory, the liberals stood for progressive ideas and the rights of the working class; they were avowedly anti-clerical, but not anti-religious. The liberal party contained most of the intellectuals, the 'professional class', businessmen and workers. In practice it is rather hard to see any difference between the rich liberal families and the representatives of conservative high society. Even in *El Tiempo* the reports of the receptions, presentations of awards, tea parties and dinners given by the spoiled darlings of the Colombian aristocracy to celebrate birthdays, coming-out parties, and so on, occupy an amount of space out of all proportion to their real importance. And it is far from sure that the liberals are in fact prepared to face the terrible problems posed by 'the age of the masses' which Colombia is inexorably entering.

In 1957 both parties were content to unite in face of the common enemy – a Péron-style military government. It had long been obvious to all thoughtful Colombians that the only possibility of a return to normality lay in working out some agreement between liberals and conservatives. The arrangement they made in 1958 was planned to last until 1974. Why only sixteen years of civil peace, one wonders? Would it prove too much or too little? Both parties agreed in advance to present a single candidate for the 1958 elections, and they also agreed certain modifications of the Constitution: votes for women, equality between the parties in the allocation of administrative and legislative posts, and the presidency to alternate between the two parties. At the end of every four-year term the outgoing president of the republic must now by law be replaced by a man from the other side of the political fence. In May 1958 Lleras Camargo, the liberal, won by an easy majority; in May 1962 Guillermo León Valencia, a moderate conservative, was the candidate presented conjointly, following the rules of a system which clearly took no note of any of the smaller political groups.

Though it had certain obvious advantages this truce contributed to the destruction of both parties. Of course there had always been differing tendencies within the traditional parties, but those differences became so marked between 1958 and 1968 that the whole established political pattern of Colombia changed. Instead of the age-old struggle between liberals and conservatives, there came a struggle between the centre – i.e. moderate conservatives and liberals – and extremists of both right and left. The Gómez old guard was not disarmed, and General Rojas Pinilla returned to crystallize the ultra-nationalist opposition. Thus the conservative party was split into three groups with the moderates, still led by Ospina Pérez, controlling about 70 per cent of the conservative vote. But the national and local elections of March 1962 proved that Laureano Gómez could still count on 20 per cent of the conservative vote, particularly in the countryside, and that Rojas Pinilla, though he could not stand for re-election himself, still controlled the remaining 10 per cent.

*

The conservatives are in a minority in Colombia, as was made clear once again in the 1958 elections, when they only won 1,262,122 votes, as against the liberals' 1,745,319. The parliamentary elections of March 1962 confirmed this trend: then they got only 25 per cent of the votes. Thus, for over fifty years, the Colombian tories had only won because the liberals were divided. Internecine dissensions and rivalries are at least equal now in the two, once enemy, camps. Eduardo Santos, Lleras Camargo and Lleras Restrepo and their liberal group have a left-wing opposition to cope with, skilfully led by Alfonso López Michelsen, son of the former president. His 'Liberal Revolutionary Movement', founded in 1959, got 16 per cent of the votes in the elections of March 1962. Obviously this was a movement which could expect to get at least half of the liberal votes in the country, and its supporters were drawn from the most dynamic sectors of Colombian society – workers, students, the middle class. But it was a movement lacking in trained leaders. López Michelsen, who derived some of his prestige from his father, believed in rapid and spectacular reforms in the country areas; to counter this the orthodox liberals placed their hope in their own plan for agrarian reform. The large landowners were resigned to the plan, since ultimately it did them little harm, being more a plan for settling unused land than a real agrarian reform. It provided for the breaking up of only a few large estates and that to the great profit of their owners. This law was fiercely attacked by the Liberal Revolutionary Movement, the Castroist leagues and the communists.

The truce looked unlikely to last, in any case. It was undoubtedly respected in Bogotá, in the legislature, the presidential palace and the ministries; it was respected too in Medellín, Cali, Barranquilla and Bucaramangaa. But elsewhere the guerrillas had started up again; Tolima, the most badly disturbed area from 1948 to 1957, once again vanished from the columns of the press. *Bandoleros* roamed the savannas, attacked farms, stole, would demand money from travellers and then vanish into the nearby *sierra*. Were they no more than just highwaymen? In the Andes some ten areas of self-defence were established – pathetic and fragile – rejecting the authority of the central government. Elsewhere, guerrillas were handing out land and attacking the army. There were not many communists in Colombia, nor had they any power, but they were well organized and extremely active. In October 1949 the Colombian communist party had called for 'self-defence by the masses' in the country; from 1950 to 1953 quite large gangs of party members had lived as peasant-soldiers, making attacks, lying low in the mountains, and then coming back to work in their villages after the regular troops had gone. Certainly not all such groups – of which there were many by 1948 – were communists, but they would be prepared to follow a communist lead. In a land now entering the age of planning and technology, the liberals and conservatives were still, as in the past, exchanging, in Parliament and the press, brilliant arguments borrowed from the leading nationalist and liberal thinkers of nineteenth century Europe. They have since come to recognize that the shadows looming over the cross-roads of the two Americas are those of two Americans – Zapata and Castro.

1965 in Colombia was a year of presidential campaigning. But, since the conservative-liberal truce, elections had become even more of a foregone conclusion than they were in Mexico, where the overwhelming predominance of the Institutional Revolutionary Party enables the government candidate to be sure of winning. From the beginning of the year everyone knew that the liberal, Lleras Restrepo, was to succeed the conservative, Guillermo León Valencia. The only new element was the ever more serious and profound dissociation between the politico-social apparatus of the regime and the people as a whole. In the local elections in March 1964 the political and ecclesiastical leaders had already had to fight desperately to persuade people to vote, and despite their efforts almost 70 per cent abstained.

President Valencia, of humble origins, presented himself as the 'poor man's president'. But after two years in office his prestige soon fell. His many and often untimely speeches were an irritation to the authorities and the representatives of 'high society'. Indeed, one unfortunate phrase he used in his speech at the reception to welcome General de Gaulle to Botogá almost led to his instant dismissal. But he succeeded in restoring a shaky situation, and in the end managed to get rid of his Minister of War, General Ruiz Novoa, one of the many officers becoming more and more restive over the effects of the almost total involvement of the armed forces in fighting the guerrillas. In the beginning of 1964 Ruiz Novoa had remodelled the army to fit it better for its fight against what the authorities called the 'independent republics', and the peasant leaders 'self-defence' areas'. According to Germán Arciniegas, the former education minister, these 'independent republics' were 'insignificant and gradually declining groups of anti-social individuals'; according to Mgr Germán Guzmán, in his well-documented book,* the peasants in these republics were chiefly concerned to 'find peace, in which they were

*Germán Guzmán Campos, *La Violencia en Colombia*, Bogotá, 1967.

thwarted by the Colombian armed forces with the help of agents from the north American military mission'.

A determined attack by the armed forces succeeded without any trouble in reducing these pockets of peasant resistance. The gradual exodus of people from the areas of Sumapaz and Río Chiquito continued painfully across the mountains. In the Marquetalia district the army could hardly hope to occupy the whole of a territory reckoned to cover 5,000 square kilometres, and their attack against Marquetalia aroused a tremendous movement of popular solidarity all over the country, contributing to a new understanding among the lower clergy, and making it clear that 'violence' would not really be eliminated if these 'independent republics' as such were wiped out by force. It is not impossible that the later resurgence of guerrilla fighting in Tolima and Santander provinces was partly the result of the Marquetalia operation.

'Violence' once again became a subject of concern with the authorities and the press. In point of fact it had never died out, but now, despite the army's really major effort at 'pacification' and soothing the restless peasants, it became clear that the left-wing opposition movements were becoming more and more well organized. And it also became clear that there was an increasing political awareness among the guerrillas, some of whom would appear unexpectedly in the villages of Tolima, Cauca and Santander, wearing their uniforms, under the very noses of the police and troops. What was absolutely certain was that it would take more than massive intervention by the army to palliate the anguish in the country and stop the bloodshed.

The old families of Botogá, whether liberal or conservative, went on as before exchanging phrases and arguments which no longer had any real connection wih ordinary life. Almost ten years of truce between the two great parties had resulted in the creation of a new Front uniting the five 'left-wing' splinters of the conservative party, and the so-called 'officialist' wing of the liberals. Valencia's successor, the liberal Lleras Restrepo, aged fifty-six, a lawyer, former Finance Minister, journalist, and his country's delegate at many international conferences, was certainly a man of presence and cultivation. But could one man, however excellent, succeed in overcoming the profound disillusionment of the Colombian people? To change the pattern of generations, which must be done, would undoubtedly affect too many people's interests and overthrow too many accepted situations, not to cause enormous upheavals.

Disturbed by the increasing poverty of the masses and, spurred on by the resolutions of the Second Vatican Council, the Church, which had so often remained silent or come to terms with the powers that be, especially conservative ones, began to show a keener anxiety. Though it did not undergo a renewal on the scale of that in the Churches of Brazil or Chile, it none the less constituted a factor of the greatest importance in analysing the political situation.

Paradoxically Colombia even provided the Latin American world with a subject for meditation, and an example: the death of Fr Camilo Torres among the guerrillas of Santander in February 1966. Torres, son of a well-off family in Bogotá, studied in Louvain, and was ordained priest in 1954 at the age of twenty-five. Through his mother he was descended from one of the founders of the Colombian republic. He got his degree in sociology in 1958 and was appointed chaplain to the University of Bogotá after doing a lot of travelling in Europe and the U.S.A.; he was a rigorous scientist and far from being a romantic or dreamer in his awakening consciousness of the sub-human conditions in which the majority of the poor in Bogotá were living.

Starting in 1962 Torres, an outcast from the ruling classes and subjected to misunderstanding if not positive hostility from the hierarchy, became involved in activity that was at once political and religious. As a member of the Institute for Agrarian Reform he set up a model farm and co-operatives. He met left-wing political leaders and active communists – though they had their reservations about the work of this churchman whose increasing popularity was reminiscent of Jorge Gaitán before 1948. With the approval of his friend Mgr Guzmán he decided to form a 'United Front', acting within the law, but bringing together all the forces of the left, including the communist party. But lack of organization, internecine jealousy, defensive reaction by the authorities – especially the Church authorities – all contributed to the paralysis and ultimately the failure of Camilo's *Frente unido.* In June 1965 he asked Cardinal Concha for permission to be laicized and that autumn, convinced 'that there was no solution other than armed struggle', he joined the guerrilla groups of Santander. The circumstances of his death are not fully known: the authorities claim that he was armed but according to his friends and biographers he was acting more as a kind of political commissar, and the weapon found on his body was that of a comrade who had been killed. Further, his friends maintain that he was killed before being captured. Thus, two years before the death of Che Guevara, a still little-known Colombian priest, impassioned, sincere, and a revolutionary, died in such a way as to provide an example that was the starting point for a movement of which the Church in Latin America is still feeling the repercussions.

Throughout the sub-continent thousands of young priests have studied, and are still studying, the words and the incredible life of Camilo Torres, as expressed briefly in his last message: 'The people know that legal ways have all been tried. The people are desperate and ready to risk their lives so that the next generation of Colombians shall not be a generation of slaves. Every sincere revolutionary must realize that the armed struggle is the only solution left to us....' The backwardness of the Communist party headquarters in

Colombia in giving unreserved support to this notion of the 'armed struggle' – clearly in line with Castroist theories as defined in the Havana conference of August 1957 – caused much heart-searching. Diego Montana Cuellar, one of the most high-ranking CP leaders, who had led Colombia's delegation to the tri-continental conference in Havana in January 1966, spoke out in May 1968 against the 'right-wing deviationism' of the leadership. Montana Cuellar had travelled through the country with Torres in 1965 campaigning for the *Frente unido.*

The hierarchy too were affected. In a pastoral letter in June 1968 the bishops demanded 'a profound change in the socio-economic and socio-religious structures to enable us to move from past selfishness into really committed activity on the plane of justice inspired by charity'.

In fact it had been on the note of the need for a 'great transformation' that President Lleras Restrepo had taken office in August 1966; he invited the presidents of Chile and Venezuela to his inaugural celebrations, thus establishing the foundation of the 'Bogotá club' in which Colombia, Venezuela, Peru, Bolivia, Ecuador and Chile – all the Andean countries whose problems and preoccupations must inevitably have a lot in common – formed into an organization for the development of the whole region.

Venezuela, alas, the richest of all the member countries of the 'Andean Development Corporation' was soon to have serious reservations and start limiting her collaboration. Bolivia, for her part, could not enter wholeheartedly into the group as long as her conflict with Chile over the question of access to the sea was not satisfactorily resolved. But the Bogotá meeting nevertheless marked the beginning of a new spirit in inter-American relations and by 1968 the 'Andean Development Corporation' seemed to be a natural body (in the same way as the Common Market of Central America) for fostering the long-term economic unification of the continent, and the foundation (by 1985, it was hoped) of a Latin American common market.

Apart from the founding of the 'Bogotá club', Lleras Restrepo's government had certain other successes in the international sphere which were far from negligible. While preserving excellent relations with the U.S. he managed to restore both business and diplomatic relations with the U.S.S.R. which had been broken off at the time of the *Bogotazo** of April 1948. The communists, who were made the scapegoats for the 1948 rising, had thus had to wait 20 years for its failure to be forgotten. However, a commission of inquiry (whose findings have admittedly not been published in detail) declared, in 1950, that the source of any foreign involvement was to be found in the direction of Caracas rather than Moscow, since according to the commission's experts, there was definite proof of dealings between Jorge Gaitán and Rómulo Betancourt. But the re-establishment of normal relations between Bogotá and Moscow aroused the ire of the Cubans.

Lleras Restrepo augumented his popularity by rejecting the advice of a special envoy from the International Monetary Fund. He had inherited a difficult economic situation, due to the ever-increasing balance of payments deficit, but refused to devalue the Colombian *peso* despite threats to block all the credits granted by American organizations and the IMF. In the end the Bogotá government worked out a compromise formula. However, his problems were not only economic; they remained primarily political. The conservatives watched with evident irritation the 'transformations' in the agrarian, fiscal and administrative spheres planned by Lleras' liberal team. Only 26 per cent of the voters had taken part in the 1964 elections and barely 37 per cent in the presidential election of 1966. The parliamentary elections of Spring 1968

* *Bogotazo* is the name given to the three-day popular uprising in Bogotá after the assassination of Gaitán.

were hardly any comfort, with 60 per cent of the voters manifestly uninterested in electoral joustings which only affected them for the worse.

Faced with such disturbing apathy, liberals and conservatives seemed more and more attracted to a repetition of the 'national pact' of 1957. But it was to be doubted whether this alone would provide the strong solutions needed for the many and varied problems pressing upon them. The abortive revolution of 1948 still had not found a leader by 1968 though, of course, during those twenty years it had been partly turned aside from its original objectives and exploited by demagogues. But the capacity of the Colombian people for revolution remains as great as ever in the towns and above all in Bogotá, chosen by Paul VI for his first meeting with the Latin Americas now 'on the road to de-Christianization . . .'

CHAPTER 6

Venezuela

STATISTICS

Area: 352,143 square miles
Estimated population in 1967: 9,352,000
Population density: 26 per square mile
Annual rate of population increase: 3·8 per cent
Annual increase in average per capita *income from 1960 to 1966:* 0·5 per cent.

PRINCIPAL PRODUCTS

Coffee, sugar, cotton, rice.
Petroleum (world's third largest producer), iron, gold, diamonds.

Venezuela is quite rightly looked upon as the millionaire country of South America. Every year the huge oil companies which drill, refine and sell its 'black gold' pay royalties and taxes to the government amounting to 60 per cent of the national income. In other words, year in and year out, Venezuela can count on an average income beyond the wildest dreams of the finance minister of any other Latin American state.

Though Venezuela has to some extent been affected like everyone else by inflation, and there is a large national debt abroad (428 million *bolívares** in 1965), the country has the largest reserves of gold, dollars and credits of any in South

* 4·50 bolívares = $1 and approximately 11·00 bolívares = £1.

America. The fantastic development of the oil industry since 1930 accounts for Venezuela's relative prosperity (with a *per capita* income of around 860 dollars in 1966, high indeed for South America), her equally relatively strong currency, and the volume of her foreign trade: 2,783 million dollars-worth of exports in 1965 (with oil accounting for 90 per cent of it), and 1,375 million of imports for the same year. These exceptional figures enable the Caracas government to manage as far as possible without foreign credits or public borrowing. They have also made it possible to invest large sums in developing the country, and to carry out a policy described by the government in the vivid term 'sowing oil'.

Venezuela's large and regular resources are not only the result of her oil; her situation at the summit of the south American continent, and at the southern point of the triangle of the Caribbean, the ease of communications among the various provinces, and her small population in relation to her size, all these are far from negligible assets. Mariano Picón Salas has compared the map of his country to 'the skin of a bull dried in the tropical sun and so oddly cut that some pieces have remained stuck to it'. The image has stuck: this bull's skin laid out to dry along the Caribbean shore extends over 352,143 square miles, making Venezuela the sixth largest country in Latin America (following Brazil, Argentina, Peru, Colombia and Bolivia). The formidable obstacles which most of the others have to face in establishing communications among their different regions are almost non-existent in Venezuela. There is a fine road linking Caracas, the capital, with all the major towns along the coast; the Transandine highway, that acrobatic ribbon of asphalt that forms part of the *carretera panamericana*, crosses the Andes passing by way of San Cristóbal, and makes it comparatively easy to get to Bogotá.

From the Guaira peninsula to the Punta Playa, near the frontier of Guyana, the coast extends for 2,813 kilometres, having at least thirty excellent ports, to say nothing of the natural harbours in the Lake of Maracaibo. West of Caracas one of the best-known and most secure ports is called Puerto Cabello – Port Hair – for it was said that all the galleons of Spain could be safely moored there by a single hair.

*

This large and accessible area is also not very densely populated. The latest CEPAL estimates give the number of Venezuelans as just over 9 million – but this has to be approximate, since there are remote parts along the Orinoco or in the *llanos* where the inhabitants are more or less nomads and it is impossible to obtain accurate figures. At the beginning of this century Venezuela had only 2,391,000 people, so the average population increase has been very fast indeed – about 3·8 per cent per year – but still, by comparison with the 19 million people in Colombia and the 12 million in Peru, each of which have land areas barely any larger than Venezuela, Venezuela is at a distinct advantage.

Her natural resources are enormous and still not fully exploited. When the great navigator Amerigo Vespucci discovered the huts on stilts of the natives on the south shore of the Lake of Maracaibo, he gave the place the name 'Little Venice' – Venezuela. But for a long time the conquistadors were not much interested in it; the *llanos* were left to herds of wild horses, and only the *haciendas* along the shoreline produced cotton and cocoa.

This type of classic colonial economy based on agriculture and a family system of working the land was soon replaced by an economy that demanded advanced technology in order to give priority to the intensive exploitation of the riches of the subsoil. After oil came iron. The immensely rich deposits of the Cerro Bolívar in the Guiana district is only part of a huge total of iron ore deposits in the Imatica 'belt', extending for almost 700 kilometres from the Delta del Amacuro territory to the Galeras del Cinaruco in the State of Apure. The total reserves are estimated at 2,500 million tons. Mining began in 1950 and production grew from 1,000 tons in 1950 to 17,400,000 tons in 1965. In that year negotiations were begun with American, European and Japanese firms on the basis of service contracts to transform the ore into semi-refined metals.

In a very short time Venezuela became Latin America's largest producer and exporter of iron, the two major deposits being worked respectively by the Bethlehem Steel Company and the Orinoco Mining Company. The U.S., taking 87 per cent, is obviously the largest customer for Venezuelan iron ore, and consequently the intensive exploitation of this new product adds to the country's dollar imports; unfortunately it does not make it possible to 'diversify' the form of Venezuela's exports to the U.S.

In 1962, the Orinoco steelworks, near Santo Tomé, 80 kilometres from the Cerro Bolívar, began production. Its position is due to the existence of a relatively small vein of ore with a very high iron content, of lime at Pertigalete, of coal at Narigual, of valuable waterfalls at Macagua (near the tempestuous confluence of the Caroní and the Orinoco) and of oil in the valleys of the east and of the Orinoco. The Venezuelans chose the hot and inhospitable site of Santo Tomé for reasons much the same as those which led the Colombians to build their first steelworks at Belencito. But though the Venezuelans had greater technical facilities because of the greater financial 'generosity' possible to the Pérez Jiménez government, the Orinoco steelworks had to deal with precisely the same problems, and suffered from the same defects as Belencito.

Apart from these iron ore reserves Venezuela also has mountains of bauxite, of gold and of diamonds, but obviously oil remains far her most important source of wealth. A veritable river of oil flows out of the country, and there is nothing to indicate its drying up in the foreseeable future. The world's largest exporter, Venezuela was also in 1968 the world's third producer, with only the U.S. and Russia producing more.

Venezuela's production amounted to 195·6 million tons in 1956. It had fallen to 138 million tons in 1958, which was a year of disturbances, uncertainty and economic stagnation, following the fall of the Pérez Jiménez distatorship. But by 1959 it had risen again to 141 million. Thus Venezuela still has a favourable – and envied – position in the world market and her resources do not seem under any real threat. With all these blessings, Venezuela should be an uneventful paradise: it has been calculated that if only the country's total revenue were redistributed equitably every citizen of the country ought to be able to live a peaceful and profitable life. But egalitarian societies are non-existent, even in the Eldorado, and obviously this is a Utopian dream rather than a reality.

In fact the impressive statistics which would seem to oblige one to remove Venezuela from any list of under-developed countries conceal a far more complex situation. The first point to be noted is that there is a huge disproportion between exports and home consumption (with only 8 million cubic metres consumed at home in 1964, as compared with 186,234,000 cubic metres exported). Venezuela's black gold is controlled by firms who keep almost all of their profits elsewhere; therefore Venezuela's wealth is only apparent and strictly relative. Furthermore, oil has created a distortion in the economy which places it more and more at the mercy of outside events and fluctuations in the market. An increased demand for consumer goods and services has led to a raising of prices, so that exports have become more and more 'expensive'. And Venezuelan industry and agriculture cannot compete with foreign products without protective tariffs which contribute to a further increase of prices on the home market. For a long time travel agents have recognized Caracas as having the unenviable privilege of being the dearest city in the world – even more so than New York – and despite a recent devaluation of the *bolívar* matters do not seem to have improved. 'Playing *bolo*,' during the Pérez Jiménez dictatorship of 1948–58 really meant getting rich quick for rich Venezuelans and foreigners.

The fall in oil prices which began in 1964 also shows that a continual increase in production does not necessarily represent an advantage to any country particularly affected by the protectionist policies inaugurated by the U.S. Of course the vast reserves of oil belong to the state, which may grant or refuse concessions to whom it will; but negotiations on the granting of concessions or the reviewing of past agreements have aroused innumerable and bitter disputes between the Caracas government and the huge foreign firms concerned, who have no hesitation in using any form of blackmail to secure their interests. The concessions at present held by such firms are among the richest deposits in the country; so the decision of the Betancourt and Leoni governments of granting no further concessions and doing all that they could to favour the national oil company (Corporación venezolana del petróleo) has made dealings with those firms more difficult and bitter than ever. Anyone who makes a careful study of how the concession areas are divided among the north American oil groups and the Anglo-Dutch groups will see that in Venezuela, as elsewhere in Latin America, American capital has gradually ousted European. In 1956 north American oil trusts already controlled almost five million hectares of concessions out of a total of about 6·2 million. Of the 17 foreign companies taking part in the extraction of Venezuelan oil the most powerful are Creole (39·9 per cent of total production), Shell (26 per cent) and Mene Grande (12·7) per cent. Note too that the petroleum industry occupies no more than

2 per cent of the country's economically active population. Wages and salaries represent an insignificant fraction of the total value of the exports of oil and its derivative products (during the past six years the number of white- and blue-collar workers employed in oil firms fell from 55,170 to 33,262). Of the fifteen refineries in operation only one belongs to the national company; and in point of fact 66 per cent of Venezuela's oil is taken out of the country without being refined at all (and thus at a lower price). All these reasons combined to make the government try to put into practice a policy for the defence of its oil, starting in 1958: the 'fifty-fifty' rule, in particular, was changed to raise the State's share in the profits made out of oil to 67 per cent. To protect prices the Caracas government created the OPEP (Organization of Petroleum-exporting countries) in alliance with the Arab nations of the Middle East, but the results were not as good as had been hoped. Another major step was the formation of the CVP (Corporación venezolana del petróleo) in 1960, which tried to work out agreements to cooperate with the foreign trusts, but obviously this could only advance very slowly, and the area CVP is working still only represents a minute part of the total concessions. It is in the new sphere of petro-chemicals that the Venezuelan government has made most progress since 1953, when Petroquímica Nacional was founded: established at Morón in Carabobo State, this industry enjoys unusually good transport facilities, and the various plants in the Morón complex were working to 87 per cent of their capacity by 1967.

*

The glaring contrast between extreme wealth and extreme poverty is a commonplace in Latin America. But it is more shocking perhaps in Venezuela than elsewhere because of the strides the country has made over the past fifteen years and the fact that the national income has doubled in the last decade.

The Betancourt government set itself the target of increasing the *per capita* income to 1,000 dollars. Yet there is little significance in thus taking a total figure and dividing it by 9 million people, for it takes no note of the abyss between the well-off Venezuelans and those, for instance, who rot away their lives in the *ranchitos* of the Ávila. Slums and shanty-towns mar far too many Latin American cities: the *favelas* can be seen above the futurist excitements of Rio de Janeiro, and there are miserable *barriadas* in the very heart of Lima; vast, depressing, monotonous working class suburbs lie all round Buenos Aires, and the thousands of destitute people in Bogotá live in *barrios* which are bogged down in a sea of mud whenever it rains.

Hovels, shanty-towns, *favelas, barriadas, barrios* or *ranchitos* – the phenomenon of urban concentrations where there is no comfort, no sanitation, no water, no light, no work, and often no hope of any improvement is not peculiar to South America. But that even Caracas, one of the finest cities in the whole sub-continent, should not have escaped this monstrosity is alarming.

Of the 1,500,000 people in greater Caracas, about 400,000 (we have no exact figure) live in the wooden huts with corrugated iron roofs put up in a matter of hours by ever more numerous, desperate and violent squatters on the red hillsides above the jewelled city. These *ranchitos* even sometimes appear overnight in the no-man's-land around the building sites of ultra-modern apartment blocks.

What really made Caracas its present size was the incredible expansion of the building industry resulting from the unbounded speculation which marked the years of the Pérez Jiménez dictatorship. In 1938 the town had no more than 200,000 inhabitants in an area of 543 hectares; in 1961 it covered 19,000 hectares, and the population was over

1,300,000. The sides of the Ávila valley rise both north and south of the town. In 1938 there were 10,900 vehicles there, and in 1965 200,000. Though the transport problem has been eased by the construction of huge motorways, it is still a pressing one, especially as regards the bottle-necks that build up during the rush hour. Equally pressing is the problem of the chaotic increase in the number of *ranchitos* (or *tugurios*): in 1950, it was reckoned that 14 per cent of the city's population lived in 'marginal' dwellings; in 1959 this percentage had risen to 35 per cent, and the tendency is for it to increase, despite the construction of 'super-blocks' (the '– 23 de Enero' block alone houses over 100,000 people) – which lack the services indispensable to concentrations of their size. In the 23 de Enero super-block, the number of people in each apartment may be anything from 1 to 22, the average (according to Pedro Cunill the geographer) being 6. Almost 90 per cent of the apartments are let or occupied illegally. Yet this tropical 'housing estate' is an enormous improvement over the huddles of *ranchitos* that stretch up above it as one enters Caracas. This is just one indication of the vastness of the problems faced by sociologists and architects with this proliferation of fringe populations: and it is not lessened by the fact that the same problem must be faced at La Guaira, the port for Caracas, at Maracaibo, and a number of other towns – for the six largest towns in Venezuela alone contain 31 per cent of the country's total population.

No one could fail to be impressed by the humming activity of the capital. 900 metres above sea level, at the foot of the Ávila mountain, which Baron von Humboldt was the first explorer to climb (taking care to avoid poisonous snakes), Caracas is huge and unplanned, a mingling of many cities in one. It developed by chance in the mud generously thrown up by the oil industry, and when Pérez Jiménez, dreaming of Mussolini-style military parades, sent his demolition men right through the city with their bulldozers, it was not done to any planned design. In the city centre the streets are still unnumbered, and the arterial roads still bear traditional names dating back to colonial times.

One of the evident signs of a certain slowing-down of business is the ageing and, even more, the adaptation to circumstances one notices in the town's vehicles: in 1958 Caracas had more taxis than Chicago, and Cadillacs were a common sight. In 1968 there was less obvious luxury in the streets: the chrome on the sumptuous American cars had rusted or come off altogether, and there were far more European cars, chosen because they are more practical and, more important, cheaper. Some French manufacturers have even established local assembly lines to make the most of this new market.

Caracas lived for ten years to the shattering rhythm of pneumatic drills and pile drivers. The gigantic tower-blocks of the Centro Bolívar, where all government offices are gathered, are an apt symbol of their furious beating, and completely overshadow the crumbling cupolas of Santa Teresa, the old colonial church. The Centro Bolívar is a collection of skyscrapers, offices, shopping centres and multi-storey car-parks; its clear-cut outlines have totally covered the traces of the old city founded by Captain Diego de Losada in 1567.

'The Caracas Indians', records the chronicle, 'attacked him so fiercely that Don Diego called on the protection of the apostle St James, patron saint of Spain . . .' He called the town Santiago de León de Caracas, and there is still a square named after the Libertador Bolívar, where the cathedral stands surrounded by streets running down to the banks of the river Guaira. Paved with mosaics, shaded by trees, with orchids providing delicate patches of mauve, and alongside it the old University now used as the Palace of the Academies, the Plaza Bolívar still has an old-world charm which comes as a surprise in the midst of the bustling city.

A vast and historic tree, the *ceiba*, similar both to an oak and a baobab, persists in slowing down the rush of traffic – it is the only tree in this whole San Francisco district, for everywhere else mechanization has won the day. To the east the Sábana Grande, the great savanna, was only a minor suburb ten years ago, but is now a new town, a new centre with its halo of neon signs, a smart business district. The many *urbanizaciones* from 1952 to 1958 led to speculation, and in places the value of land increased a hundredfold in less than five years. The fever has gradually died down but the expensive and complex follies ordered by Pérez Jiménez still give the town a special air: the Military Circle is vast, with swimming pools and artificial beaches, and drawing rooms with Gobelin carpets – a temple to the glory of the army, aggressively sumptuous with its marble halls and courtyards. In the space of a few years the dictator had built the Avenida Urdaneta, set up three television transmitters and built a 400-room palace costing 8 million dollars. Nothing, it seemed, could stop the builders and speculators in their continual efforts to extend the limits of the possible.

*

The boldness of Venezuelan architects has so altered the face of the capital that one has to go up the old road of La Guaira to discover the city's three ages. To the north the old Andalusian houses in their pastel colours, Bolívar's Caracas, with patios and little streets where the *serenos** used to make their rounds calling out the time of day. On Sundays the Creole farmers from round about used to come to town on their small, spirited *llanos* horses, crossing straight over the sugar plantations of Petare, the orchards of the Sábana Grande and the age-old mahogany forests of Los Caobos. Today Los Caobos is more like a large city park.

The second Caracas came into being around 1870, under

*Night watchmen.

Guzmán Blanco. The houses of that date have the comfortable, graceless style of Baron Haussmann's middle-class town houses in Paris. At the foot of Calvario hill, the Silencio district was rebuilt in 1942, having been ravaged by an epidemic of the plague at the beginning of the century: Silencio is quite the wrong name for it – it is the forum of Caracas, the place for demonstrations, the starting-point for processions, and the centre where popular revolts have tended to come to boiling point. Even from its heights Caracas is something of a shock, but the shock cannot fail to be softened by the coming of the splendid motorway from La Guaira, where the port installations and the international airport are situated.

That road, sixteen kilometres long, crosses three viaducts over ravines, and tunnels twice through mountains, one tunnel being 3,200 metres long. It replaces the old winding road which for so long made Caracas into something like an eyrie, and where the motorway enters it, both faces of the city can be seen simultaneously: both skyscrapers and *ranchitos*. The *ranchito* dweller, watching his television set (generally paid for in instalments which put him into debt for life), is not excited only by wrestling matches, which are Caracas' most popular form of sport, but by the whole world below which approaches him, the world of the oil men, of society receptions, of luxury hotels, of all those whose lot is happier than his. He lives on a little maize and rice; his children may earn a few coins in the town centre as shoeshine or errand boys. On Carnival days the people from the *ranchitos* come down into town and jeer at the well-off; revolutions unleash people who are violent, hardened and frustrated. If there were a flag flying over their homes, it should be the black flag of anarchy.

*

Dictators are sometimes lucky and Pérez Jiménez was outstandingly so. The oil boom coincided with the first year of his rule: production, which had been only 95 million tons in 1953, grew to 146 million in 1957. In 1956 and 1957 this man, fat, round-faced, cruel and limited, who – incredibly – managed to keep the people of Venezuela under his thumb for ten years, granted new concessions to oil companies to an estimated value of a thousand million dollars. When the dictator landed in Miami the day after the uprising of 23 January 1958, he had a brief dialogue with the reporters who met him at the airport: 'Don't worry about me,' said Pérez Jiménez, 'I have 200 million in savings.' 'In *bolívares?*' they asked. 'In dollars, of course!' The Betancourt and Leoni governments which followed him were naturally tempted to put down all their financial troubles to the dishonesty and corruption of his regime, and certainly he had left behind vast debts. He had built enormously, but he had also stolen and wasted a great deal. The foreign companies seeking contracts for government work knew that to offer large commissions to the *caudillo's* favourites and certain high officials would give them a chance of beating their competitors to the post, so a whole class of *nouveaux riches* had a vested interested in upholding the dictatorship. Luxury hotels, unnecessarily large dams, unused or inaccessible cable cars, avenues as wide as city squares – Pérez Jiménez clearly suffered from the childish compulsion common to so many Caribbean dictators to perpetuate their names in stone, marble and steel, whatever the cost.

Yet it would be ridiculous to suggest that his work was entirely negative; such vital industries as steel and petrochemicals came into being before 1958 and have developed enormously since then. Pérez Jiménez wanted to 'sow oil', in the phrase popularized in 1947 by the leaders of Rómulo Betancourt's Democratic Action Party.* All one can say is that he sowed lavishly and reaped but a small and poor crop. The Betancourt regime did not conceal the fact. 'It is true,'

* Acción Democrática.

said Betancourt, 'that Venezuela has some of the largest financial resources and best economic potential of any country in South America. But our problems have been inherited from the dictatorships. They are more or less the same as those in the rest of South America: a population growing too fast, farmland that is poorly distributed, inadequate industrial development, a low level of home consumption, and an excessive concentration of the population in towns to the disadvantage of the badly under-populated country areas.'

It is quite true that concentration in towns is not a phenomenon peculiar to Venezuela, but it is more acute there. One in every four of the population lives in greater Caracas; 80 per cent of the population is concentrated along the coastal strip.

*

What is quite clear is that the economic machine which had looked so hopeful a few years before was now giving cause for anxiety. In 1959 the figures of the major firms were all down; the State's budgetary deficit was 317 million dollars in 1960 and 562 million in 1961, whereas up to 1958 there had been no deficit in the balance of payments. The trade of the oil companies was enough to make up for the deficit in other operations and still leave an excess reckoned by U.N. financial experts at 65 million dollars in 1957. The January 1958 revolution resulted in an immediate flight of capital, and between January and December 1958 the provisional Larrazábal government made the mistake of shouldering the debts of the dictatorship: chivalrous, no doubt, but paying out 100 thousand million *bolívares* (30 thousand million dollars) made a deep hole in the treasury.

At the same time the money of the businessmen who had worked with the dictatorship had been removed to the safety of American banks. Finally in January 1959, with the coming to power of the Betancourt government – reputedly extremely left-wing – the situation deteriorated to such a point that the flight of capital between January 1959 and January 1960 was twice as great as it had been during 1958.

But it must be added that wage increases permitted by the Betancourt government (averaging 30 per cent) and increased state spending also contributed to speeding up the process. With greater expenses and fewer resources Betancourt was forced into taking austerity measures.

Beginning in 1959 imports were restricted and customs duty on all non-essentials vastly increased. For a long time the *bolívar* had been a competitor with the dollar and Caracas rejoiced in a wild and fevered worship of the golden calf. From 1948 to 1958 'making a *bolo*' was the one major concern of Caracans, whether native or foreigners (who had come in great numbers). In ten years Venezuela received 800,000 immigrants, mainly Spanish, Italian and Portuguese. The oil companies alone had some 50,000 employees there in 1958. But the oil firms gave an example of lack of confidence, cutting down their staffs and almost ceasing to invest.

*

'There's something rotten in the state of Venezuela...' as Shakespeare might have said. Venezuela has a disease of the land: that is the first obvious obstacle on the way to progress. The greatest writers of Venezuela seldom talk about the world of oil – their favourite landscape is not that of the derricks, the pontoon bridges, the refineries along beaches scattered with oil waste and salt, the well-shafts standing alongside the stiff clumps of cactus. A great novelist like Rómulo Gallegos, president of the republic for a few months in 1948, will turn his first love and attention to the *llanos* which lie at the foot of the eastern slopes of the Andes.

Settled first by Spaniards, who raised animals there, the *llanos* produced a hard people, generous, mistrustful, veering between melancholy and over-intense gaiety. The *llaneros*, white/Indian mestizos, have something in common with the *gauchos* of the Argentinian plains and southern Brazil. Their life is more or less nomad; and the *joropo*, which has become the national dance of Venezuela, with its accompaniment of the *zapateado*, the flamenco tapping of heels, was their invention.

Rómulo Gallegos tends to make his hero a young city man with a longing for the wide open spaces and blazing sunsets of the *llanos*. Another contemporary novelist and journalist, Miguel Otero Silva, is obsessed with the slow death of the villages of the interior, killed by oil fever. Alejo Carpentier sees the real Venezuela in the great forests south of the Orinoco, while Ramón Díaz Sánchez seeks to escape into the melancholy colonial *haciendas* of the Caribbean coastal area. But the poet, Juan Liscano, gives lyrical and despairing language to the thirsty soil of the Barquisimeto country:

> This earth is like a lunar plain
> roamed by the rats of the rain,
> clawed by the talons of the wind...

The determined refusal of Venezuelan intellectuals to face the ocean of oil which has flowed over their country for the past thirty-five years, and their happy but uneasy flight into regional beauties, are most significant. Venezuela is seeking the balance it has lost: for thirty years or more the fishing villages, the *haciendas* of Carabobo, the villages of the Andes, have all gradually lost their people, who have left for city life and oil, and they are still losing them. Peasants without any hope for the future have turned into specialized but rootless workers in Maracaibo or Caracas, while the land produces ever smaller and poorer crops.

At the beginning of this century Venezuela was exporting a million 60-kilo bags of coffee a year, and this represented half the country's total income from exports. Today coffee is just one of several agricultural products and not a very important one. Enormous herds used to wander under the open skies of the *llanos*, but they have been largely abandoned, for oil has also almost put a stop to cattle-breeding – in 1966 there were barely more than seven million head all told.

Agricultural production only contributes 7·4 per cent to the internal gross product, well below oil (23·8 per cent), services (16·4 per cent), and even industry (13·4 per cent) which has as yet hardly had time to develop. Apart from the special curse of oil, bemoaned by poets and novelists with perhaps too much fervour, the reasons for this failure in agriculture are of course similar to those in the other Andean countries. Only 1½ million hectares are under cultivation, representing no more than 55 per cent of the possible total. Yet the rural population is still 38 per cent of the whole, despite the enormously rapid move towards urbanization. Not merely are the yields very low (11 quintals to a hectare for maize, as against 33 in the U.S.), but the unequal division and under-use of the land results in a situation of intense poverty. Though not perhaps as desperate as the lot of the country people elsewhere in the Andes, especially Peru, the situation here gives serious cause for concern.

Approximately one third of all Venezuelans still live on the land and live very badly. Ninety-four per cent of all cultivable land belongs to large proprietors who make up only 1·5 per cent of all landowners. Small and average holdings account for a mere 6 per cent of the total, and 350,000 peasant families (over 2 million people) have no land of their own at all. Though in certain sectors of industry, especially petrochemicals, Venezuela has achieved the most advanced technological development, it still suffers from the archaic '*conuco*' system – agriculture based on using up land and then moving on. This very widespread system introduced by the peoples of the Amazon and the Caribbean is similar to that common in many parts of Africa.

It involves spending the dry season cutting down bushes with machetes, and then trees with axes; all the wood is then burnt, and the ground cleared is then sown without further preparation with the start of the rains. A long stick, the *chicora* or *barretón*, is used for sowing, and reaping is by hand. The same ground, having been thus cleared, can be used for three consecutive years, and is then left alone for ten years during which the natural vegetation reappears. There are various different forms of *conuco* in Venezuela, but it is thought that about 67 per cent of all farming follows some such pattern. Needless to say the peasants only manage to feed themselves and their families very poorly by this system, and in the course of producing what little food they do, exhaust the resources of soil, water, forest and fauna.

Even in 1816 Bolívar was anxious over the fate of the poorer Venezuelan peasants. Since then half-hearted attempts, which later petered out altogether, were made, especially in 1936, 1948 and 1949. The great merit of the Betancourt government was that it undertook a real programme of agrarian reform in 1960. The law of 5 March decreed the giving of land to a hundred thousand peasant families; its implementation was placed in the hands of the National Agrarian Institute (IAN), which shared out the land, some already acquired for the state by levies etc., some confiscated by the commission as being illicitly exploited, some brought with the owners' agreement and some simply expropriated where 'estates were not fulfilling their social function'. Pastureland however was not affected by the reform. In fact, by any standards, it was a timid, careful reform, more concerned with settling the countryside better than with any change in agrarian structures or the large-scale ownership of land. It made quite a number of cases of speculation possible, and some landowners in fact made a considerable profit by 'agreeing' to sell their land to the IAN.

Thus, though the results of the reform were in some ways more spectacular than those of similar programmes carried out in other countries, it is also easy to see its limitations. According to CEPAL, only about 1·69 per cent of the *latifundios* were affected; it was mainly land belonging to the state that was distributed. In 1964 the Institute settled 82 per cent of the peasants on public, and only 18 per cent on private, land. By the beginning of 1967 a total of 3,407,550 hectares had been redistributed among 131,250 families, and 803 million *bolívares* had been invested in the operation; hand in hand with this went the work of irrigation, road-building, and setting up schools.

Experts have reckoned that the Venezuelan reform has been 'the most costly in the world', while its positive effects have been slight, owing to the absence of agricultural technicians and the natural indolence and physical frailty of the under-nourished people involved. In any case it will certainly take years for any major changes to become evident. After 1965 it became the tendency for the government only to buy up private land under strong pressure from the peasants; and the population explosion seems to make nonsense of a reform that has been too slow, too expensive, and no more than a drop in the vast ocean of need.

Most of the peasants belong to the league controlled by the Democratic Action party, which partly explains the loyalty of the mass of country people to the regime from 1958 to 1968. Agrarian reform is a vital part of the total plan for developing the country; the Betancourt government's target was to complete it in twenty years. But voices from the exreme left were heard to declare that this was too long to wait. The union leaders were continually harrassed by peasants impatient over the delay, and took over certain estates by force. As in north east Brazil, peasants' leagues were formed, did some soul-searching, disintegrated again, hesitating over doing anything really direct and revolutionary. But from the country areas of Venezuela, which had for so long been silent, arid, parched with thirst, a rumbling was beginning to be heard.

*

The rule of oil begins at Punta Cardón on the Paraguaná peninsula. The sticky black mud which so hampered and annoyed the fishermen on the Lake of Maracaibo at the beginning of the century has been domesticated and brought under control in the canals that take it from the fields round Bolívar and Lagunillas to the gigantic refineries whose superstructures stand black against the horizon. But you can still smell it, still feel its presence. It soaks into the earth giving this 'lunar' landscape a greenish tinge, and it is the only reason that brings such numbers of men to this torrid, inhuman desert.

When the first pipelines were laid only a few Indians roamed this hell of sand, wind and water which thrusts forward into the Caribbean towards the Dutch island of Aruba. Their belief had always been that the 'mountain' of Santa Ana – a hill barely higher than the peninsula around it – was a divinity from whom they could hope for salvation. Their ancestors who handed this faith down were obviously quite right: the Indians' poor little village has become a town of 50,000: Punto Fiji. The airport's runway is at Las Piedras, and looks like a film set from *The Wages of Fear*.

Nets drying on the beach lie in front of a row of crumbling wooden huts. A huge advertising poster is stuck up in the worm-eaten remains of an old boat. Beyond this is a world of thistles and thorns, and the air palpitates with heat. Occasionally you hear the rumbling of a *mechero* – the jet from which the burnt gases come; whenever the huge white flame with its bluish tinge goes out, those whose job it is go towards the now silent stand and throw burning rags at it. It is no good throwing them from too far, since they will not catch; but nor must one go too near for a man can go up like a torch in the gas-laden air; occasionally a workman will misjudge the distance.

From Punta Cardón you can see the gleam of the oil tankers lying out to sea, but never any of the oil itself: what one Creole writer calls 'the blood of Venezuela' is one of the hardest things to catch a glimpse of, though its rule extends from the Paraguaná peninsula to the foot of Lake Maracaibo.

Even those who actually live in Maracaibo never see any oil. They see skyscrapers as fine as any in Caracas, air-conditioned hotels, the university of Zulia State, of which their town is the capital; they see flower-lined avenues leading to the modern state housing-developments, the smarter residential areas, clubs and tennis courts, an air-conditioned shopping centre: none of this existed in 1925. But of the oil itself all they see is the machines used for getting hold of it: the thousands of derricks whose metallic masts rise up above the lake, the bores, the gleaming tankers, the barges, the floating, ultra-modern equipment for re-injecting the gases.

It is a world of automation with very few people in it. The occasional white or grey figure can be seen clambering about high up in the air, his head protected by an aluminium helmet. Men and machines are in a permanent steam bath, and at midday the asphalt in the streets seems to be positively smoking. In the windswept market, either on the ground or on plain white-wood tables, lie heaps of pineapples, papayas, green bananas, shiny turtles, indigo-shelled lobsters, and fascinating pink, mauve or purple fish, with pearly scales and incredibly long antennae.

At night huge flashes of heat lightning illuminate the southern horizon. Under the roofs of the boatsheds by the port lie schooners waiting to go who knows where, with blue gulls or motionless pelicans sleeping on board.

The Lake of Maracaibo is what the Indians used to call the

lagoon of Coquivacoa; the town itself was built right at the north of the lake's western shore, just opposite Altagracia, previously a short trip by boat and recently linked to it by a metal bridge 9 kilometres long.

*

The mailboat cuts through the oily water of the lake, weighted down with parties of silent Guajiro Indians, whose wives wear marvellous pompoms of many-coloured wool on their shoes, filled with scented cargo, mountains of pineapples and papayas and cages of birds, while the steel points of the derricks rise up and up. The lake is linked with the Caribbean by a channel nine kilometres wide. In 1951 major drainage works made it possible for the largest ships to negotiate that channel by clearing the alluvial deposits which obstructed it. This has made traffic with Aruba and Curaçao very much easier.

Up to 1925 Maracaibo was merely a stopping place, a small business centre for the export of produce from the surrounding countryside: sugar and cocoa in the main. Though the first probings by geologists had indicated long before then the presence of vast layers of naphtha under the ground surrounding Maracaibo, it was only in about 1910 that the large oil companies began doing any real prospecting. The hinterland of Maracaibo is desperately dry: thin thirsty bushes manage somehow to survive among the serried ranks of 'organ-pipe' cactus. Directly above the long, sraight, empty roads, groups of vultures wheel slowly in the empty sky.

The oil-workers' camps, their bungalows scattered among clumps of flamboyants and bougainvilleas, are surrounded by high chain link fences, as though to protect their deliciously green lawns against the merciless invasion of the surrounding stones.

Here and there, behind a cactus bush, or at the bend of a red road, a mechanical pump rattles away without pause, alone in this heavy solitude, as surprising as some unknown species of animal. All along the Caribbean shore a narrow strip of yellow sand lies between the water and the Andean foothills, the refuge of the Motilone Indians who have not yet overcome their fear of the oilmen – a fear amply justified by a history of 'punitive' expeditions in the past.

*

The first well was drilled at Mene Grande in 1914 and the first oil was exported in 1917. But only in 1922 did the oil boom start to make a complete transformation in the whole appearance of Maracaibo and indeed of the very life of Venezuela. The explosion of the 'Number 2 Los Barros' well took place on 22 October 1922, but the excitement of this discovery was forgotten in the thunderclap which took place in Europe on that same day, with the march of Mussolini's blackshirts on Rome. After that development was rapid: 321,000 barrels were exported in 1932, 625,000 in 1942, and 1,700,000 in 1952.

Almost three quarters of all Venezuela's oil comes from the Maracaibo area and the rest from the east, from the valleys of Apure and Barinas, of the Cariaco near Barlovento, and of the Orinoco. The famous deposits in the Bolívar district near Lake Maracaibo alone produce 72 per cent of the total; in fact the basin of the lake is the largest production area in the whole of the western hemisphere. Up to 1958 the huge sums invested in the oil industry brought some benefits to Maracaibo but since then the new policy of prudence on the part of the oil companies has struck a heavy blow at the economy of Zulia State. The government's development plan, patterned on that of Guyana, has been unable to stop the recession. The urban centres which arose all along the eastern shore of the lake because of the expanding oil industry (Cabimas, Tía Juana, Ciudad Ojeda, Lagunillas, Bachaquero, Mene Grande), now look more like western American small towns with rings of shanty-towns around them than workers' housing developments of a standard consonant with the technological level of the industry itself. The vast majority of the homes in this almost unbroken succession of 'oil towns' are little different from the *ranchitos* of Caracas. Though the establishment in 1964 of an 'indusrial zone' to which large financial concessions were granted by the government did a lot for the town of Maracaibo itself, Venezuela's second largest city, with its modern airport of Caujarito, it too is surrounded by an ever-encroaching circle of slums. The exploitation of the wealth of oil around Lake Maracaibo has thus resulted in the creation of an industry which is controlled by foreign interests which make enormous profits, but have done nothing to contribute any real improvement to the standard of living of most of the people who actually live in the area. Quite the reverse. This ludicrous situation is not only denounced loudly by those on the far left, but also adds to the bitterness of the nationalists who, though they long to change matters, are fearful of killing what they still see as the goose that lays the golden eggs.

The monopoly of the big oil companies no longer looks as if it were absolute, for the American anti-trust law has resulted in the establishment of so-called 'independent companies'. There are sixty different firms involved in the oil business. But in reality the interests and alliances among the various groups are so complex and interwoven that the 'good neighbour' rule is scrupulously observed by them all.

The Caracas government will eventually be forced to confront the almost solid front presented by the oilmen. The last thirty years has been filled with more or less fierce disputes between them and the Venezuelan leadership. But for the most part such disputes have ended in compromise. It cannot be denied that up to 1928 Venezuela could certainly have made more capital than it did out of the terrific rivalry between the Anglo-Dutch and American companies. But at that time the country was wholly under the thumb of Gómez, the dictator, whose first concern was his own and his family's private fortune. He therefore made no attempt to set bounds to the exorbitant privileges claimed by the oilmen, but merely did what he could behind the scenes to gain personal profit by coming to terms with them. The law of 1920 fixed royalties at the low level of 7·75 per cent; on the whole, relations between the Gómez government and the oil companies were most cordial.

By 1929 there were 24,000 workmen employed in the oilfields, and in 1930 Gómez was able to pay off Venezuela's foreign debt – just at a time when most other Latin American countries were desperately affected by the great world economic crisis. Venezuela was the only country in South America to emerge from the depression years with increased power and prestige.

*

This was obviously due to a combination of highly favourable circumstances and especially to the miracle of oil – though in fact the man in the street had little share in that. It would be impossible to pretend that Gómez had any coherent policy for oil; all he wanted was to make as much money as he could. In fact it is probable that this 'tyrant of the Andes' had very little idea of the revolution that the development of this new industry really represented.

He was a countryman, a suspicious peasant from Tachira, and in fact a man highly suspicious of any spectacular advances, of social upheavals and of the stranger who might look too openly into his own house. He was in favour of extracting the oil but there could be no question of refining it on the spot. That was Gómez's attitude – though it would obviously have been in the national interest to have a refinery built in Venezuela. Consequently in 1917 Shell set about building two refineries on the Dutch island of Curaçao, just off the Venezuelan coast. In 1935 Gómez's death unleashed the Venezuelan people's first wave of anger against the oil companies for making profits out of all proportion to their investments or to their actual work.

Gómez's successors, sensitive to this indication of public opinion, set about disputing with some determination the privileges he had granted to the oil companies. The royalty rate was slowly but gradually raised after painful negotiations and the companies were obliged to build refineries.

Rómulo Gallegos, a respected member of Congress, made his voice heard for the first time to provide intellectuals with arguments and reasons to support this burgeoning nationalism. Gómez had used oil as a commodity: that commodity was contributing to the creation of a still shaky national consciousness. A law passed in 1938 laying down rules for further claims was firmly rejected by the oilmen, but the Second World War came just at the right moment to make a truce between the companies' representatives and the Caracas government desirable.

The battle began again in 1944. In 1945, on 18 October, a group of young nationalist officers organized a putsch which also had the support of the leaders of the Democratic Action Party. It was a dubious alliance and was not to prove long-lived; but the revolutionary junta formed as a result of this *coup* forced the oil companies to accept the famous fifty-fifty rule: 50 per cent of all profits must go to the state. Gallegos had been the prophet; Betancourt was the spokesman and organizer of the movement.

From 1945 to 1946 he worked out a rational and coherent oil policy. The central notion in his system was a simple one: while the oil companies had certainly taken risks and ventured their capital during the early years, they had already made enough profit to compensate for most of it; it was only right that Venezuela itself should now profit from this natural resource and thus secure its own harmonious economic development. The blood of Venezuela must at last begin to give life to its weakened body.

Thus the major lines of the oil policy adopted by the Betancourt government in 1958 were already laid down in the 1945–6 plan: social improvements, the setting up of a national company, increased royalties, refining to be extended under state control, a national tanker fleet. The man whose job it was to argue all this point by point with the oil companies was Juan Pablo Pérez Alfonso, Minister of Development, and a close personal friend of Betancourt. But hardly had he begun to negotiate with the companies when, in November 1948, another military putsch removed the Democratic Action government which had barely begun its term of office. The leaders of this putsch were officers who, as is usual in such cases, established themselves as a provisional junta. Some sinister intrigues and timely murders left Colonel Pérez Jiménez alone in power. Obviously no one could ever prove that the putsch had been organized or financed by the oil companies in their fear of the plan for nationalist reform put forward by the Democratic Action leaders; but it certainly came at just the right moment to rescue them from a very nasty situation.

*

The reforms hoped for by Democratic Action were shelved, but not wholly. Pérez Jiménez took up one idea which was also a popular slogan: 'sowing oil'. We cannot yet present an objective balance sheet for the nine years of this particularly oppressive dictatorship, and perhaps we never shall. The leaders of the Democratic Action party, having been followed, hounded, imprisoned, forced into impoverished exile if they were lucky, able only to clench their fists as some of their closest comrades were tortured, came back to Caracas in 1958 with a natural wish to settle old scores and in far too angry a state to make any calm assessment of the defeated military regime.

Unfortunately for Betancourt and his friends, they once more took up the reins of government in Venezuela just when an oil recession was beginning. The Suez crisis and the partial cessation of oil deliveries from the Middle East had led Venezuela to over-produce from 1956 to 1958; now the demand was dying down. Not only had the Middle East come back into the world market, but the other oil-producing countries of Latin America were developing at a spectacular rate; and, finally, Europe and Canada were increasing their own production as well.

These disadvantages were partly, but only partly, made up for by the fact that the United States could not really do without Venezuela's oil. Though certain of being able to sell there, Venezuela still had to face the fact that her margin for manoeuvre in any negotiations with the oil companies had been greatly reduced. It was in this context – not very favourable, but far from desperate – that the dialogue between the oil magnates and the Betancourt government began again.

From 1958, Juan Pablo Pérez Alfonso, the father of the fifty-fifty law, was once again the Minister of Mines and Fuel. The first serious dispute arose out of a discussion over collective wage contracts between the companies and a government under strong pressure from the unions. In effect the Betancourt plan of 1958 was barely more revolutionary than that of 1946. It rejected nationalization as solving nothing. But it proposed an increase in the royalties payable by the companies and refused to grant any new concessions. 'From 1947 to 1957' declared Pérez Alfonso, 'the extent of concessions granted rose from 300,000 hectares to 6 million. Such an increase indicates a total failure to consider the national interest.'

In 1958 Juan Pablo Pérez Alfonso visited the countries of

the Middle East: he met Nasser, King Saud of Arabia, the Iraqi and Iranian governments, the Emir of Kuwait. To them he said, 'Since our interests are so similar, let us work together. Let us form a producers' group which will put us in a stronger bargaining position with the oil companies.' OPEP was thus established in 1961; it has been something of a failure, not only because of the hostility of the oil companies, but also the bad faith of some of the Arab leaders.

*

The Venezuelan national company, of which the Caracas leaders had dreamt for the past twenty years, became a reality in 1960. Without skills, without experience, without organizers, almost without staff of any kind, and without much financial backing, it brought a smile to the lips of the Shell and Esso men. It was in fact highly doubtful that it would ever be in a position to control the complex operations needed, from prospecting to dealing with the international market. But at least it existed.

Its formation looked like a threat that could be freely uttered because it would never have to be used. Yet Betancourt's prudent reformism was disliked by the oil companies who lamented the good old days of the Pérez Jiménez dictatorship.

Following the military coup of November 1948 Betancourt had had to emigrate to Puerto Rico and then to Costa Rica, where his friend José Figueres was president. The Eisenhower government had insisted that the governor of Puerto Rico, Muñoz Marín, should not allow him to stay there for too long. Pérez Jiménez, when he was in turn overthrown in January 1958, was under no such ban. Four years after his fall, Caracas's demand to Washington for his extradition was unanswered. The wandering life of a political refugee led by Betancourt for ten years, and the luxurious life of an idle millionaire led by Pérez Jiménez in his new home in

Florida, indicated more than merely a difference of income. Betancourt had not found favour with the oil trusts for, despite the concessions he had been forced to accept, they still wanted someone easier to deal with, whereas the wealthy general, despite being accused of political crimes and the misappropriation of public funds, still had the benefit of powerful and barely concealed protection. By the time the former dictator was at long last extradited and the Caracas government was able to bring him to court for 'misuse of public funds', the Democratic Action leaders were already under threat from those on their left who wanted more revolutionary measures. Now, twenty years after the 1948 coup, Betancourt and his friends were in turn being accused of conniving with American imperialism.

*

Venezuela gave Bolívar to America and the world. The most revered of all heroes of South American independence was born in Caracas on 24 July 1783. Venezuela also gave its own people Juan Vicente Gómez. One of the most amazing and compelling *caudillos* of South America took power in 1908 and only abandoned it on his deathbed twenty-eight years later.

Bolívar, a man of aristocratic and wealthy family, had black eyes, a frail, almost sickly look, dark complexion, a fiery and pleasure-loving nature, long, thin arms, and enormous charm. Gómez was a thickset giant, silent, hard-working, cunning rather than clever, with the shoulders of a fighter, and a marked fondness for women, money, land and absolute power.

Bolívar and Gómez, both outstanding characters, illustrate the two deepest tendencies of the Venezuelan people. Bolívar undoubtedly had some black or Indian blood in his veins; Gómez was the son of an important Spaniard and a peasant woman. Even today it remains difficult to work out the exact proportions in which the various races have contributed to the formation of the people of Venezuela. At a conservative estimate at least one of every ten Venezualans is pure white, and one pure negro. The other eight will be some kind of mixture, for there are barely more than 250,000 pure Indians left. But there are enormous differences between the mestizos of the plains, of the *llanos* and of the hills – differences which date back to colonial times. The Indians of the high valleys and mountains were harder to conquer, stronger and more civilized than the Arawaks or Caribs of the coast and the islands. They were fighters where the latter were peace-loving and friendly.

The Spanish settlers established themselves first of all along the coast at Cumaná and then at Coro at the south of the Paraguaná peninsula. Caracas, Valencia and the other inland towns were founded some time later. But Mérida and San Cristóbal, the two cities in the Venezuelan Andes south of Lake Maracaibo, were built by Spaniards who moved on from the highlands of what is now Colombia, from Bogotá or Tunja. The real conquest of the rest of Venezuela had barely begun at the end of the seventeenth century. On the coast and in the warm, low-lying districts, sugar-cultivation developed, as in Brazil, because of the massive forced immigration of black labourers. Thus the mestizos of the coast are less violent, darker-skinned, more sensitive, and less hard-working than the men of the mountains.

*

Gómez was primarily an Andean. The Venezuelan army has always had a large proportion of officers from the Andean provinces, and the excessive role played by the military in the public life of the country in the past two hundred years is partly explainable in terms of this aggressive and obstinate element in the Andean nature.

Only the *llaneros*, with their passion for riding the prairies under the open sky, have ever been able to present their lances, their breasts, their courage or their cruelty in confrontation with the wild *guerrilleros* who rushed down from the sierra. The history of Venezuela is the ever-repeated story of the battle between industrious authoritarianism and an impassioned but dreaming liberalism.

'I have ploughed the sea . . .' murmured the disillusioned Bolívar before he died. The *Libertador* had good cause to be embittered and disappointed; his dream of a South America united in brotherhood had fallen to pieces. Greater Colombia, made up of Venezuela, Colombia and Ecuador, had only a brief existence, and Venezuela itself, as Bolívar was about to leave it, seemed on the eve of being fragmented by a flock of little dictators.

'This country,' said the anti-clerical Bolívar bitterly to the priest who was with him at the end, 'this country is bound to fall into the hands of a crazy crowd of little tyrants, almost too small to notice, of all colours and all races . . .' The shadow of Páez, the greedy *llanero*, and those of all the *caudillos* to come, flitted before Bolívar's eyes as he lay dying. What had happened to the vow he had made to his friend Carreno on his way to Italy? 'I swear before you, I swear by the God of my fathers, I swear on my honour, I swear by the country of my birth, that I shall not let my arm fall or my soul rest until I have broken the chains in which the will of the Spanish power holds us.' That dream at least has come true. And today what he did is recognized by Venezuela and not by Venezuela alone. His birthplace in Caracas is now a museum where one can follow the suffering and fevered life of this warrior-philosopher.

Simón Bolívar, young, rich, carefree, stirred by the ideas of Rousseau which he had learnt from his tutor Simón Rodríguez, left for Europe and Spain for the first time and there married María Teresa Rodríguez y Alaiza. A year later, mature and serious, seeking to forget the death of his young wife by plunging into action, a quite different Bolívar set off from La Guaira for Europe – this time Paris. There he met Laplace, Gay-Lussac, Vauquelin and Humboldt. The German scholar and naturalist had just come back from a trip to the West Indies. He spoke of Venezuela: 'The fruit is ripe, but I cannot imagine any man able to pick it ...' Yet the man who could was in front of him, impatient, alive with ambition, fêted by Parisian society, dazzled and then disappointed by Bonaparte, and in his mind already fighting on battlefields far larger than any in Europe to win South America's independence. At Notre Dame the name he hoped to leave to posterity suddenly came to him in a trance-like moment of exultation: the Liberator. And twelve years later he was in fact to be hailed by celebrations in Caracas with excited cries of '*El Libertador!*'

*

He was not in fact the first – barely even the second. His forerunner was Miranda, a man thirty years older than himself who had served in both Spanish and French armies, had travelled in Prussia, England, Russia, Turkey and even Scandinavia. He was at Valmy and his name is engraved in the stone of the Arc de Triomphe. He left Paris, where he had arrived in the revolutionary days of 1792, just before Bolívar got there in 1804. Two years later he organized his first attempt to liberate Venezuela, but it failed. At the second attempt he had young Captain Bolívar beside him. Facing them was an undistinguished Spaniard: Monteverde. Who betrayed them? Bolívar, resigning the main square of Puerto Cabello almost without a fight – or Miranda who came to terms with Monteverde? Bolívar certainly had a meteoric career: Miranda was arrested by his men at La Guiara, and he was then given a safe-conduct by Monteverde in exchange for Miranda.

In the end history has heaped the same praise on them

both. The war Bolívar began again alone, setting out from Cartagena de Indias, in Colombia, while Miranda suffered in a dungeon in Cadiz, was to last over ten years. From 1813 to 1824 Bolivar fought like the general of an empire, and at Carabobo he won so overwhelming and total a victory that Napolean himself would have been proud of it.

What has been described as Bolívar's 'splendid campaign' took him from the coast of Colombia to the capital of Venezuela which he entered in triumph. But Monteverde would not admit himself beaten. Firmly entrenched at Puerto Cabello, the Spanish general methodically set about reconquering Venezuela, sustained by the ferocity of Boves and his cavalry.

Venezuela paid a higher cost than any other country for South America's independence, with thousands of dead, buildings in ruins, and a hatred never totally to die. Bolívar was pursued, worn out, driven away from Cumaná and he set off again for New Granada, sticking close inshore in his wretched little boat. But, like Cortés, even in defeat he was already making his plans for future victory. He organized his next, and this time successful, expedition in Jamaica and Haiti; its success was due to Bolívar's realization that you can only win if you have the people on your side.

The first two attempts to liberate Venezuela had failed primarily because the mass of the people mistrusted such Creole grandees as Bolívar, who in their eyes represented a privileged class. The Second Republic was overthrown because Boves and his *llaneros* thought the danger from the Creole aristocracy was greater than that from the Spanish delegates. Once the *llaneros* had moved over to Bolívar's side, victory was assured. As long as the idealists and the populace remained in opposing camps it was easy for the Spanish to maintain their power, but once the infantry of the liberating army was filled with peasant volunteers things were very different.

A liberation movement had sprung up in Peru and set a most contagious example. The parish priest of Dolores uttered his cry to revolution in Mexico; provinces later to become Chile, Argentina, Uruguay and Bolivia were stirring; Bolívar was at Angostura, on the Orinoco, where he established his base camp, and he moved up the valley from east to west, enlisting the *llaneros* of Páez as he went, crossed the Andes, and with the help of Santander, liberated Colombia. He proclaimed the union of Colombia, Venezuela and Ecuador. Miranda's dreams had been fulfilled; now the former master and his favourite pupil, having for a time been at odds, were once again comrades in arms. After Carabobo everything was settled in Venezuela. Bolívar descended on Quito with Antonio José de Sucre, and Sucre went on alone to drive the royalist army right down to Peru.

On 9 December 1824, while Bolívar waited in Lima, Sucre routed the Spaniards on the plain of Ayacucho: this was the greatest, and final, battle in the war of independence. Bolívar had no part in it, and this may possibly have saddened him. But by then he could, had he wished, have had himself made emperor of a vast kingdom with seven capitals: Caracas, Bogotá, Quito, La Paz, Lima, Santiago, Buenos Aires; they would all have accepted him as their ruler, and even San Martín, the liberator of Chile and Lower Peru, generously deferred to him at Guayaquil.

Yet he was beginning to lose the faith that had sustained him throughout. People were conspiring against him; his best generals were abandoning him, betraying him, intriguing and trying to carve out kingdoms for themselves in an America which Bolívar wanted to see standing as a single, strong, free entity. In 1828 the Panama Congress which he called together to try to unite the various States was a failure. Yet the fact that Bolívar's name is today respected and admired by one and all, from the Rio Grande to Tierra del Fuego, is in fact chiefly because he was the first to launch the idea of the necessity of such inter-American collaboration. Panama was the forerunner of Chapultepec, Bogotá, Rio de Janeiro and Punta del Este. Yet it was only by a miracle that Bolívar escaped assassination in 1828.

Santander was governing in Bogotá and Páez in Venezuela. Boussingault met Bolívar at the time and was later to say, 'He was acclaimed because he was feared. He was adored almost as an idol because he was a great man. But in reality, nobody actually loved him.' The Bolívar he saw, exhausted, weakened by tuberculosis, was still 'that little man below average height, with a head too large for his body, but with energy, a keen glance and enormous vitality of movement'. Yet underneath it all he was a man worn out, sad, bitter, tired of fighting.

His most faithful lieutenant, Sucre, was murdered. He himself never again saw Venezuela: he stopped at Santa Marta and died there on 17 December 1830, precisely 11 years after the establishment of Gran Colombia before the Angostura Congress.

'Nothing is won without force ...' was the final despairing thought of this Liberator, whose own mind had been formed by Rousseau's *Social Contract*, with its doctrine of a return to nature and the natural goodness of man. Between the death of Bolívar and the appearance of Gómez, Venezuela was subject to almost permanent anarchy and just such tyrannical rulers as Bolívar had most feared.

*

However, from this long tale of bloodshed, violence and terror, the names of two or three *caudillos* stand out among the rest. The first is Páez. This cruel and illiterate *llanero*, once in power, whether directly or through others, became a wise and paternalistic president, governing for over fifteen years to the advantage of the landed oligarchy. For the liberation of Venezuela carried out with the help of bandits, mestizos,

Negroes and *llanero* herdsmen had certainly at first benefited only the Creole bourgeoisie.

Páez, a large, unkempt and fierce man, once a tamer of wild horses – hence his nickname of 'Centaur' – only loved two things, according to Gómez' biographer, Thomas Rourke: money and seeing his enemies die. The same could be said equally of most of his successors. Guzmán Blanco, who became president following a *pronunciamiento* in 1879, believed, to paraphrase the famous saying about General Motors, that 'what was good for Guzmán Blanco was good for Venezuela.'

Twenty years after him, anther dictator, General Castro, was to behave in so unbearably arrogant a manner that the great powers in Europe sent a squadron to shell La Guaira. Then there was Gómez . . .

Juan Vicente Gómez was probably born in 1857 though the exact date is uncertain. He was four when his mother, the wife of a Spaniard from Cucuta named García about whom nothing is now known, took him with her across the border to live with the Gómez whose name he took. The same landscape can be seen on both sides of the frontier: wooded, mountainous, cold and difficult. This mountainland of Venezuela was the cradle of a stalwart, conquering and headstrong race of men. Gómez's adoptive father was just a small farmer on the sierra, working hard to support his thirteen children, of whom Juan Vicente was one.

It was hardly surprising that young Gómez, by the age of fourteen when his adoptive father died, was a determined competitor, hungry for gain, and as hard on himself as he was on everyone else. He increased his holding, acquired others, and gradually became a kind of village squire. The Gómez family were known and held in awe from the Colombian border to San Cristóbal. But to get from San Cristóbal to Caracas and the presidency would not have struck anyone as a possibility; it certainly had not entered Gómez's head by the time he was 46. Had it not been for the chance that brought the whirlwind of civil war across his estate, La Mulera, his fate might have never have been so totally changed.

The government General in command in the State of Tachira offered to make him a Colonel so that he could lead his *peones* in the fight against the rebels. Gómez, still quite unused to political intrigues and alliances, accepted the offer. But he had chosen the wrong side: the regular troops were beaten by Crespo's guerrillas, and Gómez, in the losing camp, had to leave La Mulera and flee towards Cucuta. The entire tribe followed him, women and children, and servants who were now fighting men.

Seven years later Gómez was rich again. He still had friends in Venezuela and had given much thought to the dangers of war and revolution. He offered his sixty men and his entire fortune to General Castro, to help him in the putsch he was organizing. Castro's party made a fantastic journey from San Cristóbal to Valencia and Caracas: 1,400 kilometres of ambushes, incredibly bold manoeuvres, and narrow mountain passes to cross.

*

Having set off with less than a hundred men, Gómez arrived in Caracas with ten thousand troops. He had shown himself an able, brave and merciless commander. He had never before left his Andean retreat, but now, in middle age, he was getting to know his country for the first time.

It was a revelation. On 26 October 1899 he entered the capital. His soldiers slung their hammocks between the trees of the Plaza Bolívar, a strange lot of men, ragged, wild and starving. As a reward for his services Gómez was appointed governor first of Caracos, then of Tachira. Luck was always on his side and people began calling him the sorcerer, *el Brujo*. He was sent into the plains of the Orinoco to deal with rebellious local leaders, whom he quickly subdued.

In July 1903 he returned to Caracas in triumph as a conqueror, though only four years earlier he was an Andean peasant who had never even seen the sea. Castro's presidency was filled with tension and his friends persuaded him to seek relaxation in Europe. He set sail from La Guaira. Gómez waited no more than twenty-seven days, and then acted.

A cousin by marriage of his, Eustoquio, had been arrested for murder. He had him freed and gave him a senior post in the San Carlos prison where he had been in the cells. It could have been a challenge, but to Gómez it was a joke, and a declaration of intent for the future. 'Funny, is it not?' he said. And the silent Gómez did indeed begin to play jokes upon Venezuela. He decreed the dismissal of Castro, and himself seized power, without causing the slightest reaction.

In April 1910 Congress legalized his coup. Gómez was appointed Commander-in-Chief and president until 1914. He settled his mother on an estate in Macuto, his sisters in towns near the Miraflores palace, his second wife in a fine house on El Paraíso, and his sixteen-year-old mistress, Dolores Amelia, he kept in his own house. But the only woman he really feared, and feared until the end, was Dionisia Bello, whom he had abducted when he was still the master of La Mulera. She was the only woman he ever really loved, and by her he had seven children, whose name became Gómez Bello. Children, grandchildren and cousins all grew up in the shadow of the presidential palace just as they had earlier shared in the good and ill fortunes of La Mulera. One curious thing about Gómez was his incredible physical likeness to Stalin.

In four years the budget for the army had increased by 180 per cent. He flattered his officers, corrupted them, showered gifts of money on his favourites, just as, forty years later, another Colonel, Marcos Pérez Jiménez, also from Tachira state, was to do. Gómez the president still had about him some elements of Gómez the farmer. He took part in cattle-dealing. He had enormous admiration for Bolívar – and also for Kaiser Wilhelm II. He falsified dates to make his birthday the same as Bolívar's, and the press published a picture of Gómez alongside one of Bolívar with the legend: 'The Father of our country, and the Saviour of our country.'

As the years went by Gómez came to be feared and eventually hated. He was given the nickname of *Gregorio el Bagre*: he was the ogre, the barbarian, the vampire, the bird of prey come down from the mountaintops into Caracas. He took possession of vast estates, but he administered the country just as he had run his own farm: methodically, patiently, carefully and competently. He brought order into an administration that had been completely at sixes and sevens. Members of his own family were given the key jobs and the army was handed over to officers who were, like himself, men of the Andes. There was now no question of elections or re-elections: Gómez was in power and there he stayed. He arrested all who objected, tortured them, sent them to lay roads through the jungle, or locked them up in the fortress of Puerto Cabello or in San Marcos, near Maracaibo. To the outward eye Venezuela was a relatively prosperous and orderly country, but thousands of prisoners were slowly rotting away in gaols which were totally submerged when the tide came in, fettered to the iron ball and chain to forestall any attempt at escape.

*

But what really made Gómez rich was oil. The profits of the dictator and his favourites rose in proportion to the barrels of oil exported. In 1930 the income from oil alone was four times as large as the country's entire income had been in 1915. The Gómez clan grew with almost the same rapidity. (He had 97 bastards!) He had always the same impudent good luck, stamping out all conspiracies and having those responsible hanged alive from meat-hooks. He went to live out in Maracay, leaving his henchmen in charge in the capital, but in his final months Gómez became a suspicious man who would only leave his home with a police escort, and machine guns trained on the empty streets.

His death on 15 December 1935 was met with an outburst of delight and excitement among the people. Eustoquio was massacred by a mob in Caracas and all the family had their property confiscated. Fourteen tons of lead – balls, chains and bars – were removed from the Puerto Cabello dungeons. And the sisters, cousins, friends and colleagues of the dead tyrant fled along the La Guaira road as fast as they could.

Will the history of Venezuela always have the same pattern? Twenty-three years later, on 23 January 1958 at 3 a.m. another convoy of cars was speeding along that same road as Pérez Jiménez, his relatives and friends, fled from the revolutionary mob. In the streets of the capital they were besieging the headquarters of the Seguridad Nacional.

In 1935 the people were hunting for Eustoquio, a man feared even by Gómez himself; in 1958 they were hunting for Estrada, the organizer and commandant of Pérez Jiménez' Gestapo. Police were massacred. Altogether more than 300 people were killed in the revolution. Another dictatorship had fallen.

In a sense Pérez Jiménez was even worse than Gómez, for the latter had at least insisted on a measure of honesty from his officials. Pérez Jiménez perfected the system of government by corruption. Fictitious companies were invented to enable his favourites to make vast fortunes out of public funds. The campaign against the secret organizations of Democratic Action was carried out at vast cost and quite shamelessly – indeed three of the major leaders, among them Carnevali, were murdered in cold blood in their prison cells. Concentration camps, deportations, tortures: only the army seemed immune. Students who sympathized with the communist Democratic Action Party and the COPEI (Christian

Social Party) were so bold as to murmur objections in 1956: the central university was promptly closed down for two and a half years. High schools and other educational institutions were also closed on various occasions. The monolithic trade unions imposed by the regime were so obviously controlled by the police that Venezuela was forced to withdraw from the International Labour Organization in Geneva.

From 21 November to 31 December 1957 members of the university undertook a systematic campaign of public protest, supported hesitantly by the clergy. A secret Patriotic Junta was formed with members of the Democratic Action Party, of the communist party, of the Democratic Republican Union and of the COPEI, none of them over 35. This revolutionary group took its inspiration from the European resistance movements against the Nazis during the war. It had a propaganda section and a commando group, and it provided a focal point for trade unions. Manifestos and statements were printed at night on more or less secret presses. This opposition, intellectual and relatively ineffective, would certainly not have succeeded by itself in overthrowing a highly armed and equipped military regime, had it not been for the fact that the business world and parts of the army no longer supported Pérez Jiménez.

*

At dawn on 1 January 1958 there was mutiny at the Maracay air base. It was apparently put down quite fast. But the Patriotic Junta ordered a general strike. Shock troops from the working-class districts were for several days in uncertain confrontation with the sub-machine guns of Estrada's police. What finally tipped the balance was a strike by the oil workers. Caracas bristled with barricades but the army stood firm, and twenty per cent of the officers were arrested. It was the navy that gave the longed-for signal after hope had almost gone: the warships in the port of La Guaira raised anchor, and Pérez Jiménez ordered the air force to bomb them. The air force refused and made common cause with the navy. There could now be no doubt as to the outcome and Pérez Jiménez decided to flee.

The popular hero of the revolution was Admiral Wolfgang Larrazábal, the naval commander-in-chief, and he was acclaimed by all as president of the provisional junta. It looked for a moment as though this dynamic, democratic and sincere man would find it easy to make use of the situation to snatch the victory away from the secret political groups of the Democratic Action Party. His uniform and presence would have made him an ideal *caudillo* in the eyes of people accustomed to think in such terms. Whether from conviction or tactics, Larrazábal gave a number of pledges to the left. It was into this highly-charged atmosphere that the American Vice-President Nixon had the clumsiness or ignorance to fall in April 1958.

Larrazábal did not even try to prevent the students from demonstrating: '*Fuera Nixon*', and '*Muere el imperialismo yanki*'.* He said in fact, 'If I were younger and not in an official position, I too would be out in the street telling Mr Nixon what we all think of the collusion between the U.S. and Pérez Jiménez ...' The communists and other leftists chose Wolfgang Larrazábal as their candidate for the presidential election of December 1958; but the exiles, with Betancourt in the van, had come home, and ultimately the network of the Democratic Action Party proved itself stronger than the newly popular Larrazábal. The evening the votes were counted a crowd gathered in front of the Admiral's house to beg him to stay in power, but he refused. He had joined in the Punto Fijo pact made before the election among the major parties, stipulating that the leaders of the AD, the COPEI, and the URD all promised to give their support to whomever was elected.

*Out with Nixon, Death to Yankee Imperialism.

Betancourt gave some seats in his cabinet to members of the URD who had voted for Larrazábal, but he gave the key ministries to his own friends – Juan Pablo Pérez Alfonso got Mines, José Antonio Mayobre Finance, and Manuel Pérez Guerrero Planning.

Betancourt was born in Guatire in 1903, the year Gómez came to power. His father, an unknown provincial journalist, moved to the capital, and there Rómulo was taught psychology in the high school by a man called Gallegos. As a law student in 1927 he took part in the students' struggle against the Gómez regime and this was the turning point in his career. Wanted by the police, exiled, Betancourt began his long journey from place to place in an endless search for a haven, from Mexico to Bogotá, from Puerto Rico to San José de Costa Rica. He also spent the time working out a coherent theory of government – something which had up to then been completely lacking in all Venezuelan political movements. He flirted with Marxism, like his Peruvian friend Haya de la Torre, and for a time actually joined the Party. But, like Haya, he broke completely with the communists because he could not agree to the rules laid down by the Caribbean CP Bureau.

His movement was to be a nationalist and reformist party, supported mainly by the peasant working class and the middle class in the towns. But only in 1941, after two further years of enforced meditation in Santiago de Chile, was Betancourt allowed to appear again in public to carry on the fight. The Statutes of the Democratic Action Party were altered, and Rómulo Gallegos became its president, with Rómulo Betancourt its secretary general.

His first experience of power in 1945 was brief. Between 1945 and 1948 the AD certainly gave proof of its popularity and won over 80 per cent of the votes in the elections. But the 1948 coup forced Betancourt once again into exile. He returned unchanged – he was certainly no extremist. It would seem that from 1945 to 1948 he had terrified the business circles and upper middle class of Venezuela with his programme of agrarian reform. If so, then all one can say is that it did not take much to alarm that most privileged class in the richest country in South America! In any case, from January 1959, Betancourt did his best to reassure those who most opposed his government, and to some extent he succeeded.

*

This man whom the middle class saw as an agitator quite prepared to blow up all the oil wells in Venezuela was in fact a moderate liberal. In August 1960, at the inter-American conference in Costa Rica, the Venezuelan delegation, by his orders, was the first to move a condemnation of Castro's regime in Cuba. Though it was done to please Washington, this did not seem to Betancourt any abandonment of his own principles. Like Haya de la Torre, like Figueres, like the governor of Puerto Rico, Muñoz Marín, Betancourt still believed that support from American democrats and liberals would be enough to counterbalance the demands and pressures of the American oil companies.

One could, and indeed one must, he thought, fight the oil companies every inch of the way; but it would be bad tactics to show hostility to any American tendency to democracy. Arcaya, Venezuela's Minister of Foreign Affairs, leader of the delegation at San José and a member of the URD, did not agree and resigned. His going caused bloody rioting in Caracas, led by the communists and others on the left. Betancourt had then to undertake a hard battle with the pro-Castro and the extreme left in Venezuela. The resignation of all ministers with URD tendencies forced Betancourt to lean more on the Christian COPEI party – in other words, further to the right – than he could possibly have wished.

There was more rioting in the streets of Caracas in November 1960: students occupied the university buildings, as in the last moments of the Gómez regime, defying the police who tried to get them out. After several days' fighting the students capitulated. But this trial of strengh only served to hasten the collapse of the left wing of the AD. A number of members had already broken with the party leadership during the course of the previous summer and in 1961 further cracks appeared in the structure.

The new AD leaders took a definite stand on the side of the opposition – while Betancourt's friends were almost open in their regrets over the failure of the American Bay of Pigs expedition in April 1961. In 1965 the AD seemed more divided than ever before. The split to the right of the ARS people – decided on just before the general elections of December 1963 – had hung fire owing to their little group's lack of success to date, but the MIR leaders were still unwilling to come to terms with the headquarters of the old guard, and even within that headquarters there were increasingly conflicting tendencies and individual rivalries which grew even more marked after Raúl Leoni became president in March 1964. Betancourt, settled first in London, then in Berne, and writing his memoirs, still controlled the policies of the party and the country through the good offices of his friends in Caracas, chief among them Carlos Andres Pérez. It was evident that the AD, established in power, middle class, all too ready to think 'things were now running quite smoothly', was in fact undergoing a gradual process of disintegration which might well be fatal to it in the 1968 general election.

*

Betancourt, now abandoned by the left, got little support from the right. His best ally was Washington. To cope with ever-growing pressure from the opposition he resigned himself to a considerable swing to the right. Soon a hundred

American experts with some thousand assistants and workers arrived in Caracas at the beginning of 1962 to 'collaborate' with the service chiefs of the various departments of the administration. This technical aid was paid for wholly by the American government, which shortly afterwards offered scholarships of up to 400,000 dollars for Venezuelan students to follow courses in administration in Puerto Rico.

Fiat of Italy had signed a contract at the end of 1961 to build an assembly plant in Caracas; but early in 1962, under American pressure, the contract was annulled, and the Ford company were given preference.

Thus a regime which had come to power in 1959 with a reputation for being revolutionary had, in less than three years, become one of the U.S. government's most faithful allies. There were certainly a number of human reasons for this change: it may be thought that Betancourt and the other AD leaders had suffered exile for too long and could hardly be expected to risk the mammoth upheavals which would result from attempting fully to carry out the principles they held in their youth. But Betancourt had undoubtedly always been a reformist. His new friendship with Washington was dictated by economic necessity, certainly, but it was due primarily to his categorical rejection of the Cuban solution which he could only see in terms of triumph for communism.

Similarly, faced with the growing menace of Castroism, Washington could not stand by and watch a pro-Castro regime established in Caracas. Betancourt served his full term of office, despite the gunfire heard in Caracas at night and the attacks of the guerrillas. But he was despised by the left and received no special sympathy from economic circles on the right.

Despite the increase in guerrilla activity organized by the leaders of the FLAN (Armed forces for national liberation), despite the recrudescence of terrorism in Caracas itself, despite finally an increasing hostility in Venezuelan business circles and the U.S. State Department, Betancourt remained where he was. In the elections of December 1963 the left-wing leaders, communists and MIR-ists both, fought tooth and nail, and on 1 December firing could be heard all over Caracas, while thousands of people waited patiently outside the polling stations. But for all their efforts the elections were barely affected at all, and that first of December was probably one of the darkest days ever experienced by the Venezuelan left wing. There was a vast turnout of voters, and even allowing for the inevitable pressures from landowners in the country and the normal amount of falsification, it had to be admitted that the majority of the people of the country were opposed to the kind of violent action advocated by the MIR and the CP.

*

This by no means meant that they unreservedly approved the policies of the Betancourt government. The AD certainly remained in first place, but only just, and in Caracas itself it was defeated. Raúl Leoni, a Corsican by birth, who had been selected as the party's candidate after much hesitation and endless consultations with the prophets of the old guard, won 33 per cent of the vote – far less than the proportion won in 1958. The real winner was a certain Rafael Caldera, a lawyer and a close friend of Chile's Eduardo Frei, the leader of the Christian Social Party (COPEI) which had been allied with the AD in the final months of the Betancourt government. COPEI won 21 per cent of the votes and thus became the second largest party in Venezuela. Though COPEI commandos had taken part in the fight against Pérez Jiménez alongside the secret AD groups, the progress of the Christian Democrats in Venezuela was hampered by the history of compromise between the Church and the military between 1948 and 1958. But, as in Chile, the new stand being taken by some of the clergy against social inequality had at last made it possible to breathe new life into this movement – created before the war by rightists, and since then totally remodelled by young trade unionists and the 'young employers' groups of Caracas and Maracaibo.

As soon as the election results were known Dr Caldera decided the wisest course would be to spend his time in opposition as constructively as possible, strengthening and organizing all the forces of COPEI to fight the elections of 1968.

Those who really suffered in December 1963 were the leaders of the extreme left wing. The working class districts, *ranchitos* and modern housing developments, voted for the candidates of the URD (Republican Democratic Union) of Jóvito Villalba, and the Democratic Front of Arturo Uslar Pietri – both of which were anything but left wing. Pietri's party also won all the conservative votes in Caracas. The indecisiveness (right up to the last moment communists and socialists hesitated as to what their tactics for the election should be) and ill-conceived activity of the far left had the paradoxical result of weakening the Democratic Action Party and strengthening the ranks of the conservatives. The left-wing leaders set about the painful examination of their mistakes and tried to work out a new plan of campaign. A number of communists and socialists began to favour a 'policy of activating the masses' – in other words, an implicit abandonment of guerrilla activity. But dissensions among the leaders made it impossible to arrive at any clear and unanimous definition of such a policy.

The communists seemed more inclined than the left-wing socialists of the MIR to return to peaceful and legal action. Certainly Pompeyo Márquer, the imprisoned secretary general of the Venezuelan CP, continued to defend the idea of direct action, but most of the other communist leaders, obliged to live more or less in hiding, opted for some solution of compromise with the Leoni government.

This policy of friendship came up against an obstacle in 1964 which had not been surmounted by the middle of 1965. Officers and civilians in the Leoni government could not agree on a reply. Inside the cabinet as constituted in March 1964 by Leoni, men like Gonzalo Barrios, the Minister of the Interior, though directly responsible for fighting the guerrillas were in favour of dialogue with the left-wing leaders. The military however opposed any such policy, and throughout 1964 and during the first months of 1965 the army intensified its so-called 'pacification' operations against the guerrillas, chiefly in the western states of Lara, Falcón, Portuguesa and Barinas. But Venezuela in 1965 was very different from Cuba in 1957. Castro's followers had managed in a relatively short time to gain control of large sections of the island while Batista was still dictator, and to enrol larger and larger numbers of landless peasants in their forces. Six years of 'leftist' insurrection in Venezuela had made no major change in the political picture of South America's millionaire country. The guerrillas were still an irritation to the government and a source of anxiety to the industrialists, but it would be hard to imagine so limited a movement ever seizing power – either by intensifying an armed intervention which already presented enormous problems, or by managing to achieve a legal status by returning to the old politics of 'mass action'. What seemed most likely was that Venezuela would still have to put up for some time with this painful – but by no means fatal – sore.

The only question before the general election of December 1968 was whether Caldera's Christian democrats could repeat the victory won by their counterparts in Chile in March 1965. Though their origins had certain similarities, the two parties were by no means identical; there seemed no possibility of a COPEI landslide but Caldera's personal chances were good because the Democratic Action Party was exhausted by its ten years in power, and Betancourt's successors had so little prestige. Caldera was born in 1916 in Yaracuy state; he had got his doctorate in law, and had been a barrister, a politician, a professor and a writer, attorney general in 1945 (resigning from that post under the junta), and presidential candidate in 1947. A determined opponent of Pérez Jiménez, he was imprisoned for several months, and then lived in exile in New York, where he met Betancourt, returning to Caracas in 1958. His party won 16 per cent of the votes in the 1958 elections and 21 per cent in 1963. This modest advance hardly suggested the likelihood of an absolute majority in 1968, but on the eve of the elections the general impression was one of such general disintegration among all the other political parties, as to make it possible that COPEI might take the lead.

AD supported Gonzalo Barrios, former Minister of the interior, and a member of the 'old guard'. Even in his own party his candidature was looked on with reservations and in mid-December Luis Beltrán Prieto, a former AD president, launched a new group, the MEP (Electoral People's Movement) with the avowed purpose of defeating Barrios. Discreet but significant contacts were made between the MEP and the CP which had chosen a new name in order to be able to enter the electoral contest: Union for Advancement (UPA).

Other groups appeared which were scarcely more homogeneous – independents following Uslar Pietri, the AD–ARS of Ramos Jiménez which had broken away from the AD in 1961 following personal divergences, the FDP (Democratic Popular Front) of Larrazábal, the hero of January 1958, and the URD of Villalba. Throughout 1968 endless alliances were formed and dissolved and it was quite impossible to foretell how the major leaders would behave when the election actually took place. The reactions of the people were equally inscrutable, with the AD influence diminishing among trade unionists and peasants and that of the COPEI increasing.

In the central university of Caracas, where armed forces were put on guard at the end of 1966 (and in fact in February 1967, a new regulation was brought into force to restrict the traditionally autonomous and extra-territorial status of the university, because it was said in parliament to be 'the major guerrilla base'), COPEI got almost 40 per cent of the votes in the June 1966 election of delegates to the council of the Federation of University Centres (FCU), while the communists and MIR-ists between them got 52 per cent. Evidence of this kind, however, is too fragmentary and specialized to admit of any generalizations.

Guerrilla activity was still a thorn in the government's flesh, and a major cause of discord on the left. The MIR had in 1964 organized its own revolutionary *foco* at El Bachiller, east of the capital. After a period of relative calm, there were fresh outbreaks of revolutionary violence in 1966 and 1967. The brother of the Foreign Affairs Minister, Dr Irribaren Borges, was murdered on 3 March 1967 by a group of terrorists near Caracas just after the Leoni government had restored the constitutional guarantees suspended the previous December. This murder, described in some left-wing circles as a 'mistake', was indirectly to bring about the public break between Fidel Castro and the political bureau of the Venezuelan CP.

Actually the divergence between orthodox Venezuelan communists and the Cubans had been increasing all the time since December 1963. In 1966 Fabricio Ojeda, former UDR deputy who had organized the guerrillas, and Douglas Bravo, the commander of the Falcón guerrilla movement, attacked the attitude of the CP political bureau to the Havana government. In particular they demanded, in line with the doctrine of Che Guevara, that the political and military leadership of the revolution should centre in the operational areas themselves and not in the towns. The bureau responded by expelling Bravo from the party. On 13 March 1967 Castro, in a resounding speech, deplored the 'treason' of the Venezuelan CP. They replied by accusing Castro of trying to play at being 'pope' of the revolution; and Jesús Faría, the new secretary general in exile of the party, condemned Bravo in an attack on 'the tiny anti-party group led by a former member of the central committee, a man of militaristic and dictatorial leanings'. The break was public and total. It led to a relative friendliness between the communists and the Leoni government but did nothing to stop guerrilla activity nor to solve the profound problems which had brought the guerrilla movement into being in the first place.

Following in Betancourt's footsteps, Raúl Leoni managed to produce a reasonably good record in the sphere of economic development. One of the most spectacular things on the credit side was the exploitation of the Guiana valley: the complex of barrages on the Orinoco was providing 1½ million kW by the end of 1968. The Guiana basin, now seen as Venezuela's great land of opportunity, seems to offer endless possibilities: hydro-electric power, iron, manganese, oil, natural gas, asphalt, sulphur, diamonds, bauxite and gold. But the Matanzas steelworks did not live up to expectations and was unable to satisfy all the demands of the Venezuelan market, though the oil companies were forced, somewhat against the grain, to use part of its output of seamless tubing.

In the Andes a 'corporation' was formed, similar to the 'Corporation of the Guianas', to exploit the riches of an area which had up till then suffered a similar neglect. But the real problem for all Venezuelans was a rather different one: how might they, in the Andes or the Guiana, or anywhere else, halt the increasing penetration of foreign business interests? Was it possible to opt for a path of 'non-capitalist development' as the most revolutionary among the Christian democrats had defined it in Santiago? Almost 40 per cent of all north American investment in Latin America was in fact in Venezuela. In 1962, according to the figures given by the

Central Bank of Venezuela, the profit level of the oil companies had risen to 37·8 per cent – whereas even in Pérez Jiménez days it had not been more than 33 per cent. In March 1968 the *Chicago Daily News* stated that 'American businessmen calculate that the profits available in prosperous Venezuela are so great that investments are amortized within only five years'. Obviously such optimistic estimates take no account of the 800,000 Venezuelans without regular work, the 2½ million illiterate, landless peasants, or the mushrooming slums. American capital invested in Venezuela earned twice its own original value from 1957 to 1967. It is reckoned that north American businesses will have taken three thousand million dollars or more in profits out of the country during the following five-year period. It could hardly be claimed that the democratic and reformist experiments in Venezuela have been a success in terms of stemming the increasing pressure from American imperialism. Certainly the means chosen were not the most suitable; yet it is very possible that they were the only ones that could be used, and the relative failure of the attempt at armed revolution would seem to support this idea. But it has become clear that there are more and more Venezuelans who are resolved by some means or other to shake off this restrictive and humiliating foreign control.

CHAPTER 7

The Dominican Republic*

STATISTICS

Area: 18,703 square miles
Estimated population in 1967: 3,754,000
Population density: 200 per square mile
Annual increase in average per capita *income from 1960 to 1966:* 1·0 per cent.

PRINCIPAL PRODUCTS

Coffee, cocoa, tobacco, maize, sugar, bananas.

On 30 May 1961 on a deserted road at 10 in the evening the *Benefactor* was killed like a dog: his corpse, unrecognizable, riddled with bullet-holes, was found the next day in the boot of a car which belonged to one of his attackers; it had been hidden in the garage of an abandoned villa in the residential area of Santo Domingo. Where the ambush had taken place there were still some pieces of glass, a pool of blood and the General's cap. This – which sounds like the end of a commonplace thriller – in fact describes the murder of Rafael Leonidas Trujillo Molina who was for thirty-one years the most powerful and most feared of all the Caribbean

*The large island that lies between Cuba and Puerto Rico in the Caribbean was originally called Hispaniola by the first Spaniards who landed there. Only later was it divided into the two separate states known today as Haiti and the Dominican Republic.

dictators. From 1930 to 1961 Trujillo was the absolute and undisputed ruler of the Dominican Republic, the first American soil to have been settled by Spaniards (though Columbus, on his first voyage, landed in the Bahamas and then Cuba, before discovering Hispaniola).

*

When the Spanish lawyer Jesus de Galíndez went to the consulate of the Dominican Republic in Bordeaux, after the Civil War, to ask for a visa, he saw the official portrait of Trujillo for the first time, showing a cruel, thin-lipped smile on a fat face.

'Is that the president?' he asked.

'No, *señor*, he is the Benefactor of the country,' replied the official.

At that date it was true for there was a lay figure in the president's chair, and Trujillo was ruling from behind the scenes; but of all his titles, the one Trujillo himself liked best was that of *Benefactor*. Whenever his name appeared in the press the type-setters had to take the greatest care to get it absolutely right: S. E. Generalísimo Dr Rafael Leonidas Trujillo Molina, Honourable President of the Republic, Benefactor of the country and Reconstructor of its financial independence.

Having appointed himself the Republic's permanent representative at the United Nations, Trujillo was received by President Eisenhower at the White House. The visit was scheduled to last five minutes, and Dominican satirists will tell you that the entire five minutes was spent by the interpreter in reading out Trujillo's virtues and titles. Galíndez certainly did not suspect that the man whose portrait he saw in Bordeaux would turn out to be his murderer: but in 1956 he was in fact kidnapped in New York by paid killers and executed by order of the *Benefactor*. This incident did great harm to Trujillo's reputation in the United States; but there was more to come. Not until after his death did the revelations really begin.

*

The terrible SIM, Trujillo's secret police, never had the smallest inkling of this incredible plot, planned, organized and put into operation by a group of Dominican businessmen, lawyers and doctors. The SIM had discovered endless previous attempts at such plots, arrested thousands of people, and deported some hundreds of the most representative members of the Dominican intelligentsia. The attack of 30 May was only successful because the conspirators were so few in number.

Five days before he died Trujillo invited several friends to visit him on his estate in San Cristóbal. This man of seventy, still in good health, though perhaps slightly slower than in the past, cynical and amusing, though he knew he had been virtually abandoned by the United States, was still quite convinced that his position was impregnable, and could still make sarcastic jokes about his opponents, despite their dangerous increase in numbers. His most formidable opponents – Castro to the west and Betancourt to the south – he spoke of with the utmost derision. On the evening of 30 May he left his home as usual and asked Commandant Zacarías, who had been his chauffeur for twenty-five years, to drive him to San Cristóbal. He himself only had a revolver, while the chauffeur had a sub-machine gun. So cocksure was he that he did not bother to order the military escort which usually went everywhere with him and that was his mistake. In some mysterious way his killers found out and they got into three cars to ambush him. By the time Zacarías caught sight of the first of the three in his rear-view mirror, it was too late. The first shot through the rear window wounded Trujillo slightly.

'I've been hit,' he cried. 'Stop. We shall have to fight it out.'

Zacarías tried to persuade him not to try but to drive as fast as possible; a second shot, however, caused him to swerve. The commando car overtook on the right, almost going into the ditch, and stopped crosswise on the road in front, making escape impossible. The official account stated that Trujillo got out of the car and still had time and energy to empty his revolver among his opponents before collapsing in the middle of the road. A different account has it that Trujillo begged for mercy, promising his murderers money and power if they would spare his life. What is certain is that the chauffeur was so seriously wounded that he was left for dead on the road, though by some miracle he did in fact recover. It is certain also that one of the attackers was wounded and taken by his comrades to a clinic where the police found him.

Only two members of the group managed to take refuge with trustworthy friends; all the others were speedily arrested, tortured and finally killed.

*

Only very slowly was the veil drawn back; only gradually was the true face of the Trujillo regime discovered. What happened in the Dominican Republic in the weeks following the ambush was unlike anything previously seen in any Latin American country suddenly rid of a dictator; it indicated to what point the Trujillo clan had control of the minds and hearts of the Dominican people. In Venezuela, for instance, the death of Gómez – charged with the same kind of bloody crimes as Trujillo – caused outbursts of joy everywhere. In Santo Domingo Trujillo's death caused astonishment, stupefaction, grief, and above all a fear of further reprisals from the rest of the Trujillo family. No one dared to throw hats in the air outside the oldest cathedral in the western hemisphere in the Plaza Colombo; on the contrary, processions of thousands came to pay their respects, both men and women weeping. Trujillo's eldest son 'Ramfils' was in Paris at the time of his father's death. He had the unexpected good sense to charter a plane and was back in Santo Domingo only twenty-four hours later in company with the diplomat-playboy Rubirosa. This, which looked at first like a piece of impudence, was actually more an indication of the panic of a proprietor faced with losing his strong-box in a fire, and succeeded in prolonging the apparent power of the Trujillo clan for some months. The father-myth, created, fostered and carefully kept up by Trujillo for thirty-one years, only lost its hold the following December. Then the departure into exile – with help from the Americans – of the eldest son, his two brothers, and finally the rest of the Trujillo family, unleashed passions long held in check, and for the first time sent the people in their masses out into the streets.

*

The 2,000 statues of Trujillo, built by himself for his own glory, in the squares of Santo Domingo, San Cristóbal, Santiago de los Caballeros and elsewhere, were destroyed, as was the memorial stone set up on the site of the ambush which had for weeks been decorated piously with floral tributes. 'Daddy's republic' was at last dead. It now remained – and indeed still remains – for the Dominicans to try to produce an objective balance-sheet of the life and work of this, the most praised and most hated man in the country. Not an easy task.

For over a quarter of a century the merits of the *Benefactor* had been expatiated upon by every writer in the country – either for love or money, but unambiguously in either case. Before Trujillo, they said, there was anarchy, poverty, fighting inside the country, total control by foreigners. Under Trujillo there was happiness, economic recovery, order and genuine independence, sealed by the 1936 agreements with Cordell Hull. The most outrageous comparisons caused no surprise: Trujillo was ranked with Simon Bolívar, the *Libertador*.

The 'glorious era of Trujillo' had begun in 1930. This was no meaningless statement, for the jurists of the country set about ensuring that it had a solid content: official documents and State laws all spoke in terms of Trujillist chronology. Thus the year 1955 was also the twenty-fifth year of the Trujillo era. There were sometimes lapses and mistakes that could be quite comic: in 1944 the bust of a heroine of the Independence, who had died a century earlier, was solemnly unveiled with the legend: 'María Trinidad Sánchez, *Era de Trujillo*'! In the streets of the capital the covers of the drinking-water fountains were all marked 'era de Trujillo'. The highest mountain on the island, the airport, streets, squares, villages were all christened Trujillo. Even the capital 'besought' the *Benefactor* to be allowed to change its name to Ciudad Trujillo – which was granted after a quite unbelievable press campaign. Every night the sign in front of the War Ministry was illuminated with the words: *Trujillo es mi Norte*.* The patients in the country's hospitals could spend their wakeful nights meditating on the phrase heard on all sides, 'Only Trujillo can cure people'. Many homes, wealthy or humble, were decorated with hideous coloured portraits: 'In this house, the head is Trujillo, symbol of the Nation'. The two largest daily papers, *El Caribe* and *La Nación*, rivalled one another in their search for superlatives to praise the president. Trujillo was successively appointed the republic's best lawyer, best doctor, best teacher, best scholar, and naturally of course also Rector of Santo Domingo University. The best everything, still greedy for more glories and greater homage, Trujillo felt it necessary to write his fame into the laws of the country – even though outside it that fame was barely known.

A law of 11 November 1932 recognized as official his title

* Trujillo is my lodestar.

as Benefactor of the nation, and the Dominican party, the only party in existence under the regime, used his initials R. L. T. M. as their inspiration for choosing their major principles: *Rectitud, Libertad, Trabajo, Moralidad.** In 1956 Trujillo wanted his world fair. Modern and functional buildings were put up on the George Washington Boulevard. The most interesting things in the exhibition were an obelisk, a carved stone *mappa mundi* with Ciudad Trujillo in the centre of the world, and a theatre of fountains with ultra-modern machinery. It was only used once, but Trujillo opened it with great ceremony and enjoyment; he even began the ceremony several times over, first in an overcoat, then in a jacket, then dressed in the successive uniforms of an admiral, a general and a polo player. He then grew tired of the whole thing but this *eau et lumière* show went on; every evening at 9 o'clock illuminated fountains and pools flowed exquisitely before thousands of empty seats to the tune of Chopin's *Grande Polonaise.*

*

This obelisk-builder was born on 24 October 1891 in San Cristóbal. Though he never fought on any battlefield he declared war on Hitler, Mussolini and even Hirohito; and he adopted the title of General. His father was an ordinary clerk in the postal service, and Trujillo's lyrical biographers, so fulsome over his years in power, have the tact to cast a cloak of discreet silence over his childhood. Thus we do not actually know whether the young Trujillo, the fourth of eleven children, was also some sort of minor official. What we do know is that Lieutenant-Colonel Trujillo was in command of the national police when the American military occupation which had begun in 1916 came to an end. In 1928, at the age of thirty-seven Trujillo was appointed commander-in-chief of the army – a key post and in fact the necessary

* Rectitude, Liberty, Work, Morality.

springboard to any political career. To the Americans, who had favoured his rapid rise to power, as to his less enthusiastic fellow countrymen, Trujillo declared with confidence: '*No hay peligro en seguirme . . .*'* However his first months as president – a post to which he was elected by more votes than there were electors to cast them! – were punctuated by summary executions and a wave of surprise attacks which sent his opponents packing to a better world. In September of the same year a hurricane almost totally destroyed the town of Santo Domingo.

*

Up until 1930 the history of the Dominican Republic had been no more than an endless series of disturbances, revolutions, civil wars, of chaos quite as desperate as any in South America. The treaty of Basle in 1795 had extended French domination to the Spanish-speaking part of Hispaniola. Toussaint Louverture then occupied the eastern part against the will of the French commissioner Roume de Saint-Laurent and of the First Consul. From 1809, when the eastern section got rid of the French troops who had sought refuge there after the Haitian rising, until 1844, French soldiers, Toussaint Louverture's black forces, and Spanish troops played a bloody and destructive game of hide-and-seek which only really ended when the two States were formally separated into Haiti and Santo Domingo. It must be noted that the new republic was for a long time hesitant over its future. The division of the two parts of the island was totally arbitrary, mainly growing out of rivalries among the colonizers. For a very long time this frontier, as theoretical as it was indeterminate, had men on both sides of it trying to bring together again the separated halves of Hispaniola. On the Spanish side there was a tendency to form secret societies; the *Trinitaria*, led by Duarte, Sánchez and Mella, opposed the

* There is no risk in following me.

Haitian attempts to win back Santo Domingo. The skirmishing went on until 1861, when in March of that year President Pedro Santana made a decision unique in the history of American colonial independence: he proclaimed the Dominican Republic re-annexed to Spain. This step provoked another revolution. On 11 July 1865 the Spanish government was forced to give up Santo Domingo for good, but it seems that the Dominicans found their independence difficult to cope with, for in 1869 President Báez offered the country to the United States. The American Senate refused this surprising Trojan horse of a gift; but the idea remained alive.

The last decades of the nineteenth century saw a succession of dictators and petty tyrants, who between them got the country's finances into such an unhealthy state that the great powers threatened to intervene to get what was owed to them by force.

In 1916 Washington was the first to act. The marines landed in Santo Domingo on the excuse of the need for the U.S. government to see that American creditors got their money back. Customs, finances and administration all went under direct control of an American military government established in Santo Domingo, and in fact it was not long before American forces were running all the republic's affairs, with all real authority in the hands of Vice-Admiral Thomas Snowden.

*

Eventually the fury of the Dominicans at once again losing their independence reached the ears of the American senators. In 1921 there was a plan for evacuating Santo Domingo but it came to nothing: not until the 1924 agreement did the marines slowly begin to depart. But the customs remained under north American control until the Trujillo–Cordell Hull agreement of 24 September 1940 whereby the U.S. lost all its authority over administration.

In 1930 Trujillo therefore moved into a situation established by military governments during the American occupation – but at least it was a very familiar situation as far as he was concerned. Few Dominicans had been willing to collaborate closely and genuinely with the American forces.

Rafael Leonidas Trujillo was among those who had. On 9 December 1918 he had applied for and got a position in the national guard, whose major work was pursuing gangs of Dominican guerrillas as they moved from one area to another protesting against their country's being occupied by the marines. The mysterious murder of Commandant Lord, head of the national guard, left that post unfilled; when the marines left, President Vásquez called on Trujillo, whose forcefulness was well known, and made him Lieutenant-Colonel. Though he did not realize it, Vásquez was actually setting the seal on his own abdication. At the first sign of rebellion against the old, blind and over-confident President, Trujillo organized only a token resistance by his men, and Vásquez was driven out, leaving the way to the presidency open.

It is hard to isolate the good from the bad in his thirty-one years of rule. Certainly it was to Trujillo's credit that he got rid of American control over the country's customs and excise. By repaying 9,400,000 dollars owed to the U.S. he also made Santo Domingo the only Latin American country without a foreign debt. Economically the country improved beyond all knowledge under Trujillo, especially by comparison with its neighbour, Haiti. Barrages were built and land irrigated; exports went up from 18 million to 140 million dollars; no one disputes the statement that though sinister, Trujillo's Santo Domingo was relatively prosperous. It is also fair to put on the credit side of one of the most appalling of all Latin American dictators the construction of cheap housing for the working class, some 3,000 kilometres of asphalt roads, a hundred or so new bridges, canals, and magnificently equipped hospitals. (Though Dominicans are still quick to point out that the roads were built with the needs of himself and his family chiefly in mind.) In fact the 'Trujillo era' was first and foremost the gradual and almost total spread of one family's power all over the country. Here Trujillo is very reminiscent of Gómez in Venezuela: like him, he governed his country as though it were some kind of model farm. Gómez died poor and detested; Trujillo was murdered with cries of hatred and his personal fortune has been reckoned, probably accurately, at 800 million dollars. A yacht he had built in Germany before the war cost him 9 million dollars and he called it after one of his daughters, Angelita – yet he only used it for short cruises in the Caribbean.

*

By the end of his life, Trujillo was effectively and totally the owner of Santo Domingo. Either in his own name or those of members of his family he owned or controlled the whole of the country's economic activity, apart from those sectors in the hands of American firms. He certainly had control of the mass media – of radio and television. All beer drunk by the citizens of the republic was the *cerveza presidente Trujillo*. All trade in salt, meat, sugar cane, cocoa and coffee were Trujillo business.

Air transport, tobacco, the national lottery, insurance companies, banks – even the artificial insemination of cows – were all so many Trujillo monopolies. Directly or indirectly, the dictator owned over a third of all cultivable land. 'Here,' Dominicans will say, 'everything belonged to Trujillo ...'

When he first made his appearance on the political scene Trujillo was a man of forty, imposing in appearance, his complexion dark, his face forceful; he had a thin black moustache. In a very short time he could be recognized as a complete megalomaniac, practising nepotism and fostering a personality cult of the most incredible kind. Each month a small town or village would be chosen to pay homage to the *Benefactor*: the programme was always the same – a parade composed of notables, of sporting teams, of Trujillist trade unions and local leaders of the Dominican Party. Little girls in white dresses, one for every year he had been in power, and society ladies would pass smiling before the viewing stand where the *Jefe máximo* stood with his right arm waving almost mechanically, and no hint of a smile on his face. 'Ramfils', his eldest son, was appointed a colonel at the age of three, and 'protector of unhappy children' at the age of six. At nineteen he was an ambassador and attended an American military academy. It was common gossip that the presents he gave to two Hollywood stars cost more than America gave in aid to the Dominican Republic in a year. Angelita, Trujillo's eldest daughter, was chosen at the age of fourteen to represent her country at the coronation of Queen Elizabeth II, with ambassadorial rank. London turned her down and the English ambassador in Santo Domingo lost his job over the affair, for Trujillo could never forgive an insult. Similarly he withdrew all Dominican cadets from American military academies because 'Ramfils' had not got high enough marks to satisfy his shooting instructor.

Nor could Trujillo forgive even a hint of opposition. He organized the Dominican Party, dissolving the eight other existing political parties. He set up a well equipped and trained modern army of 25,000. Following the example of the totalitarian regimes in Europe for which he had a great admiration, he established four separate bodies of secret police, employing nearly 15,000 informers – the *caliés*. These spies worked directly for the dictator himself. When Trujillo was dead and the Dominicans felt quite sure that there was no risk of his being replaced by another member of his family, they were the object of deadly pursuit all over Santo Domingo. A great many police informers managed to hide in police barracks and elsewhere, but a lot more were recognized and lynched by enraged demonstrators.

The Dominicans who had been arrested and imprisoned during the Trujillo regime left no one in doubt as to the kind of training his secret police had received: they told of subtle tortures in the famous *cuarenta* prison – so called because it was in Calle Cuarenta – arbitrary arrests and summary executions. The SIM had one speciality: their victims were often run over by cars which could never be traced. The press, by order of the government, would accuse many of them of homosexual practices. In 1937 Trujillo ordered the execution of several thousands of Haitian agricultural workers in the border areas; the official figures given vary between 15 and 20 thousand victims.

*

Throughout his reign the *Benefactor* continued to use the same office in the palace, even after 1952 when his brother Hector was actually the President. He remained relatively in the background, pulling strings and thwarting the ever-growing numbers of conspiracies. Dominican refugees in Venezuela, Puerto Rico, Mexico, Costa Rica or Cuba sought desperately for some way of removing this man who had been in power for over twenty-five years, with the support of Washington, the armed forces and the Church. Yet, even the latter did not take a different tack until 1959, after the Constanza affair (the landing of an expedition organized by some young intellectuals, whose survivors were to found the '14 June Movement') and the arrest of hundreds of liberals by the SIM. A pastoral letter then for the first time condemned the police-state methods of the regime, and most of those who had been arrested were set free.

'We pray that the Trujillo family will never have to suffer in their lifetime the sufferings which are today agonizing the hearts of so many fathers, children, mothers and wives in our country ...'

This pastoral, read in all the churches in the country on 31 January 1960, was an official indication of the Church's public condemnation of the regime. One of the firmest pillars on which the dictatorship rested had collapsed; there were three left, of course, but for the first time serious cracks began appearing in a structure whose total perfection had been its great boast.

Trujillo's fall was precipitated by the intense hostility of the rest of Latin America. In June 1960 he tried to get President Betancourt of Venezuela assassinated: a bomb went off on the route taken by the President's car near Caracas. Betancourt himself was badly burnt, and three of his party died. The whole affair was conducted with such clumsiness – or perhaps merely cynicism – as to disgust public opinion all over Latin America. Colonel García, Trujillo's agent and head of the Dominican Security Police who had organized the incident, was soon found out. It was not just an attempted assassination, but a major error on the part of a man who was obviously desperate.

The OAS decided to vote for sanctions against the Santo Domingo government and Washington approved. Nevertheless the Americans still bought 400,000 tons of their sugar in 1960, which was the surest way of helping the regime, and Sinclair Oil went on delivering petrol in January 1961, in spite of the official OAS embargo. Nemesis was near, however. Already condemned by the clergy, hated by the liberal middle class, despised by the working class, the dictatorship was officially left to its fate by the Kennedy government which took office in January 1961. The American press, hitherto very discreet where Trujillo was concerned, was suddenly filled with fantastic revelations about his crimes. It appeared that Betancourt was not the first man of that stature to be selected as a victim; it was recalled that on 12 March 1956

Professor Galíndez, mentioned earlier, had vanished mysteriously from New York on the eve of defending his thesis on '*The Trujillo Era*' at Colombia University. Galíndez had lived for nearly a year in Santo Domingo and collected evidence that would discredit the regime completely. He was kidnapped by Trujillo agents, taken to Santo Domingo in a private plane, piloted by an American named Murphy, and there murdered in circumstances not yet fully discovered – for Murphy and everyone else who took part in, or witnessed, the kidnapping, were immediately killed themselves by the SIM.

The episode was typical of this pitiless, bloodthirsty, outrageously daring man – one of the last true *caudillos* of the Caribbean. From mid-1960 it became clear that his day was almost over, yet even so, his death took everyone by surprise: the conspirators themselves, the Dominican people, the opposition parties and foreign opinion. There was even a period of several months during which the fate of the Dominican Republic swung between the threat of continued dictatorship and a hesitant democracy.

*

In August 1960 Joaquín Balaguer, a shy, self-effacing lawyer, had replaced Hector Trujillo as President. Balaguer, whose political career had begun well before Trujillo came to power, had had several very important jobs, among them that of Foreign Minister. His appointment as president was purely a cover-up operation, not unlike the kind carried out by Trujillo himself. The real power obviously continued to rest in the hands of the *Jefe Máximo*. It is said in Santo Domingo that the dictator actually hit Joaquín Balaguer in front of the whole Council of Ministers. After the tyrant's death the long-suffering Balaguer clung to his power with a stubbornness which might at first seem curious. Though deeply compromised with the Trujillo regime he was himself a man of integrity, and in America's plan for the gradual and careful democratization of the republic, he became a key piece. For Washington could not permit the fall of Trujillo – so long their faithful ally – to result in any kind of Castroist regime coming to power. From the American point of view Balaguer was the man to facilitate a smooth transition from dictatorship to a regime which though liberal, would be hostile to the radicalism of Castro.

The Dominican people had taken no direct part in Trujillo's overthrow. Sociologists nowadays explain that for several weeks they suffered from a revolutionary frustration complex. Then the patient who had for thirty years been anaesthetized, indoctrinated and mystified, suddenly came to life again. The first riots did not take place until 7 August, over two months after Trujillo's death. Demonstrators set fire to the radio and television station, Radio Caribe, which belonged to the dictator's family. On 24 August there were further demonstrations, when a sub-commission arrived from the OAS to study the as yet far from clear situation. The people took to gathering at the international airport of Cabo Caucedo, Trujillo's old airport, to welcome foreign notables or returning political refugees with cries of 'Libertad, Libertad!'

On 21 October thousands of people came into the capital to welcome Juan Bosch, leader of the revolutionary party, on his return from twenty-five years in exile. Something like a political life was beginning to develop out of the apparent apathy and indifference that had followed the death of the *Benefactor*. 'Ramfils' was far from being the man his father had been; he recognized at once that protecting the family fortune was far more important than any attempt to shore up his rapidly failing power. When he had transferred the equivalent of 200 million dollars to foreign banks he resigned from his post as Commander-in-Chief of the Army and took a plane into a well-cushioned exile.

Then Santo Domingo had a shock: Trujillo's two brothers, Generals Hector and Arismendi, suddenly returned there in early November 1961, after a period in the United States. Dominicans love nicknames: Arismendi was generally known as 'Petén'; though more self-effacing than Hector, he was quite as fond as Rafael Leonidas had been of splendid uniforms and carrying automatic weapons. Both brothers were ill-informed enough to believe that it might still be possible to achieve a coup d'état – but their illusion was soon shattered, shattered in the time it took for American warships to appear off the Dominican coast. And for the first time since 1930 a section of the army made it quite clear that they would do everything possible to prevent any return of the Trujillo family. The unrest began at the San Isidro base, the air force headquarters, 15 kilometres from the city by a motorway cut straight as an arrow through the bougainvilleas and coffee plantations. The airmen unanimously voted to get rid of Arismendi and Hector as soon as possible. This body, so beloved and favoured by the dictator, and on whose loyalty the family would have expected to be able to count, did a sharp about-turn, and its spokesmen let it be understood that their wish was to take part in the new movement in the country. Undoubtedly the majority of the armed forces still favoured the old regime, but a great many of the younger officers had got in touch with leaders of political parties who had come out of hiding or returned home after prolonged exile.

*

By the end of 1961 there were three major political movements in evidence: Juan Bosch's Revolutionary Party, the National Civic Union, a collection of leading men under Fiallo, and the '14 June Movement', headed by Manuel Tavárez Justo. They all had their party offices within a stone's throw of one another in the Calle del Conde in the middle of the city. The question that needed to be tackled first was whether a genuine democratization of the Dominican Republic might not lead to a rise of Castroism in a country whose capital was less than two hours' flying time from Cuba. In the months before Trujillo's fall young people were seen for the first time in the streets of the city wearing the Cuban colours; some even wore Fidel-type beards to indicate their sympathy for the Cuban revolutionaries. The most resolutely Castroist elements in the Dominican Republic were drawn from among the children of the liberal bourgeoisie: lawyers, doctors, teachers, architects. The most outstanding and excitable of them were deported before the end of 1961, and the Castroist threat removed for the moment by combined action from the Balaguer government and the United States. But the authorized political parties still faced a political scene upon which everything still remained to be done. Their immediate objective must be to gain supporters; offices for this purpose rose up in the town centres as well as in the more distant shanty-towns and suburbs. Juan Bosch and Dr Viriato Fiallo made tours round the country, but Manuel Tavárez Justo's 14 June Movement decided to boycott the elections altogether. The new politicians spoke of 'democracy, the dignity of the people, and raising the standard of living'. The 14 June Movement, which took its name from the abortive Constanza landing, was already considerably more to the left than the other two, and its activists, on the first floor of a corner building in the Calle del Conde, had a far more revolutionary air about them than their counterparts in the Civic Union.

Juan Bosch, leader of the Revolutionary Party, seemed to be the steadiest, and his class origin was evident. He had quite a gift for public speaking, and his years in exile had taught him the need for political work to be carried out in depth. But he himself defined his movement as a Dominican version of Betancourt's Venezuelan Democratic Action Party. He had in fact spent the last few years of his exile in Caracas, and when he returned to Santo Domingo in October 1961 he was welcomed with delight by thousands. It looked for a moment as though he could have led a vast popular movement which would have insisted on the immediate removal of all traces of Trujillo's regime, and carried the overthrow of the *Benefactor* to its logical conclusion, both at home and abroad. But in reality Bosch's chief wish was to get his men into the key posts in his Revolutionary Party as quickly as possible, and his own tendency was to make the first step in his programme a fight against the influence of Castroism.

The National Civic Union could in theory count, to start with, on the largest number of supporters. Its leaders were representative of that middle class which had suffered worst under the Trujillist repression, especially during the final years of the regime. But the friends of Dr Viriato Fiallo described themselves primarily as conservatives. Their trump card was the fact that the problem of foreign investment – and especially U.S. investment – existed less in the Dominican Republic than anywhere else in the Caribbean. From this point of view Trujillo had unwittingly rendered his country a real service. Since 1952 he had fought the Americans for the monopoly of the sugar industry; he had had some new factories built, notably in San Cristóbal, and, using methods which had proved their worth on other occasions, he forced such American firms as the West Indies Sugar Corporation to sell him others. So when the new government came to confiscate the property of Trujillo and his family it took over in doing so an economy free of foreign constraints and actually based on its own well-established infra-structure.

*

The first public demand of the Dominicans was expressed in the angry cry, 'Balaguer out!' During the whole of December 1961 demonstrators fired by speeches from the leaders of the Civic Union, the Revolutionary Party, the '14 June Movement', faced the army and all its tanks to demand the removal of a man who symbolized a survival of the Trujillo regime. Once again there were dead bodies in the streets of Santo Domingo, yet Balaguer tried to hold on, using such supposedly vote-catching weapons as giving free cars to out-of-work taxi-drivers. But it is questionable whether he really wanted to remain in power. He seemed a worn-out man; there were pressures from at least two directions which explained his amazing staying-power: both the U.S. and the army wanted him. But divisions in the army became more obvious until General Etcheverría, felt by everyone to be the 'strong man' since the Trujillo family had gone, made the astonishing decision to try to overthrow the provisional civil and military six-man junta. The putsch lasted for twenty-four hours. The U.S. frowned and American cruisers speeded up their vigilante operations around the coast. General Etcheverría was arrested by his own subordinates in the San Isidro base. Once again the people filled the streets and from dancing and shouting crowds came the cry of 'Libertad! Libertad!'

Yet another section of the Trujillist edifice collapsed. The Balaguer–Etcheverría tandem, with the discreet support of the United States, had succeeded in containing popular pressures and preventing their developing into bloody revolution. But now keeping the colourless Balaguer in office came to appear more dangerous than useful, and he retired and chose as his refuge the Nunciature. The provisional appointment as president of Bonelli, a liberal lawyer, quite moderate enough to worry no one, enabled the OAS at last to lift their sanctions against the republic. Despite possible future changes, it was clear by the middle of 1962 that the *festina lente* policy followed by Washington had been wholly successful.

But the painful coming to birth of a liberal regime concealed for some time the true problems of the country free from Trujillism. Two thirds of the peasants owned no land. 40 per cent of the population and three quarters of those living in the capital were wholly or partially unemployed. The building-up of the Trujillo family fortunes over thirty years had ended by impoverishing the country; and the permanent and difficult problems of finding a rational economic solution could not be seen to be basically the same as those facing other Caribbean countries: too much land left undeveloped, or insufficiently developed – too many peasants without any land.

The rising of 24 April 1965 took everyone by surprise, in a way even the conspirators themselves. Rumours of a *coup* had been rife in the narrow streets of Santo Domingo with increasing precision and certainty since February, but no one thought the trouble would start before mid-May. Nor had anyone any idea of the scale of the events brewing up, nor of the repercussions they would have all over the world.

There were prophecies of a right-wing military *coup*, to be led by General Elías Wessin y Wessin, a man of Lebanese descent, commandant of the training centre of the San Isidro air base. The 'San Isidro generals' spoke almost openly of their desire to overthrow the triumvirate led by Donald Reid Cabral which had been trying to manage the country's business since the fall of Juan Bosch's democratic government in September 1963. Reid Cabral, a businessman (importing English cars into the country) was intelligent but without great character, and on advice from the American Embassy he set about trying to hold back the appalling wave of corruption sweeping over the higher echelons of the armed forces and the business upper middle class. 'Donny's' position was ambiguous: as leader of the triumvirate he himself benefited from considerable tax exemptions which enabled him to sell his cars at huge profits. Then, too, such a policy of austerity, introduced so late in the day, could not fail to enrage the corrupt army officers, nor did it even have the advantage of being popular elsewhere. The middle class, crushed by indirect taxation, and the mulatto and negro working class, all felt nothing but intense disgust for the men in power. Certainly Juan Bosch's Revolutionary Party, its leader in exile in San Juan de Puerto Rico, and the leaders of all the left wing movements, especially the '14 June', made attempts to draw their forces together. But the crushing of the guerrillas, who had been organized in November–December 1963 by the leaders of the Marxist-Leninist 'Popular Movement' and the nationalist and progressist '14 June Movement', had decimated the leadership of both parties, and Manuel Taváraz Justo of the 14 June Movement lost his life among them. Ultimately it was the almost universal condemnation of this established and organized corruption which proved to be the catalyst in the 24 April rising.

*

As in every well-ordered *pronunciamiento*, everything began in the barracks near the capital. General Rivera Cuesta, the Army Chief of Staff, having been ordered by President Reid Cabral to dismiss four high-ranking officers suspected of subversive activities, was arrested by a group of liberal young officers and n.c.o.'s. The rebels immediately demanded a return to the democratic constitution of 1963 which had been observed for less than six months. (It is quite a thought that in forty years there were only six months during which essential freedoms were guaranteed!) It is easy to understand why the Dominicans took this Constitution – more symbolic than perfect – as their number one demand. At San Isidro General Elías Wessin y Wessin, with only a single armoured battalion, was not unduly upset to hear of the fall of the Reid Cabral triumvirate which he had himself hoped to overthrow; but the demands for a Constitution by the rebels in the 16 de Agosto barracks – soon to be reiterated by those in his own headquarters – soon made clear the threat that existed to the civil and military Trujillists. The re-establishment of the 1963 Constitution involved the return of ex-President Juan Bosch, whom he had overthrown, and implied also a breath of democratic air entering the stuffy atmosphere of San Isidro. Wessin presented the rebels with an ultimatum. It may well have looked like a foregone conclusion, this confrontation: generals and colonels with tanks and planes on the one side, against a handful of young officers with three thousand men and a stock of automatic light weapons on the other.

What completely changed the course of events was the rebels' decision to come out of their barracks on the evening of 24 April and establish themselves in the old town – and, more important, their decision to hand out arms to civilians. From Sunday 25 April it became clear that all the tanks and planes of the San Isidro generals could not defeat a whole nation, armed, inflamed, and believing in their cause. Their gamble was certainly to cost the revolutionaries dear: the confusion in the streets of Santo Domingo for twenty-four hours was enough to cause the U.S. embassy to ask for American armed intervention 'to protect the lives and property of their nationals'. However by Monday evening the rebel colonels and other superior officers, chief among them Colonel Francisco Caamano Deno and Colonel Montes Arache (commander of the Frog-men commandos), had matters under control, and had brought some organization into this rabble of civilians – reminiscent of some revolutions of the past – whose goodwill and enthusiasm were beyond doubt, but whose military skill was non-existent. In Washington, Thomas Mann, former Under Secretary of State for Latin American Affairs, and a personal enemy of ex-President Juan Bosch, urged upon President Johnson a 'massive armed intervention to prevent the communists taking power'.

*

Up to Wednesday 28 April everything hung in the balance. Wessin had massed his tanks on the left bank of the rio Ozama, opposite the old town which was now more like a fortress. At four p.m. the U.S. ambassador, William Talley Bennett Jr, believing Wessin to have won the day, countermanded the armed intervention ordered by Washington. At five Wessin's tanks, under a barrage of thousands of Molotov cocktails even before they got as far as the crossroads of the Avenida Duarte, were beaten back by this astonishing people's army led by a tiny group of determined and honourable officers. They went back over the Duarte Bridge. Wessin, overwhelmed, appealed for help to the U.S. Ambassador; within a quarter of an hour a message reached Washington: 'The authorities are no longer in a position to guarantee the safety of foreign nationals.' The 82nd airborne division, which had left the U.S. at dawn, speeded up their movement towards Santo Domingo. In the early hours of the next day, two battalions of the 82nd division took San Isidro without any trouble. 'If you had not come,' declared Wessin, 'they would have killed us all...' Hardly could the San Isidro generals have admitted a more total defeat, realizing too late that they had the whole nation against them and not merely a few troublesome junior officers. The naval gunners of the 'assault ship' S.S. *Boxer*, who had begun evacuating American and other foreign citizens at midday on Tuesday the 27th, also landed, somewhat west of Santo Domingo. Thus, forty-nine years after their first occupation of Hispaniola, American troops were once again coming to the rescue, this time of the counter-revolutionary forces led by General Wessin. But the incident provoked a wave of protest which threatened the stability of a number of Latin American governments.

This was only the start of a revolt among the armed forces, and what had begun as an internal Dominican crisis, now became a matter of international concern. Washington published a list of 'fifty-three Communist figures' who were preparing to seize power in Santo Domingo as a result of the rising. By mid-May American troops in the country had reached the astounding total of 22,000 marines and parachute troops; add to this the ordinance services, and the crews of some thirty-seven naval vessels cruising off-shore, and we find more than 40,000 American servicemen involved in the operation. This angry and utterly disproportionate response to a threat whose seriousness can now never be really gauged, gave rise to a certain uneasiness in the White House, and indeed all over the world. It soon became evident that Kennedy's successor was trying to extricate himself as best he could from this Dominican wasps' nest which was proving even more uncomfortable than the sands of the Bay of Pigs.

When it was clear, and admitted even by the American government, that 'the communist threat was greatly reduced', a number of arbitrators tried to work out a political compromise. On 16 May President Johnson in despair sent four of his chief advisers, among them McGeorge Bundy, White House Special Adviser on matters of security, and well known as a supporter of a 'hard line' policy in Vietnam. But in Santo Domingo McGeorge Bundy was intelligent enough to realize at once that the most profitable thing the United States could do would be to help get a moderate government 'hostile to both right- and left-wing dictatorship' into office as soon as possible. The revolutionaries' leader, Colonel Caamano Deno, elected president constitutionally on 5 May by Congress (the same body that had been dissolved in September 1963), agreed to this formula after a dramatic private interview with McGeorge Bundy. But General Imbert Barreras, the leader of a so-called Government of National Reconstruction set up on 7 May with the help of Bartlow Martin, former American ambassador to the republic, rejected this compromise. The U.S., victim of its own naïve Machiavellianism, could see no other solution than to hold a watching brief while hoping for things to return to some kind of peace and quiet.

*

America's first mistake was intervening on such a massive scale, taking a sledge-hammer to crack a nut; its second was to persist in the fiction created in Washington of 'two rival factions'. Colonel Caamano and his men, established in the twenty *cuadras** of the old city, having lost the industrial districts in the north after a military attack by the Imbert junta supported by American troops, may have appeared to be on the defensive; but they could count on the support of the large majority of the ordinary people. Despite a repression reminiscent of the darkest days of the Trujillo era, despite the vast-scale arrests and executions of students in the 14 June Movement, the Imbert junta had little real control of the countryside. But the junta could claim to 'control the country', which from the American point of view has always been the most important reason for granting recognition.

However, it was no longer a question of the United States standing alone between Colonel Caamano, on the constitutionalist side, and General Imbert, spokesman of the privileged Trujillists. Washington had certainly managed to get its armed intervention in the republic sanctioned by the OAS, traditionally ready to follow any line demanded of it by its powerful northern neighbour which controls the purse-strings of the Alliance for Progress. But this Pyrrhic victory over the Pan-American Union – largely due to certain procedural tactics and pressure from Ellsworth Bunker, the U.S. delegate – also provoked violent upheavals all over Latin America.

Few governments managed to conceal the anxious state of public opinion in their countries. One of the most remarkable examples of this was Argentina. There the armed forces were

* Blocks.

in favour of sending contingents to Santo Domingo, but Congress, in which the Illia government had a comfortable majority, was firmly opposed. Caught between military and civilians, Dr Illia played for time, in the hope that the whole matter would gradually lose its urgency. Countries like Chile and Uruguay, traditionally allowing more freedom of ideas and expression in regard to the U.S., adopted a courageous attitude of opposition which made it obvious what a fiction the unity of the OAS really was. That organization, already weakened by its embargo on Cuba, proved over Santo Domingo that it was not an independent regional organism, but a heterogeneous assembly subject to the will of the United States. The successive OAS 'peace missions' displayed a partiality which was hardly surprising, given its long history of ineffectiveness, but was all the more shocking in view of the scale of the tragedy affecting the Dominican people. The United States might make much of the fact that a certain number of Latin American countries had accepted collective force. But a closer look was enough to show that governments of such participant countries as Honduras or Nicaragua were not themselves in a situation so very different from that of the Cabral junta before 24 April. None of the major democratic nations of America – Mexico, Chile, Uruguay, Venezuela or Peru – would agree to support this pretence to an inter-American 'peace force'. Finally, the most significant humiliation for the United States was the intervention of the United Nations. For the first time in the history of Pan-Americanism, the U.N. entered a dispute which the U.S., in the terms of the long outdated Monroe Doctrine, had hoped to be able to 'keep within the family'. This intervention by the U.N. was clearly, though prudently, signified by the arrival in mid-May of the Venezuelan economist José Antonio Mayobre, a member of the CEPAL commission of experts. From Santo Domingo Mayobre tried most courageously, and with the support of the Indian General Ryckie, to inform the U.N. secretariat general of the daily and absolutely flagrant violations of the Charter. General Imbert and the hard-liners from the American embassy made it as obvious as they could that his presence was unwelcome; 'spontaneous' demonstrations were organized outside both his house and those of the U.N. delegation. Unemployed men were brought there from the poorest areas of the city to loiter and society women were heard loudly declaring their wish for 'independence'.

Not until 3 September and the establishment of García Godoy as provisional president did the constitutionalist forces of Colonel Caamano leave the entrenched positions they had defended with such courage since April. There was obviously no comparison between the fire-power of the besieged and that of the American besiegers; the American high command, wearing from May onwards the armbands of the OAS, must surely have often been tempted to use force to get rid of these 'constitutionalists' whose real power lay in having the genuine support of the people. On 15 June a forceful but short-lived thrust by the marines enabled the 'Inter-american' high command to narrow down the already small area controlled by Caamano Deno's forces. Several foreigners, among them the Italian Capozzi and the Frenchman Rivière, were killed by American bullets on that occasion.

The September compromise brought the first phase of the popular uprising to an end. Basically it settled nothing. The American forces were certainly gradually evacuated: by the beginning of 1966 there were no more than 7,000 left, as compared with a one-time record of 42,000. But the Dominican people, exhausted after four months of appalling suffering, could now only look forward to the return of a conservative regime controlled and supported by that same United States whose action had succeeded in destroying the impetus of the April revolt.

General elections took place on 1 June 1966. Now, after the major crisis of the previous year, every political office in the country was due for renewal: the supreme magistrature, as well as those of 4 deputies, 27 senators, 77 mayors and 417 municipal councillors. As expected, the campaign began immediately after García Godoy's installation as provisional president. He was a moderate man, a former ambassador, and member of the Juan Bosch government, and the director of a huge tobacco company in Santiago. The major job to be done by his team, all appointed with the approval, if not at the express wish, of the U.S., was to enable the election to take place in the best possible conditions.

Despite his own good will and the proclamation of a general amnesty, the elections were held in an atmosphere of intense restlessness, and there were a mass of irregularities which cast grave doubt on the validity of Balaguer's election. Three candidates were competing: Rafael Bonnelly, leader of the National Integration Movement, and previously a member of the 1963 Council of State; Juan Bosch, leader of the Dominican Revolutionary Party, President of the Republic from February to September 1963, the man whose name had become a symbol and a war-cry for the April constitutionalist revolutionaries the year before – which was in one way his trump card, but also a considerable handicap; and finally, Joaquín Balaguer, who seemed as if he must inevitably to some extent represent traces of Trujillism even if only faintly.

No one could seriously envisage Balaguer's winning when he presented himself as a candidate at the beginning of 1966. Logically the favourite was Juan Bosch, who had returned to Santo Domingo in triumph. The leader Bosch certainly had cause to feel that the echoes of the constitutionalist movement had reached a large majority of the population. He could also guess at the basic hostility of the Dominican people to the armed intervention by American and OAS forces. Yet it seems as though some of those one would have naturally expected to support Bosch held it against him that he had only returned on 25 September 1965, after the conclusion of the truce that in theory put an end to the conflict. In any case Bosch was not able to carry out a proper electoral campaign. While Balaguer's electoral caravanserai travelled the country, handing out promises and gifts, Bosch had to make do with a few speeches on the radio – and he could not even always get to the radio stations in the capital, because of his opponents' threats to kill him (and that they were no idle threats was proved by the fact that several of his bodyguards were killed on various occasions).

Juan Bosch, ever honest, did not set out to charm anyone. He spoke firmly against the American intervention, though in fact on the eve of polling day he did attempt to moderate his attack. The orthodox (pro-Soviet) Communist Party, the Dominican Popular Movement (pro-Chinese) and the 14 June Movement (Castroist) all advised their members to vote for Bosch, but he rejected their support. This was certainly a mistake, for he could not possibly hope to win with no support except that of the Dominican Revolutionary Party whose part in the April rising had not been heroic. Making his platform one of a return to peace and tranquillity, declaring himself the spokesman of the mass of the peasants, terrorized and bullied by the army and the police, Balaguer won the election despite his 'Trujillist' past. He won 760,000 votes as against only 495,000 for Bosch. On 1 July he was sworn in, and the 'constitutionalists' might well consider that the blood shed between May and September had been shed in vain. Balaguer's first move was to ask Bosch to take office in a government of national union, but he refused; on the other hand, a number of other leading members of his party agreed to accept ministerial posts.

Balaguer's first year was a difficult one. Some of those most obviously active in the 1965 crisis had certainly been got rid of. General Wessin y Wessin had been appointed and actually physically forced to go to Miami as Consul General. Commodore Rivera Caminero, another right-wing leader, was made naval attaché in Washington. Caamano, Montes, Arache, La Chapelle, Aristy and various others of the 'constitutionalists' had also been sent off to various diplomatic posts abroad. Colonel Caamano Deno was made military attaché to the Dominican Republic's embassy in London, where he stagnated until October 1967 when this formerly influential constitutionalist leader, disappointed by the way things had gone, and not caring to remain inactive indefinitely, decided to leave his job. In the spring of 1968 some of his friends thought it possible that Caamano might be somewhere in the Caribbean – probably Cuba – preparing to make a triumphant comeback. But in any case, among those who remained, the bitternesses of 1965 lingered on. Balaguer suggested that those who had settled for the 'constitutionalist way' be restored to their old ranks and allowed back into the army; but this operation, accompanied inevitably by innumerable incidents, delays and humiliations, actually served to discredit the constitutionalist officers – which made it fairly clear which side had really won the day.

The economic crisis was equally serious. Draconian austerity measures succeeded in reducing the balance of payments deficit considerably (12 million dollars, rather than the 45 million predicted in 1967). The internal public debt was reduced in a similar proportion. But social unrest was not lessened: since July 1966, restrictions on the right to strike coupled with wage freezes had given rise to a number of protest movements, any of which might have developed into a violent confrontation and broken the truce of September 1965.

Balaguer had to guard his left flank, so to say, but possibly there was even more danger from the right. Those who supported Wessin and the military leaders – whose outrageous privileges had been almost totally suppressed in 1965 – made it clear on several occasions that they had 'learnt nothing and forgotten nothing'. Well-based rumours of a coup were denied by the presidency, but it is likely that the 'vetoes' of the American embassy, now a state within a state with its own vast civil and military staff, were more effective here than all Balaguer's carefully worded statements.

Significantly, Balaguer was in no hurry to punish the crimes of certain members of the armed forces or the police against defenceless civilians or constitutionalist activities. Though considerably reduced by the end of 1966, the wave of political murders still continued. Alongside this was a wave of left-wing terrorism beginning in June 1967 which gave Balaguer and the conservatives an excuse to issue warnings of the 'threat of communism'. By the end of 1968 Balaguer's reformist party still did not represent a powerful or coherent political force, despite holding the majority of seats in the legislature. Bosch's PRD, though split into varying tendencies, undoubtedly remained the most important political group. Under the leadership of José Francisco Peña Gómez, who had become its secretary general after Bosch's departure to Spain, the PRD adopted a more radical line, refusing all invitations to collaborate with the Balaguer government.

Balaguer himself seemed in 1968 chiefly concerned with strengthening the country's economy, with the help of large American loans. In 1966 he had had 10 million dollars in 'direct aid' from Washington. In 1967 90 per cent of the 40 million dollars provided as 'essential subsidies' were used in agriculture and public works. Washington consequently agreed to increase its quota of Dominican sugar imports (600,000 tons from the 1967 harvest), with the result that sugar sales brought 70 million dollars into the Dominican treasury in 1968. The United States' willingness to make exceptional efforts to help the Dominican Republic can be seen from the weekly discussions between President Balaguer, the U.S. ambassador and the AID officials. This openly admitted dependence on the U.S., attacked fiercely by all the left-wing groups and the Dominican Revolutionary Party, causes some reservations even within the reformist party itself.

At the end of 1968, three years after the last death rattle of the 1965 crisis, it was clear that anything might happen in the republic. The slight progress that had undoubtedly been achieved in the economic sphere was not enough to conceal the growing discontent of the military, still clinging to their memories of the *belle époque* they knew under Trujillo.

CHAPTER 8

Haiti

STATISTICS

Area: 10,714 square miles
Estimated population in 1967: 4,577,000
Population density: 427 per square mile
Annual rate of population increase: 2·3 per cent
Annual increase in average per capita *income from 1960 to 1966:* 2·9 per cent.

PRINCIPAL PRODUCTS

Coffee, sisal, sugar, cocoa.
Bauxite, salt.

The tubby boats with their heavy much-patched sails leave the steep banks of the island of Gonâve at nightfall. They go slowly across the Saint Marc channel, and arrive to land their sacks of charcoal on the sticky docks of Port-au-Prince. Selling begins on the spot. Lengthy bargaining takes place amid the dead fish lying on the quay and with the sweetish smell of rotting twigs of sugar-cane all around. Men stripped to the waist, their bodies running with sweat, are bent almost double by the weights they bear. The first picture the visitor sees of Haiti is extraordinarily colourful, but also terribly revealing: the fuel Haitians normally use is the same that was used three or four centuries ago – charcoal, the poor man's anthracite.

In the Port-au-Prince market, which spreads out along the

pavements and down the tiny streets round the port, trade is slow. The market-women sit on the ground, their skirts tucked up round their thighs, in front of their tiny baskets.

A human tide, with here and there a pink or mauve head-scarf standing out from the rest, flows endlessly in this noisy and almost permanent market. The heaps of pottery, the multi-coloured blouses and skirts, the sharp smells and shouting and general exuberance are all reminiscent of something in Africa. It is perhaps an over-simplification to describe Haiti as some do as a scrap of Africa in the heart of the Caribbean; but it is certainly true that there is nothing here to suggest America.

*

Haiti is unique in the western hemisphere. To start with, this first black American republic has kept French as its language; its doctors and lawyers and architects speak the French they have learnt in France. But ordinary people have stuck to Creole: Haitian Creole is not a dialect, nor a *patois*, nor a French that has developed along its own lines, but a kind of musical abbreviation, almost as hard for a foreigner to learn as the most obscure secret language. Yet to look at Haiti on the atlas would give you no hint of any such thing: there you find the well-known names so familiar from childhood pirate stories, and the coasts both of Les Cayes and the north west are studded with names that sound like Normandy: la Dame Marie, la Grosse Chaudière, le Port à Nanette, le Mouillage Fouques, le Bord de Mer and la Baie du Môle. The lowlands are still called Limonade or Marmelade because the Frenchmen who landed found them swampy, and indeed they still remain so. There is even a Saltrou, divided from the world of the capital by the wooded heights of the la Selle range. The somewhat salacious humour of the first colonizers gave villages names like 'Belle Dondon' and 'Marie Galante'. In the towns, Port-au-Prince, Cap-Haïtien and Saint-Marc, the brightly coloured buses in which passengers sit opposite each other on long wooden seats bear such religious titles as: 'The Infant Jesus of Prague', 'Thy Will be done', 'The Son of Mary', or 'What God wills'. But the descendants of Toussaint Louverture have altered the phrases to a point at which they have become totally incomprehensible to the keenest ear. Educated Haitians themselves can move with ease from the most perfect academic French to local Creole.

Port-au-Prince has roughly half a million inhabitants. The town cannot expand in area with the bay on one side and mountains all round the others, and flickering lights to be seen every evening from the huts in the north and south corners of the town reveal the presence of such masses of people as one could barely imagine living there. Yet week after week fresh waves of penniless peasants come in from the countryside to swell the flood to be seen pouring down the Avenue Dessalines every Saturday night. No one, even in Haiti itself, has yet found a satisfactory answer to the question: just how do all these men and women huddled together in the capital manage to survive?

*

How can they live, these destitute peasants hanging onto their tiny squares of ground on the bleak hillsides, or in the swampy plainlands of the interior? The republic extends for 10,714 square miles; but a large part of that is made up of mountains and hills which are eroded, de-forested, carved into a mass of gullies by the rain. The land that is cultivable in any real sense has thus been reduced to the barest minimum. Furthermore, Haiti even exceeds Salvador in population density, and is in the unenviable position of having the largest number of people per square mile anywhere in Latin America. It is hardly surprising that the average Haitian standard of living is one of the lowest in the world. A recent U.N. figure estimated the average *per capita* income at 77 dollars – really appallingly low: the great majority of the peasants grow no more than the things they and their families need to survive: bananas, yams, cassava, Caribbean cabbages and maize. But the almost total lack of trade between one village and another explains the inadequacy of the basic diet of nearly everyone, and the fact that its lack of balance leads to serious nutritional problems. One out of every two children in Haiti comes into the world with hereditary diseases resulting from malnutrition.

Another disadvantage is the fact that properties get fragmented into the tiniest units. Half of all farmers have less than a hectare to support their family – as compared with what is reckoned the indispensable minimum in this part of the world of seven hectares. Large and even moderate-sized properties are the exception rather than the rule. So Haiti has not even the possible solution of some kind of radical agrarian reform which might extricate it from its impasse. It is not a matter of taking from the rich and dividing among the poor, but rather of joining up what has been broken apart, and then of mechanizing. The over-population of the countryside is primarily due to the full or partial unemployment of a million small farmers and landless farm workers. In 1959 92·3 per cent of the population was rural, and the level of illiteracy reached the record figure of 93 per cent (CEPAL statistics). The population, estimated in 1968 at five million, has an annual rate of increase of 2·3 per cent which is far from being the highest in Latin America; but one gets some idea of how few resources are available to this intense concentration of people if one realizes that only 370,000 hectares are under cultivation. They produce coffee (40,000 tons), sisal (25,000 tons), cotton (1,000 tons) and cocoa (about 2,500 tons). In effect this most Negro of all Caribbean countries is dominated by the United Fruit Co. (known here as Haitian Bananas), the Haitian-American Sisal Company, and the Hasco sugar company.

Haiti's land problem is, or ought to be, a problem of loans, technology and goodwill. But the various governments that have held office since Independence (the Duvalier government not excepted, despite its claim to concern for the masses and 'négritude'), have given little or no thought to the situation. On the other hand, ancestral beliefs and electoral considerations have both positively worked against the needed reforms: thus, however little profit they may make, the peasants divide it into four, of which the first part goes to the *hongan*, the voodoo witch doctor, a feared and fearful figure who is thought to have the power to cure sick children and ensure good harvests; the second goes to the mayor of the village; the third to the chief of police; and only one quarter is kept for themselves.

*

In the southern 'jawbone' of this ragged mouth of rocks and peaks which constitutes Haiti, as well as in the north west between Gonaïves and Port-de-Paix, where the rainy season takes place at least two months earlier, the villages of straw huts are reminiscent of the more remote areas of black Africa. Streams from the mountains around the cape will suddenly turn into torrents and rush down, cutting off towns like Bassin Blue or Chansolme, so that priests and doctors can only reach them after hours of difficult travelling by jeep along roads which have become rivers of mud. In such circumstances the battle against illiteracy, as that against tropical diseases, poses peculiarly arduous problems. Nine of every ten school-age children attend no school: there is only one doctor for every 15,000 people – and yet some of the best Haitian doctors have joined United Nations teams working in the former Belgian Congo because if they stay at home their living is so precarious.

The republic of Haiti is in fact in the state of a pressure-cooker with the valve blocked, and diplomats, American and

U.N. experts are all waiting anxiously to see it explode. Port-au-Prince, the capital, gives a most illusory picture: as one approaches the fragrant hillsides that lead to Pétionville, the garden city, attractive California-style villas stand out from among clumps of bougainvillea; higher still, towards Kenskoff, luxury hotels, where a room for a night would cost as much money as is to be seen in a Haitian village in the course of a whole year, stand waiting for American and Canadian tourists. This is where the happy few live: foreign experts, officers from the American naval base, diplomats, middle-eastern businessmen, members of Haitian high society. Such residential areas as this, and the traffic jams of American cars in the centre of town during the rush hour, bear no relation to the deeper realities of the country.

*

The precise percentage of mulattos in the population is uncertain. The official census of 1950 makes no mention of it. A U.N. estimate made in 1958 gives these figures: 95 per cent blacks, and 5 per cent mulattos. All such statistics must be treated with caution since generally speaking no census of Haiti can ever be more than approximate. In 1919 the number of inhabitants was estimated at 1,600,000; but it seems probable that even then it was in fact considerably larger. In point of fact most of the peasants in the more remote regions have always managed to evade census-takers because of their atavistic fear of authority and the police. In 1940 the population was estimated to be 3 million; in 1950 over 3½ million, and in 1962 it was reckoned to be near the 4 million mark. What is quite certain, on the other hand, is the major part played by the mulattos in politics and economic life. Directly or indirectly, it may be said that since the country achieved independence they have been in control of it.

However, there is no rigid distinction between 'black' and

'mulatto', nor do the terms reflect purely racial differences. The colour of a man's skin is in fact far less important than his position in society. Ninety per cent of Haitians are black, poor and illiterate. So to be poor is first of all to be black. A few drops of white blood will not stop a Haitian's being considered as belonging to the 'pure Negro' group if he is illiterate and without money. On the other hand, rich and cultivated black men are almost automatically admitted into the mulatto class.

The latent opposition between the two groups is something that has characterized the whole history of the republic. The old cry, 'Down with the mulattos!' has often punctuated the riots in Port-au-Prince. For 150 years the Haitians who would define themselves as members of the elite have been generally mulattos. They were, and still are, very cultivated people, speaking impeccable French and conversant with all the most recent French books. Well-off lawyers, teachers, doctors, poets and government officials – this body of under 2,000 people virtually ruled the country up until 1958.

It is a body that has at times tolerated if not positively encouraged 'black' presidents – but only on condition that they respect the rules of the Haitian game of never threatening the political and economic dominance of the 'mulattos'. Since 1958 however the game has broken down. For Duvalier, as 'black' as any president had ever been, has waved on high the old banner of 'négritude' and begun a patient, insidious and at times brutal fight against the whole 'mulatto' caste. The change could not be a sudden one. There are still a great many mulattos in Port-au-Prince in key jobs in the government or the army. But whenever possible a 'black' is substituted for a 'mulatto'. What could be the Haitian people's overthrow of the group which has for so long produced the country's pampered few has not yet had any very profound consequences. This struggle for power has not in fact affected more than a tiny number of people, and the vast majority of Haitians, enormously peace-loving, still present the world with an example of what looks like a limitless power to tolerate the most desperate poverty.

*

The first people who lived on this western part of the island of Hispaniola with its difficult interior and ragged coastline, were Arawak Indians. When Christopher Columbus, during his first journey in 1492, landed at a spot not far from what is now the Baie du Môle on the north-west coast, he estimated the aboriginal Indian population at a million. He described them as 'remarkably friendly, peaceful, fine-looking and praiseworthy in every way'. As a result of their exploitation by the first conquerors and the arrival of smallpox from Europe, these 'gentle Indians' were soon largely wiped out.

To replace the decimated Indians black slaves were brought over from Africa. But before the almost total disappearance of the Indians and the arrival of the first slave ships, there was a picaresque, exciting, romantic and perhaps unique episode which has delighted generations of schoolboys as they pored over the map of the Caribbean: the epic of the pirates.

They were also known as the 'Brethren of the Coast' because only their total loyalty to one another made it possible for them to resist all the attempts to annihilate them made by the Spanish. For the most part they were of French origin, and they made their headquarters on the Île de la Tortue, just off the north-west coast; there they could tend their wounds and safely divide their loot. From a hiding place in one of the few sheltered spots on this island – with its sheer cliff of a north coast – they would set out to find convoys of Spanish galleons on the way home with their cargoes of gold. But they could never have succeeded as they did without help from cattle thieves: stolen meat from wild bulls or boars after smoking* would keep for four or five months – the time it took to get right round Hispaniola or Jamaica, or travel along the shores of the Bay of Campeche. To attack the men who provided them with meat would destroy their entire operation.

The Spaniards were well aware of this, and their first attempt to defeat the pirates was by making war on the cattle thieves. But their crack corps of *lanceros* met with failure. The Brethren of the Coast, well established on the Île de la Tortue since 1632, ceased being merely nominally subject to the King of France and became so in fact. In 1665, Louis XIV ordered an Angevin nobleman, Gouverneur Bertrand d'Ogeron, to turn these scavengers of the Caribbean into law-abiding colonials, 'I will bring chains for them from France', he added; and a royal ship set off for la Tortue with numbers of female passengers, some willing, some not. They were girls from Brittany or the Loire Valley, and having been sold by auction to the pirates, were alas, often to be found manning the guns against the Spanish galleons alongside their husbands, instead of keeping them at home as they were expected to.

But there now remain few traces of those turbulent and heroic times: a few rusty cannon, the remains of some walls at Basse-Terre where the pirates used to repair their ships after the ravages of battle. But there is still a certain mystery and magic about la Tortue. It stands up out of the sea, solid, covered in trees, above the 15 kilometres of channel between it and Port-de-Paix and Saint-Louis, on the Haitian coast. The water is infested with sharks and there are sudden storms which can cut the island off for days at a time. Even in fine weather there are dangerous currents and one is wise to

* The word 'buccaneer' derives from this. *Boucaniers* were people who smoked meat and the word was first used of the cattle thieves who stole meat to smoke it. By extension it came to mean our word buccaneers.

make the trip in the morning. Haitians do not set off for la Tortue in sailing boats from Saint-Louis without a certain apprehension. Yet set off they do, in vast numbers, for this intensely remote island is both an ideal home for the sick and a great centre for smuggling. Fr Riou, a French missionary, has built a hospital, a dispensary and a maternity home at the foot of the highest hill on the island: Our Lady of the Palmettos. This Caribbean Schweitzer is a truculent and athletic man with the kindest of hearts: from every part of Haiti hundreds of patients come by boat to his hospital every year. But at nightfall boats of a very different kind slip silently out of the island creeks; they are laden and at times dangerously overladen with Haitian emigrants setting out to try their luck in Nassau and the Bahamas. In good weather it is a four-day run. Traffic in men always seems to follow the routes of the cyclones! The men, some criminal, others merely workless, get false passports which they must hand over to the organizer of the trip after they have landed. This is a racket from which a small number of boat-owners earn huge profits, for their boats, having landed their human cargo, usually come back with arms and ammunition. Occasionally a police launch will land on la Tortue and a sailor or two will be arrested. But in general the old pirates' island goes about its business in peace and with impunity.

*

In the eighteenth century the pirates, who had in fact never ventured around the eastern part of the island (what is now the Dominican Republic) had won almost total control of the western part near their headquarters. Santo Domingo, the gem of the Antilles, then became the richest of all France's colonies. Some 40,000 planters ruled over 30,000 people of variously mixed blood and half a million negro slaves brought over from Dahomey and Sénégal. Their fate hung in the balance one heavy oppressive night in 1791. From plantation to plantation the drums beat out an ever more mournful order to revolt; the slaves massacred 2,000 French people, all the plantations were destroyed, and the handsome wooden colonial houses burnt to the ground. It was the beginning of an appalling struggle. The Haitians had a formidable and highly competent leader, Toussaint Louverture, who succeeded in beating back the French troops as well as those sent to help by the English and Dutch. In 1801 Napoleon, probably on the advice of Josephine, a Creole from Martinique, sent 40,000 crack troops who had fought in the Egyptian campaign to Haiti under command of General Leclerc. Leclerc, and after his death Rochambeau, set about the difficult task of reconquering the lost territory, with endless setbacks. Toussaint Louverture, captured in an ambush, was sent to France where he died, but his deportation simply enraged the Haitians further and in 1804 Rochambeau, having lost three-quarters of his army, had to take to his ships again, after endless and unsuccessful fighting against Toussaint Louverture's lieutenants – Dessalines, Pétion, and Christophe. In the Plàce du Champ-de-Mars in Port-au-Prince, statues of the three heroes of independence, Toussaint Louverture, Dessalines and Pétion, stand facing the presidential palace. Dessalines and Pétion, who succeeded one another in power, the first from 1804 to 1806, the second from 1806 to 1818, undoubtedly exhibited the finest statesmanlike qualities. But in the north, Christophe declared himself emperor, establishing a court modelled on that of Louis XIV; he exploited the black labourers most cruelly and had the Laferrière citadel built, a gigantic fortress which Lindbergh christened the eighth wonder of the world. This black Pharaoh of Cap-Haïtien finally committed suicide in 1820, using a gold bullet he had had specially made for the purpose.

The Haitian guerrillas cost France something in the region

of 40,000 soldiers killed – either in fighting or by epidemics. French troops still remained for some time in the eastern part of Hispaniola but eventually departed completely from what had been the gem of their empire. All that was left of them is what one historian has described as 'a vast ruin'. The new leaders, totally untrained, were forced to improvise at every step and a series of economic crises sent the black republic hurtling into a succession of brief dictatorships, of civil wars and of racial conflicts. There was a serious drop in the value of commercial production and coffee became by far the most important crop. In addition the north and Cap-Haïtien lost much of their importance, to the profit of the south. Up to 1915 there were endless disturbances on an alarming scale and only the American military occupation put an end to what was by then a real orgy of violence and terror.

It is perhaps interesting to give a brief list of the basic reasons for the decline of the republic of Haiti for they determined later developments, and they are the same reasons which paralyse the country's development now. Daniel Arty, quoting the work of Leyburn, declares that the decline in agriculture of what was the richest land in the West Indies was primarily due to the maldistribution of the land. The small farmers always got the least fertile areas as their share. He gives these basic causes for the decline: 1. the excessive militarism whereby far too large an army cost much more than the country could afford; 2. archaic methods used in farming; 3. the debt which it took the Haitian government sixty years to repay to France; 4. the whole system of import duty, in which embezzlement was the norm; 5. a failure to understand the rules of the international market; 6. the top-heavy importance of coffee; 7, the chronic political instability; 8. the failure of the upper class to undertake any kind of lucrative work. It is clear enough that these 'seven plagues' of Haiti have not really changed apart from the recent establishment of a Haitian Institute for Agricultural and Industrial Credits, and the upsurge of tourism.

*

Since 1905 the United States had really had control of the Dominican Republic. But on 27 July 1915 renewed disturbances gave them an excuse to intervene directly in Port-au-Prince. President Guillaume Sam, who had refused to sign an American Military Aid treaty, had just had over 200 political prisoners executed. The people rioted and captured the palace, and Guillaume Sam was murdered in the French embassy where he had taken refuge. The president's body was borne in wild triumph through the streets of the capital. The American admiral, Caperton, was waiting off shore, and at once ordered two companies of marines and three of infantry to land.

The United States took matters in hand quickly and energetically. In record time they gave Haiti a new Constitution, minus the clause which existed in all the sixteen earlier constitutions forbidding foreign citizens to own or rent land in Haiti. The American military occupation, wholly organized by officers from the southern states, naturally annoyed the Haitians with its innumerable psychological errors of judgement. But it did have some advantages: it put an end to the gangs of bandits working from their hiding places in the hills, and indirectly fostered the country's development. Most of the roads were built during this period, for example, and a telephone system – though its inadequacies and peculiarities are the subject of endless jokes in Port-au-Prince – was installed by the marines. The exchanges they built have since been damaged by torrential rains and when a diplomat says he is going to make a telephone call, what he means is that he is going to call on someone in his car, normally a quicker and more reliable means of contact. The Americans also – setting an example which was to be followed by Nicaragua and Santo Domingo – set about the training and organization of a national police force, the nucleus for an efficient modern army. This so-called 'big-stick' policy (strong arm methods were used to repress a rebellion in Haiti) continued until F. D. Roosevelt became president. He made a courtesy visit to Cap-Haïtien in 1934 and ordered the marines to lower their flag and go home. But in practice America's indirect control of Haiti continued until 1941 because it kept total control of the whole customs system.

*

Creole has a wonderful phrase to describe the Haitian style of *pronunciamiento*: the 'coup de langue'. This 'attack with words' starts with rumours, carries on by way of animated conversations in public squares etc., and, if necessary, ends in a general strike which results in the fall of the president. This kind of classic 'coup de langue' put an end in turn to the political careers of all the presidents during the thirty-year period before the coming of Duvalier; Stenio Vincent, Elie Lescot, Dumarsais Estimé and Paul Magloire.

Stenio Vincent was a splendid speaker – as indeed Haitian politicians so often are. He was elected in 1930 after an election organized by the American occupying forces, and the young lieutenant he chose to help him was Paul Magloire. In 1937 Stenio Vincent was faced with a tidal wave of anger and emotion which swept across Haiti after the massacre of 15,000 Haitian farm workers by the troops of the Dominican dictator Trujillo. As they did every year, the Haitian sugar workers had crossed the border to find work on the fertile plantations on the other side. For reasons which are still not clear the Dominican *Jefe Máximo* ordered them to be killed in cold blood. The figure of 15,000 is only an estimate: the Haitian government demanded a compensation of 550,000 dollars, which would have meant, if it were correct, the derisory sum of 37 dollars a head. Stenio Vincent, in doing this, made several mistakes at once. The Haitians could not forgive him for this kind of bargaining over a massacre, and his government collapsed with no regrets from anyone in 1941.

His successor was Elie Lescot, a man well known for his anti-Negro attitude – a paradox in a republic which claimed to be the blackest in the western hemisphere. Whether true or false, the general accusations against Elie Lescot were magnified with increasing vigour throughout the noisy markets of Haiti and the age-old cry, 'Down with the mulattos' could once again be heard beneath the dusty, musty arcades of the Rue Dessalines. In 1946 popular rumour accused Elie Lescot of a crime which no Haitian could forgive after the fearful executions of 1937 which were still very much alive in everyone's memory. He was accused of having been given 35,000 dollars by Trujillo. The Negro market women who normally came down every day, their heads erect beneath their baskets, stayed in their huts on the hills above the capital. In town the shopkeepers closed their iron shutters. The commandant of the presidential guard was Stenio Vincent's one-time aide, Paul Magloire, a graduate of the police training school run by the American marines.

*

Magloire and the chief army officers accompanied Elie Lescot to the Port-au-Prince airport to ensure security; they then became the leaders of a provisional junta and organized elections which brought to power a lawyer whose health was somewhat frail, and whose ideas, attitudes and objectives were the complete opposite of those held by his predecessor. Dumarais Estimé was the son of poor Negro peasants who lived in the wild and very difficult area of the Selle hills in the south. He was the first in Haiti to produce that official apologia for 'négritude' which Duvalier was to take up in 1958. Estimé considered that the real, the authentic Haitians were first and foremost the poor peasants living in the inland countryside. It was his dream to raise their standard of living and to establish a new ruling class – black, rich and educated. The Creole language was given an entirely new importance, and a whole generation of writers and poets who believed in it set about expressing themselves in its simple but poetic phraseology. The practice of voodoo, which had persisted despite the scorn of the upper class and the laws of official Catholicism, was openly tolerated. Estimé also dreamt of industrialization, of building schools, dams and hospitals. He did indeed succeed in increasing the basic wages of farm labourers but the only major achievement of his government was a modest international fair which took place in 1950. Its buildings, covered in painting and splendid rainbows, still stand all along what could be a splendid seaside promenade. They remain despite the repeated assault of torrential rains, strictly functional and perhaps somewhat pretentious in this landscape of tiny houses and pastel-coloured colonial homes, being partially occupied like those other ambitious buildings which Trujillo put up for a single ceremony on the other side of the island.

Then once again, there appeared in Port-au-Prince what seemed to indicate the approach of another 'coup de langue'. Stories about corruption in high places were going the rounds in the markets – hotbeds as always for any evil rumours. It was said that almost half of the funds voted for setting up the stands in the world fair had gone into the pockets of certain ministers. To deal with the mounting wave of hostility in the country Estimé considered it a wise move to plan an alteration in the Constitution that would enable him to serve as president for a second six-year term. Once again Magloire and the army entered the scene, and the drama carried out to depose Elie Lescot was re-enacted to send Dumarsais Estimé into exile. The army leaders courteously asked him to leave his white palace, whose empty windows looked out over the enormous Place du Champ-de-Mars, and this idol of the black peasants was taken by air to New York, where he died in 1953.

*

This time Magloire felt his time had come and that it must be he and no one else who dealt with the situation. After a quick and light-hearted electoral campaign he was elected president with over 151,000 votes as against only 20,000 for his opponent. Paul-Eugène Magloire was a northerner, born in a village near Cap-Haïtien where the memory of the exuberant and forceful emperor Christophe was still alive. His father had been a general who died in an accident while still quite young. For Paul-Eugène, after attending a religious school, the road to power went via the American officers' military academy in Port-au-Prince. He certainly started off with the best intentions: he considered that neither Negroes nor mulattos should hold exclusive power in the republic's political life. But respecting the *status quo* in fact amounted to supporting the leadership of the mulatto elite. Magloire brought back the same old receptions with their almost royal protocol to the presidential palace. He tried to be the kind of father figure president to his people who would embody on earth the 'bon Dieu bon' in whom the peasants believed so firmly; and to some extent he succeeded. He got considerable loans from the U.S. Import-Export Bank, for a well-thought-out plan to irrigate the valley of the Artibonite, Haiti's major river, which flowed into the sea between Saint-Marc and Gonaïves. He supported an intensive programme of school-building in the countryside. But nothing could really in the end conceal from everyone the fact that the Magloire government's policy worked in favour of the mulattos, and was therefore being fought tooth and nail by the 'authentic' movement of Estimé's men. The Haitian school of primitive painters – comparable to the school that arose in Mexico after the 1910 revolution – had received great encouragement from the Estimé government. Indirectly it became a symbol of opposition to Magloire. The ambitious and dynamic Magloire hoped to escape the fate that had befallen his predecessors by depending on the firm friendships he had made in the armed forces. But in September 1957 he too had to settle for exile on the advice of officers whose ears picked up the growing murmurs on all sides.

In his place, the army favoured a small country doctor with huge round spectacles: François Duvalier. Later developments proved what a mistaken choice they had made. Breaking with a well-established tradition, this president whom the men behind the scenes expected to manipulate with ease, managed after two-and-a-half years as president to get himself re-elected in June 1961 for a further six-year term, and there is no indication at the moment of any threat to his continuance in power.

*

Mistrusting an army which had for too long been the tool of one class and one caste, Duvalier decided it would be better to train and control his own security forces. The Haitians had to add to an already highly imaginative political vocabulary yet another new term: the 'tontons macoutes' became a new feature of life in the capital. *Tonton macoute* is a Creole phrase meaning something like the 'bogeyman' used as a threat to naughty children. The expression itself has a certain charm but the people it describes are anything but charming. Any Haitian who, rightly or wrongly, feels himself in trouble, lives in fear of Duvalier's army of *tontons macoutes*. No one knows exactly how many of them there are – 10,000 perhaps, or 15,000. Wearing a blue boiler suit and often large sunglasses, the *tonton macoute* is quick on the draw, and his almost unlimited power is the terror of all peaceful citizens. There remains hardly one of the old 'elite' families that has not got at least one member held in prison without having ever been charged and for no reason anyone can give. The familiar old stories of corruption and embezzlement by the administrative officials have been replaced by alarming stories of tortures and summary executions. Duvalier is under attack from the former governing class, whose privileges are slowly but surely being withdrawn; he is criticized by the Catholic Church and detested by the majority of students; he draws his support basically from two sources: his militia and the United States. It is said in Port-au-Prince that Duvalier had communist sympathies in his youth and that he is not unresponsive to the example of his neighbour, Fidel Castro: after all, the American Guantanamo base is only a stone's throw from his capital.

Whether this is so or not, his government has on several occasions skilfully fended off American fears. When the dispute between Washington and Havana came before the U.N. general assembly the Haitian delegation did not attend. At the Punta del Este conference in January 1962 Haiti surprised everyone by opposing all sanctions against Cuba, but then did a *volte face*, and voted with the U.S. to exclude the Cuban republic from the OAS. The very next day it was learnt that America was giving a further loan to the Port-au-Prince government.

Duvalier still faces the same desperate problem as his predecessors: finding dollars to finance major construction work. During the past ten years American aid, in various forms, has reached a total of 40 million dollars. It is true that of the funds allotted to technological cooperation almost 40 per cent represent the salaries and expenses of the American experts involved. But Duvalier has none the less received far more than Magloire ever did.

'My country,' Duvalier will say in measured tones to his visitors, 'is a semi-colonial one. It needs dollars for its agriculture.' That is quite true; but if you travel through the countryside you do not observe any very spectacular changes. Estimé wanted a world fair; Duvalier decided to build a garden city thirty kilometres from the capital, near Cabaret, christened Duvalier-ville. The tradesmen in Port-au-Prince were ordered to contribute to the price of this future metropolis whose foundations are gradually emerging. Parades are sometimes organized, oddly reminiscent of those to be seen in the streets of Santo Domingo in the days when Trujillo wielded absolute power. The uniforms of the militia, the banners expressing loyalty, the waving arms, the little girls with bouquets of flowers – it is all quite impressive but should not allow us to forget the profounder realities of Haiti.

In the agricultural schools diplomats and other notables are occasionally invited to watch a student grafting a plant. But today Haiti is producing less coffee than it did a century ago. At the end of the eighteenth century it was exporting 80,000 tons of sugar, whereas today the harvest is barely 60,000 tons. Coffee remains the prime source of wealth, yet tourism must also hold a high place: for the voodoo which is still practised fascinates the visitors who tour the Caribbean in search of all the magic and mystery it holds.

*

Voodoo is a religion, with its rituals, its priests, its chapels, its sacrifices and its mysteries. In theory voodoo is defined as a mixture of Christianity and paganism; but in fact voodoo is far closer to Africa than to Europe. Its rites certainly involve candles, small bells rung by altar boys and even prayers said in Latin – but its basis is African. Needless to say Creole has outdone itself in finding names for the gods of voodoo: Papa Legba, St Pierre, Tetard-l'Etang (the god of the sea), and Ogoun Ferraille – the Haitian version of Mars. Only in the depths of the forest or on the far side of the mountains can voodoo rites be carried out without interruption from onlookers. So great is its power that missionaries make no attempt to attack it openly. But they do try by other means: in their chapels and schools they do not try to find out whether all their converts or pupils are sincere; all they try to do is to get as many black priests as possible to work with them. One of the priests in the Montfort Fathers' mission in Port-de-Paix, in northern Haiti, is a Negro. He runs the college. Though Port-de-Paix is only a quarter of an hour by air from Port-au-Prince, the town looks more like some lost village in the heart of the African bush. But the presence of this missionary, as black as the blackest Haitian, is an outstanding example of what could be done, and what still needs to be done, in Haiti.

In March 1965, Duvalier once again considered having himself declared emperor of Haiti, as François I. The flowered floats in the Port-au-Prince carnival have been decorated several times with that title. The idea may seem ridiculous, but it was obvious that 'Papa Doc' and his followers were trying patiently and tactfully to prepare public opinion to accept it. Nor was it anything new. In 1964, the year of his 're-election' as 'president for life', Papa Doc had thought in terms of some kind of coronation which would secure his power, thus restoring the old dream of the 'emperor' Christophe who ultimately killed himself with a golden bullet. But it would seem that the response of the governors was not favourable. The unhappy attempt by 'commando-group of Thirteen', led by Villedrouin, a young pilot of twenty-four whose father had vanished into Papa Doc's prisons, made it clear that the exiles, chiefly settled in the U.S., were still active, despite all their personal rivalries and differences of outlook. Villedrouin's force landed in early August 1964 on the Cap Dame Marie on the west coast. The thirteen men had been issued at short notice with automatic arms and grenades. Their hope was to advance gradually through one poor village after another, causing the people to rebel. As soon as news of the landing got through, thirty political prisoners in the dungeons of Fort Dimanche were killed. Villedrouin met with success in his first moves of ambushing the regular forces and the *tontons macoutes*, but on 13 August the body of Yvan Laraque, one of the members of his expedition, was strapped to a chair and left in a public square in Port-au-Prince for two days, and by November the last two rebels, Numa and Druin, were arrested and executed in the national cemetery, in front of a mass of students and workers.

For some weeks there was a peculiarly unpleasant repression against the friends and relations of the thirteen young men who had dreamt of overthrowing one of the last and most eccentric of all the Caribbean dictatorships simply by their courage and their example. For instance, in Jérémie and the surrounding area the whole of the Savaricq family was shot without any pretence at a trial. There were a number of other such summary executions, but the problem of finding the precise facts in places where the 'Arab tom-tom' was the only real source of news, as well as the fear which totally paralysed the observers and diplomats in Port-au-Prince made it quite impossible to arrive at any precise figure. One thing was sure: the Duvalier dictatorship was more firmly established than ever, despite the increasing disapproval of the Church, the attempts against it by Haitians exiled in the U.S. or the Dominican Republic, and mounting doubts from Washington.

Back in 1961 Papa Doc deported Archbishop Poirier of Port-au-Prince, and the Vicar Apostolic whose job it was to administer the property of the dioceses was put under house arrest during the summer of 1964 for having dared publicly to demand an amnesty. In May 1963 the Duvalier regime succeeded in surviving even what looked like a death blow: on 7 May the U.S. government ordered its citizens to leave Port-au-Prince. At the same time groups of guerrillas from the Dominican Republic, with the approval of the liberal President Juan Bosch, a personal friend of President Kennedy's, invaded Haiti. It looked impossible for Papa Doc and his *tontons macoutes* to stand out against America's determined opposition – supported also by the Latin American nations as a group. On 15 May the U.S. broke off diplomatic relations with Haiti and announced their intention to reconsider their recognition of Duvalier as president. Duvalier's response was to have all former army officers arrested, as well as all the political detainees who had been allowed out on bail. The *tontons macoutes* created terror in the streets of the capital and hundreds of people sought asylum in the various embassies. Washington may have thought that they had only to frown to get their way, but Papa Doc appealed to the Security Council and laid complaints against the Dominican Republic and the United States. The Bosch government had to make up their minds to disperse the Haitian refugee camps in the Dominican Republic, and once again the storm died down leaving Duvalier intact. On 22 May Duvalier had himself re-elected for another term, and his militia had no trouble in repelling the small groups who tried to invade Cap-Haïtien. On 12 June an OAS Commission recommended that Duvalier respect 'basic human rights'.

This was clearly no more than a pious hope. Faced with the failure of the operation from Santo Domingo, the United States decided to return to 'normal routine relations' with the dictator, and the rights of men were still cheerfully ignored in this land of voodoo. The terror inspired by the *tontons macoutes* and the lauding of 'négritude' still do not seem an adequate explanation for the survival of a regime so openly flouting the principles of the Charter of American States. The number 22 is of special importance in voodoo mythology. A great many Haitians are convinced that the fact of Kennedy's having been assassinated on 22 November was due to Papa Doc's having announced some time earlier on the radio that 'he was putting a curse on the president of the United States'. And it was on the 22nd day of every year that François Duvalier always announced his major decisions to the people. However the facts are more simple and prosaic. While Duvalier obviously had nothing to do with Kennedy's tragic death, it is evident that the Johnson government showed a tolerance and patience which made it quite easy for this megalomaniac to stay in power. Washington's view in 1965 was that 'Papa Doc is no worse than anyone else'. The coast of Cuba and the Guantanamo base face the rugged and romantic shores of Haiti with their endless inlets where landing is no problem. By his proclamation of a principle of anti-Americanism Papa Doc had certainly given the Washington leaders food for thought. The Cubans obviously had not the slightest desire to provide assistance for a man who spoke in glowing terms of the black Middle Ages while oppressing a people he was claiming to lead to a brighter future. It was equally obvious that Washington in 1965 had no intention of risking a confrontation which might result in the establishment of a 'popular and socialist' regime in Port-au-Prince.

In 1964, after the restoration of diplomatic relations with the U.S. (broken off from 17 May to 3 June 1963), the BID and the AID gave Duvalier credits of six million dollars. On 21 July 1967 Washington received the astounding news that Duvalier had been assassinated. For a short time the State Department's Caribbean experts were worried that they had let themselves be caught unprepared by an event that they had decided impossible in May 1963, and of which they felt considerable fear. The joyful haste with which they rushed to deny the news as false was immensely indicative of the real feelings of the American government: Duvalier was clearly preferable to a crisis in Port-au-Prince which might have quite unforeseeable consequences. In effect a political upheaval in Haiti would place the U.S. and the OAS in an even more unpleasant situation than had the Santo Domingo uprising of 1965. 'In Haiti the authority of the law has been replaced by a reign of terror,' declared the international commission of jurists in September 1967. The absence of Papa Doc at the Punta del Este conference in April 1967 was significant: it showed how totally the black Caribbean republic was cut off from the rest of Latin America and how haunted Duvalier was by the fear of being assassinated. The July 1967 conspiracy was put down with peculiar ferocity: Duvalier had nineteen officers suspected of having been involved in the plot arrested; he then sent the police in the middle of the night to awaken the army Chief of Staff General Gérard Constant, his son-in-law Colonel Dominique, and seventeen other superior officers considered to be troublemakers. The group was taken to the prison at Fort Dimanche where the nineteen accused were tied to stakes on the firing range. Each officer was handed a rifle, and Duvalier himself gave the command to fire. The victims were all close friends of Constant and Dominique, and though one might suppose Dominique to have fairly strong nerves after supporting the Duvalier regime since 1958, he did in fact decide to escape and seek exile abroad after taking part in an execution that must have felt so much more like a crime.

Needless to say the dictator's troubles had increased over ten years of ever more absolute power. All the dithyrambics of the Haitian press and news services could not conceal the number of Haitian ambassadors who had resigned in horror as they saw the increase in bloody disorder (between June 1967 and June 1968 there were three such resignations). The 'left-wing game' intended to impress Washington and rekindle the enthusiasm of the American loan companies is a well tried method, but beginning to lack novelty. Every day, from New York and Havana, speakers representing either the 'Haitian Coalition' or the new revolutionary movements are working to defeat the propaganda Papa Doc puts out among the poverty-stricken and ill-educated masses of Haiti. The 'Coalition' has this weakness – it is supported by the 'former presidents' clique', especially Paul Magloire, one of whose aides is Luc Fouché, once the Haitian ambassador to the U.N. But it can count on the benevolent tolerance of a number of highly placed State Department officials, and its paper, *Combattant*, is well presented. The revolutionary movements, starting with the Popular Entente party, consider that the Coalition has had its day and that the fall of Duvalier would force it to reorganize its structures from top to bottom. In other words the 'gifts' from the loan companies of the IMF (the latter rushed through a five-year loan of 1½ million dollars to Duvalier at ludicrously low interest in August 1968) and the efforts of the monopolies like Reynolds Metals or the Haitian American Sugar Company established in Haiti cannot go on indefinitely keeping Papa Doc's reign of terror and bloodshed in existence. In August 1968 it even looked as though, were Duvalier to go, there might be an even more fearful explosion among the people than the troubles that burst on the Dominican Republic four years after Trujillo's death.

CHAPTER 9

Cuba

STATISTICS

Area: 44,218 square miles
Estimated population in 1967: 8,033,000
Population density: Nearly 182 per square mile
Annual rate of population increase: 1·6 per cent.
Annual increase in average per capita *income from* 1960 *to* 1966: 4·6 per cent.

PRINCIPAL PRODUCTS

Sugar, tobacco, coffee, rice, citrus fruit, maize, sisal.
Nickel, chrome, manganese, cobalt.

On 31 January 1962 at Punta del Este the Foreign Ministers of all the OAS member states approved a resolution virtually excluding Cuba from the American family. Naturally the Cuban delegate took no part in the voting; but there were six abstentions – Argentina, Chile, Brazil, Mexico, Ecuador and Bolivia.

The following day contradictory and significant rumours were running wild all over Latin America. In Buenos Aires the army presented President Frondizi with an ultimatum demanding that he break off diplomatic relations with Fidel Castro. In Quito the Minister of Foreign Affairs Francisco Acosta was disowned and expelled by his own party, the Christian Social Movement.

Eight years earlier, in February 1954 in Caracas, the American Secretary of State, John Foster Dulles, had had no trouble at a similar OAS meeting in getting the Guatemalan government of Arbenz Guzmán condemned for its supposedly communist sympathies. The accusation was one based merely on certain presumptions, and the massive vote of the OAS was no more than a moral sanction for the U.S. to use indirect military intervention – which it did five months later to get rid of a government legally elected, and guilty only of having threatened the power and monopoly of the all-powerful United Fruit Company.

*

In 1962 the isolation of Cuba, which had committed a far more outrageous crime than tiny Guatemala, looked like being equally easy to achieve. And in fact thirteen countries, including Rómulo Betancourt's Venezuela, had already broken off diplomatic relations with Castro by the time the OAS representatives met round the table at Punta del Este. All the more so in that the ebullient Cuban leader made no secret of his communist sympathies. A month earlier in Havana he had formally condemned the hypothetical 'third force' so beloved of such democrats and moderate liberals as Figueres of Costa Rica, Betancourt of Venezuela, Santos of Colombia, and Haya de la Torre of Peru. In his view there could be no solution for any under-developed country engaged in the revolutionary struggle except opting for the most extreme means. 'I have absolute faith in Marxism,' he had said in December 1961. 'At first I did not understand Marxism without revisionism; but now I become daily more convinced of the genius in Marx's vision.'

It was certainly noteworthy that he referred expressly to Marxist-Leninist and not to the Soviet Communist Party as such. But this distinction seemed of little significance to Washington and indeed to most Latin American governments, especially Bogotá, which demanded an immediate meeting of the OAS. By proclaiming his faith in the communist system, Fidel Castro had provided his detractors with an unhoped for weapon: to them he had finally unmasked his true self. This seemed all the clearer in that his statements followed a series of positive actions: at that time almost 3,000 young Cubans were enrolled in Soviet universities and 1,500 skilled workers were doing further training in Russia. In the faculties of medicine in Prague and Budapest forty Cuban doctors were attending courses. In Cuba itself two professional training centres for engineers were being run by Soviet instructors.

*

Nevertheless one may still be drawn to wonder about the real reasons for Castro's committing this obvious psychological error of publicly indicating that Washington's accusations were quite justified. Most surprised of all, perhaps, were the Cuban communists themselves. And Marinello, one of the Cuban party leaders, then in Paris, expressed his perplexity: 'Fidel is a fine man. Without him we could achieve nothing. But neither can we count on him a hundred per cent. He is quite unpredictable.' A number of governments were wondering about him as well, especially in Mexico City, in Brasilia, in Santiago and in Buenos Aires; for in fact the rulers of these four key countries of Latin America did not dare to condemn the Cuban revolution outright.

Politically there is an abyss between the more and more left-wing Cuban revolution and the paternalist reformism of a Perón or the sentimental slogan-mongering of a Getúlio Vargas. But the masses in Brazil or Argentina, in Chile or Mexico, care little for such ideological subtleties, and whatever his theories, any champion in the anti-Yankee campaign will always get their vote. The fact that his name may be Castro, that he may be a Cuban, that he may be suspected of playing the communist game – all this makes no difference. By stressing agrarian reform Cuba delighted a continent in which the vast majority of the population are peasants. Apart from Argentina, Chile, Venezuela – and soon Uruguay – the rural population is larger than the urban population everywhere. Yet despite more or less major agrarian reforms undertaken in a few places, large landholding remains the general rule. According to the estimates of one Colombian expert, 65 per cent of the cultivated land in all Latin America – some 469 million hectares – is still in the hands of a minority class of landed proprietors. The permanent hunger for land among Latin American peasants explains why the contagion of Castroism is always a risk in every country, especially among the Indians where social inequalities are most appalling. Yet it is in the most developed countries – Argentina, Uruguay, Chile, Mexico, Venezuela and Brazil – where there is an organized proletariat and unrest among intellectuals, that Castroism arouses the most active sympathy. Its first appeal is certainly to the peasants, but it is also advancing slowly but surely in both academic and urban working-class circles. In Ecuador, Uruguay, Argentina, Brazil, Peru, groups describing themselves as Castroist are stirring up interest in the unions and universities. No government in Latin America can risk ignoring or underrating this phenomenon. The Guatemala affair caused a certain emotion and some regrets. But Castroism has already become a serious internal political problem for most of the nineteen other Latin American republics. That Castro bases his actions on Marxist-Leninist theory, or calls on Soviet Russia for economic and military aid, makes no difference. Governments all over Latin America have to steer a careful course between their wish to have good relationships with the rest of America and the risk of arousing revolutionary groups at home.

*

However it is impossible to grasp the force of the impact of Castro on Latin America without taking account of the emotional factor. It is a romantic continent. Even those leaders most loud in their demands that the Cuban revolutionary regime be outlawed will often have a soft spot in their heart of hearts for Fidel. The death of Che Guevara, an Argentinian by birth, was celebrated with real fervour in Cuba in 1967, but also with genuine emotion in Buenos Aires, despite the fact that General Onganía's government was one of those most determinedly opposed to the Cuban revolution. The Cubans' reputation for high-flying oratory and the magnificent gesture long antedates the arrival of Fidel. Most of the great *Libertadores* of Spanish America were soldiers: but the liberator of Cuba was a nineteenth-century poet and a writer, one of the most representative of all America, José Martí. As was the fashion in Latin America at that time, José Martí in the literary and philosophical spheres still clung to a Hugo-esque romanticism of the most fulsome kind. He did more for Cuban independence through his speeches abroad than by any strictly political activity, and his example is one that Cuba has never forgotten. In the 1930s one of the most determined opponents of the Cuban government was Eduardo Chibas. He waged a violent campaign against corruption. This impassioned spokesman for the public good made a speech on Radio Havana which he concluded by shooting himself in the head. As he had no doubt hoped, the shot resounded all over the city. Cubans came in their thousands to take part in his funeral cortège, and Chibas' astonishing gesture did more to discredit the government than all the hundreds of articles of impassioned polemic he had written.

If a certain Cuban Lieutenant Saria had not chosen in the early hours of Saturday, 1 August 1953 to conduct himself as a soldier, there would have been no Castroism. Fidel Castro, José Suárez and Oscar Alcalde, escapees from the group which had failed in their attempt on the Moncada barracks of Santiago de Cuba on 26 July, were caught asleep by Sarria's patrol. Others of Castro's comrades, captured by Batista's army, were summarily tortured and executed. Fidel was spared by Lieutenant Sarria – even in Cuba history has its hair's breadths. And Castroism, which insists that it is a rigorous adaptation of Marxist-Leninism, a revolutionary adaptation of the strictest principles to the circumstances of the western hemisphere, began with a very human incident.

Far more than Leninism, Trotskyism or Maoism, Castroism is a personality rather than a doctrine. This is not because America is supremely the home of *caudillos*, for the Cubans in theory reject personality cults, though in practice they unwittingly accept one. But it is clear here that the handful of Castroist revolutionaries played a role totally out of all proportion to their numbers and that their chief, the 'Líder máximo', exercised an exceptionally powerful grip over the whole history of the revolution and its development into what is now called Castroism. From Madero's appeal in 1910 up to the constitution of 1917 the Mexican revolution came into being with the bloody but natural violence of the land. That first great social revolution of Latin America was inexorably built into the realities of the situation and the balance of the various forces concerned. The success of the Cuban revolution, on the other hand, has always depended on imponderables and on the decisions of a few individuals. Agrarian reform and freedom from the control of foreign capital were the slogans and clear objectives of the Mexican revolutionaries from the very first, whereas Castroism grew out of an idealistic and overwhelming protest against corruption and injustice. Its doctrine, its revolutionary tactics and strategy, its political intentions, its economic and social purposes only became clear gradually, and grew out of the pressure of events. The need to work out an ideology only appeared after it had achieved power. This is a highly important point: the entry of the Cuban revolution into the socialist camp and Fidel's adoption of Marxist-Leninism in 1961 were not the result of any intention expressed beforehand, but a development the logic of which only became clear afterwards. For Castroism to be faithful to its own essential nature meant without doubt a determined battle against the interests and influence of the United States, but this inevitability was far from evident to anyone in the United States, to whom at the beginning the Cuban revolution looked like a battle between a Cuban Robin Hood and the stupid and cruel dictatorship of Batista. Another equally important point: the neutralizing role played by north American public opinion towards the Cuban revolution in its first stage was far from negligible, and it was the rapid change in that quarter that did most to improve the chances of Castroism elsewhere in the continent. The victory of the Cuban revolution proves beyond a doubt that the establishment of a socialist government by armed struggle is *also* possible in America, but the way in which that victory was won did a lot to alter the image of Castroism. Guevara, one of Fidel's first comrades, the great theorist of guerrilla warfare and believer in the capacity of revolutionary *focos* to create the conditions for revolution, declared that 'after Cuba American imperialism will never again let itself be taken by surprise'. What was a heroic and generous epic when played out on the narrow stage of the Sierra Maestra foothills among a few bearded guerrillas became greed for power and an evil expansionism the moment it tried to strike at the economic and social structures of the island and at the strongholds of north American imperialism in Latin America. The Cuban David became a formidable dictator and Castro-communism – a term coined as a kind of ironic scorn – now became the embodiment of the subversion which had been denounced ever since the conquest of political independence by all those concerned to maintain the *status quo*. From Robin Hood to communist dictator – that these two extreme judgements could be delivered within so short a space of time by the very same people illustrates the problems of making an objective assessment.

*

Though it can be seen at once as a victorious venture, the triumph of an intelligent revolutionary avant-garde, a style of government, a bewitchment by words, a desire for direct democracy, tactics and strategy worked out on a basis of Marxism-Leninism as adapted for the third world, a search for the genuine socialist man, the establishment of a society freed of materialistic stimuli, a fiercely independent and arrogant diplomacy, Castroism is still not really fundamentally anything new. Guerrilla warfare and the armed struggle are traditional components of the history of Latin America. But for the first time – and here lies the real novelty of Castroism – *armed violence has become part of a whole international context* which is logical, if not coherent. By becoming a potentially important element in worldwide conflict and in a cold war that is for the moment being played down, Castroism has brought Latin America into the total world picture.

Not that it was not part of it before 1959 – but it was not seen as a coherent whole before that time. It was no mere chance that the rocket crisis of autumn 1962 brought the world to the brink of a thermo-nuclear war.

Another innovation of Castroism is the radical nature of its structural reforms. Mexico's agrarian reform pre-dated Cuba's, and the reform decreed in Bolivia in 1952 by Dr Paz Estenssoro did something to alter the power structures in the country which Guevara chose in 1967 as the starting point for an agrarian revolution that was intended to spread all over Latin America. But the Mexican reform took a fairly long time to get going; it had its surprises, its periods of unhampered advance and of equally obvious checks; it was enthused over and institutionalized but also modified. Its – far from negligible – results only became evident after some years, and by the time the first impetus of the revolution had died down considerably. The inevitable bureaucracy and a determination to stick closely to the main principles of the 1917 constitution combined in planning – half a century after Zapata – an agrarian reform granted by law and not won by pressure from the masses. In Bolivia the 1952 agrarian reform, which certainly did produce some improvement in living standards, also resulted in an even more terrible isolation of the tin miners. Yet in Cuba, only a year after the revolution had succeeded, there were over six hundred agricultural cooperatives with 'people's shops' where peasants could buy the necessities of life at moderate prices. Seven years later the 'people's farms' are attempting to do away with wage-earning altogether, and the first 'integral communist society' is undergoing its birth pangs on the Isla Pinos where thousands of young pioneers have settled. New generations of agronomic engineers and agricultural supervisors are being trained in the new technological universities, while the Camilo Cienfuegos school, near the Sierra Maestra, has been set up for the children of the *guajiros* – the hopeless, landless peasants of pre-revolutionary days.

The great mass of Latin American peasants live in precarious and often positively sub-human conditions. The scourge of the *latifundio* combined with that of the *minifundio*, illiteracy, oppression, feudal systems of exploiting labour, hunger, a fearful mortality rate, cultural underdevelopment: all these factors, which the ruling class are quick to minimize, present in theory an exceptionally favourable forcing ground for propagating Castroist ideas. It is significant that plans for agrarian reform have increased enormously in Latin America since 1959. In fact such plans, however dynamic, generally come to a full stop against the opposition of the property-owning classes and from only a tiny item on the balance-sheet of Castroism's successes and failures in the western hemisphere. But as attempts to stem the tide of unrest they are in fact not very effective; that those responsible for them overvalue the effect they are having is only due to the fact that the unrest has not spread in quite the conditions, or at quite the pace, foreseen by the Castroist revolutionaries. Guevara wrote in 1959: 'There is one lesson which our American brothers in such mainly agricultural countries as ours ought to learn: that is that one cannot try to start by making the revolution in the towns where its social spectrum is necessarily incomplete. They must make agrarian revolutions, fighting in the fields and hills, and carry the revolution from there into the towns....'

The Castroist thesis of the revolutionary *foco* developing first of all in the countryside and growing gradually stronger until it is ready to form a revolutionary army and win power – this quite evidently grew out of the experience of the Sierra Maestra. But though later rationalized by the French philosopher Régis Debray in *Revolution in the Revolution?*, it was already implicit in the speech Fidel Castro made before his judges on 16 October 1953 in Santiago de Cuba. 'These are the six problems for whose solution we shall make immediate decisions, together with the restoration of civil liberties and political democracy: the land, industrialization, construction, unemployment, education and health. 85 per cent of the small farmers in Cuba pay rent and live under constant threat of losing the land they are working on. Over half of the best land belongs to foreigners. In Oriente, our largest province, the holdings of the United Fruit Company and the West Indian Company stretch from the north shore to the south. There are two hundred thousand peasant families who do not own even a tiny scrap of land to grow vegetables for their starving children. The strength and prosperity of the country depend on the health and vigour of the peasants, men who love the land and will tend it well given the existence of a State that can advise them and protect their interests. ...' Castroism, though it is in a state of continual development politically, though it has moved from a liberal Christian humanism to a communism inspired by European examples, and on from that to an attempt to work out a revolutionary communism appropriate to under-developed countries, has never (since 1953) wavered in its endeavour to achieve a society in which the peasant majority of the people could leave behind the horrors of the Middle Ages. Since 1959 the areas in which Castroism has appeared to be in a position to alter the *status quo* have always been rural: the eastern area of Guatemala, the mountain regions of Colombia and Venezuela, the high valleys of Peru.

And to Lenin's question: 'What is to be done?', Castroism responds with its theory of the *foco*, the revolutionary cell whose development has been described by Che Guevara; he considered that 'the Cuban revolution has provided three fundamental contributions to the working-out of revolutionary movements in America: 1. If the people will only fight they can win a war against the army. 2. You need not always wait for all the conditions of revolution to be present: the revolutionary *foco* can create them. 3. In under-developed America the terrain where the armed struggle takes place must be the countryside.'

The Cuban leaders, like those of all Latin American countries having to face movements of armed insurrection, have an equal propensity (though certainly for different reasons!) to overestimate the impact of Castroism properly so-called. Thus it should be noted that the wave of Castroism, though it certainly appeared to extend enormously from 1959 to 1968, with numbers of both successes and failures, was often revealing or re-kindling sparks that had long been in existence or had barely been extinguished. The armed movement in Guatemala, following the failure of a rising by some young officers, was quite as much inspired by the local progressist experience (to which direct U.S. intervention put a stop in 1954) as by the Cuban drama. The psychology of the Guatemalan peasants – even those living along the Motagua river or on the Pacific coast – has only the most distant likeness to that of the *guajiros* of the Sierra Maestra. In fact the most significant successes of the Guatemalan guerrillas were actually achieved in Guatemala City, while the insecurity of the agrarian system made possible the establishment of paramilitary police in the countryside, and an extension of the 'white terror'. In Colombia armed movements inspired by Castroism developed alongside movements of self-defence among peasants who had been suffering the most rigid repression since 1948; they were led by young intellectuals from the towns, Bogotá in particular, and from 1964 onwards the crushing of the peasant self-defence areas – where the communist party was trying to establish a foothold – left the Castroist *focos* with a terrain, and possibilities for action, very similar to those existing in Venezuela since 1961. In five years the movement of armed insurrection in Falcón, near Maracaibo, never managed to become as fully established as the Cuban revolution was only two years after *Granma*'s landing in Playa Colorada. The Castroist movement in Venezuela was better known for such spectacular but unprofitable acts as the kidnapping of important figures (the footballer Di Stefano or Colonel Smollen) than for any rapid or firmly-based extension in its arenas of rural guerrilla fighting.

In the Peruvian highlands, where Luis de la Puente and Guillermo Lobatón tried to develop the ground prepared by Hugo Blanco's trade-union activity, the Castro-inspired movement of armed insurrection in the spring of 1965 was very quickly put down by a forceful counter-attack by the Peruvian armed forces. From 1959 to 1961 there were other minor set-backs to revolutionary Castroism – in Argentina (the Tucumán movement), in Paraguay (the 14 May movement), in the Dominican Republic (the destruction of the guerrilla group led by Jiménez de Moya, which gave birth to the '14 June movement' whose part in the April rising of 1965 was considerable), in Colombia (the first failure of the MOEC – Movement of workers, students and peasants), and in Ecuador (the Revolutionary Union of Youth).

The Ñancahuazú revolutionary *foco* in the Bolivian province of Santa Cruz is the most recent example of the failure of a Castroist guerrilla attempt in South America. Set on foot during the autumn of 1966 it was discovered in March 1967 and crushed by Bolivian armed forces in October 1967 after the capture and execution of Che Guevara; this *foco*, established in a rural area near oilfields was, according to Guevara's campaign diary, thought of as a future starting base for guerrilla operations in neighbouring countries – northern Argentina, Brazil, the Peruvian highlands, Paraguay. It is hard to assess Guevara's final effort because it would seem that he must have been involved in armed action in Bolivia even before the date he first planned for, and in somewhat different conditions. 'Bolivia', wrote Debray in 1965, 'is the country where the objective and subjective conditions exist in the closest combination; it is the only country in south America where the socialist revolution is possible, despite the reconstitution of an army that was totally destroyed in 1952.'

In point of fact the one constant element in all the Castroist experiments in south America, from 1959 to 1968, was the general lack of adequate support from the peasants. Guevara complained most bitterly of this several times in his Bolivian Journal. One of the reasons for the success of the Cuban revolution, on the other hand, was the gradual rallying of all the peasants to the armed movement, which began on a small scale but eventually held back the regular forces of the dictatorship and put into practice the agrarian reforms promised in each zone as it was liberated. For different reasons – varying too in the different countries under consideration – it has not been possible to achieve such a rallying of the peasants anywhere else: the lack of political consciousness, the speed with which the armed forces counter-attacked, sometimes with the help of American anti-guerrilla experts, the frailty of the revolutionary *focos*, a lack of liaison between the 'peasant base' and the 'urban networks', disputes among left-wing leaders, some of whom support the armed struggle out of sheer opportunism. Each experiment really requires its own individual study in depth.

It does not follow from this that Castroist theory as regards the priority of the armed struggle in the countryside is false. But after nine years of a movement which Washington calls 'subversive' and Havana 'revolutionary' there is one inescapable conclusion: purely and simply copying the Cuban pattern has not lived up to the expectation of the Castroist leaders. Since the disaster of the guerrilla *foco* in Bolivia, the tendency in Latin America has been in favour of seeking formulae appropriate to each country in relation to its own peculiar historical, political, economic, sociological and cultural conditions.

*

'I have never seen a land more beautiful. Palm leaves large enough to serve as roofs to houses. On the shore thousands of glittering shells. Clear water. And everywhere the same astounding symphony of birdsong. Human nature, on the other hand, is no different here from the other islands. ...' On 20 October 1492 Christopher Columbus could not say enough in praise of the eastern coast of Cuba which he discovered for the first time that day, and along which he sailed until 2 November. He became certain that Cuba was merely a continental province of the empire of the Great Khan and on 12 November he left the shores of a land he christened *Juana* after the Infanta of Spain.

The Indians Columbus found were peaceful men belonging to two major groups, the Tainos and the Siboneyes. According to Fr La Casas the population amounted to about a million. It was soon decimated by massacres, forced labour and imported epidemics. The black slaves brought over from Africa took the place of the Indians. Baracoa, at the eastern end, was founded in 1512 and from 1590 on, Havana was the centre of the Caribbean ship-building industry. The seventeenth century was marked by the development of stock-breeding and the extension of sugar and tobacco plantations: three elements which still preponderate in present-day Cuba's economy. At the same time the activities of pirates soon proved the island's strategic value. The occupation of Havana by the English during the latter half of the eighteenth century was a result of rivalries among the great European powers, while sugar production occupied a Negro work force of something like a million people. In 1816 the Cubans managed to get rid of the tobacco monopoly and in 1818 trade generally became free, but there were increasing incidents between the bureaucratic Spanish administration and the local population, among whom the Creoles especially became weary of waiting for reforms, while the emancipation movement among the Spanish colonies on the mainland was proceeding so rapidly.

A *Cuba libre* is a mixture of rum and coca-cola, in whatever proportions you fancy. Even in the darkest hours of the Batista dictatorship the Cubans never lost their sense of humour. The largest island in the Caribbean, four times the size of Belgium, was not as lucky as its neighbours, Haiti and Santo Domingo; in fact Cuba was the last American country to get rid of Spanish dominion. The Cubans' struggle for independence dragged on with varying success from 1820 to 1898. After the death of Ferdinand VII of Spain the governors of Cuba established a reign of terror and any attempts at revolt were crushed unmercifully. At the entrance to the port of Havana, on a rocky promontory, the citadel of El Morro, built in 1597, stands out, sinister and ponderous. The arrested rebels were dragged there and usually strangled by garrotting. Thousands of Cubans sought refuge in the U.S. and secret societies with such poetic names as the *Mina de la Rosa Cubana*, or *Sociedad libertadora de Camagüey* conspired to carry out desperate and ineffectual revolutions. Around 1868 some more effective leaders came on the scene. Carlos Manuel de Céspedes and Aguilera were the leaders of a real guerrilla war which lasted for ten years. But even then the emancipation movement in Cuba was actually developing under the diplomatic and military protection of America. In 1854 the Ostend manifesto had made clear the United States' wish to annex the island, unless it were possible to negotiate a purchase arrangement. The War of Secession put off all plans of this sort but in 1895 they again came to the fore. American opinion became fired by the Cuban insurgents, and their ideological leader José Martí. A committee of émigrés was formed in the U.S. – the first of many.

*

After Martí's death Cuba revolted. In two years Spain was forced to send 200,000 men to reinforce the 100,000 already on the island. The groups of active revolutionaries never amounted to more than 25,000 all told but their leaders were killed and replaced one after another. In May 1897 President McKinley demanded that Spain put an end to the war. The Spanish government had already decided to effect a gradual plan of increasing autonomy but this decision provoked the most violent reaction among the Spanish colonists settled in Havana, resulting in fearful riots and confrontations.

On 15 February 1898 the cruiser Maine, sent by Washington, was blown up in Havana with its crew. This provided an excuse for intervention (though a later inquiry proved the explosion to have been accidental) and marked the beginning of the short-lived Spanish-American war. The Spanish fleet was destroyed in Santiago harbour and the town captured on 16 July. In the treaty of Paris, on 10 December 1898, Spain renounced all claim to Cuba (as also to Puerto Rico and the Philippines).

After the departure of the Spanish the government of Cuba was carried out for three years by American governors with the assistance of certain leading Cubans. The new Constitution, painstakingly worked out and adopted in 1902, included the Platt amendment (demanded by the United States) granting Washington 'the right to intervene in Cuba to secure the lives and property of Americans'. The amendment also granted the U.S. a right of surveillance over the country's public health system and customs and excise, as well as a naval base at Guantanamo. The Platt amendment aroused such protests in Cuba that in 1934 President Roosevelt decided to modify the more humiliating clauses in it.

On several occasions, particularly from 1906–9 and again from 1917–19, American marines landed in Cuba, and up until 1925 Cuban presidents were for all practical purposes subject to control by Washington. Machado, who seized power in 1925, certainly proclaimed his liberal intentions loudly enough, but the Cubans were not slow to recognize that he had exactly the same failings as his predecessors, as well as a pronounced fondness for political murder. He had been elected for four years and clung obstinately to his post.

His authoritarian methods, the universal corruption, but also, and above all, the crisis in the sugar market, finally brought about his downfall. The protective tariffs insisted on by the American sugar-beet farmers had the most disastrous consequences for Cuban sugar exports from 1929 to 1932. The price fell to less than one cent a pound and the volume of exports was reduced by two thirds. Even a loan of fifty million dollars from the Chase Manhattan Bank could not save Machado.

The sugar market has always closely determined politics in Cuba. Not merely does Cuba's whole livelihood depend on the production and sale of this one product but it is a product with a very restricted world market. Thirty million tons of sugar were available in 1959, when all the major exporters had added their totals. In 1939 the figure was no more than 27 millions tons. Thus more sugar is being produced in the world today than twenty years ago yet barely any more is actually being consumed.

On an average Cuba sells three million tons of sugar on the open market – in other words half its normal production. The rest used to be exported to the United States with preferential tariffs. Thus the U.S. was subsidizing Cuban sugar, just as the Soviet Union does that of its satellites, and France that of its former colonies. Obviously this had to be a unilateral decision on the part of the United States, and the Cubans were obliged in return to lower certain duties and preserve a free exchange. The Americans, with their enormous consumption of sweet things, could obviously satisfy all their needs (which their domestic production could not wholly meet) by buying sugar from Cuba, the Philippines, Peru or the Dominican Republic. Until 1960 Cuba was their appointed supplier, but the U.S. could in fact manage quite well without Cuban sugar. If the U.S. were to boycott Cuba, which in fact it did, Cuba would be forced to find an outlet in Europe, Russia or elsewhere.

In 1933 relations between Washington and Havana were politically splendid but the deterioration of trade relations was certainly the starting point for the crisis which led to Machado's fall. It is true that the Cubans were from all points of view fed up with Machado and his methods. The secret societies which had proliferated under Spanish rule suddenly burgeoned afresh in Havana, and once again you could see in Miami those committees of Cuban refugees which have always made their presence felt at moments of crisis in Cuban history. Young officers joined the ranks of the malcontents, and there were student demonstrations in the streets of Havana.

*

After Machado's police arrested Enrique José Varona, a University professor who was universally respected, American public opinion suddenly and violently switched to the side of the opposition, and President Roosevelt told Sumner Welles to soothe the Cubans by persuading Machado to resign. He tried to hang on to his position but in August 1933 he finally decided to take a plane to Bermuda. Sumner Welles then proposed replacing him with Carlos Manuel de Céspedes, who took office on 12 August and was turned out again on 5 September! A junta led by Ramón Grau San Martín followed him from 5 to 10 September. Grau San Martín became head of government and in four months had set up a Ministry of Labour, nationalized electricity, given the University back its autonomy, re-opened the secondary schools and decreed votes for women.

When he left Havana to give way to Colonel Carlos Mendieta he was accompanied to the port by a crowd of Cubans who considered him as a great liberator. Mendieta only remained in office from Janaury 1934 to December 1935; in fact the strong man in the government was already the army's commander in chief, Fulgencio Batista. Mendieta was replaced first of all by Miguel Gómez and then by Federico Laredo Bru. This amazing game of musical chairs only indicated one very superficial aspect of Cuban politics, which were basically dominated from behind the scenes by the rivalry between the civilian Grau San Martín and the soldier Fulgencio Batista. Until 1940 Batista considered it wiser to stay in the background and get his officer friends into the forefront for several weeks or months. He then offered himself for election in 1940 and won.

In 1933 he was simply a sergeant-stenographer; he was promoted to Colonel in one night and commander in chief in an hour, and now had at last come to the very front of the Cuban scene. Short, solid, with a wide nose and a wide smile, friendly and at times shy, he astounded everyone by his vitality. What astounded the Cubans still further was that he accepted the verdict of the 1944 election which went against him and withdrew to Florida. His career might well have ended there and no doubt he would have left no unpleasant memories with anyone. But on 10 March 1952 a putsch which he organized deposed the Prio Socarras government – of which the least one can say is that it did little during its time in office to get rid of the enemies in its own house. Batista had formed some odd friendships with Americans who ran gambling-houses and other such establishments during his stay in Miami. Before his return Havana was certainly no monastic retreat but during his second term as president the systematic exploitation of vice there took on alarming proportions. The national lottery, fruit machines, cock fighting, horse racing: everything became a source of quick enormous enrichment for the few and the object of protection rackets run by some of the best-known 'wide boys' in the United States.

The national lottery used to be drawn monthly but now became a daily event. All the hotels were allowed to set up their own casinos and night clubs provided they paid a licence fee of 25,000 dollars. Batista's brother-in-law was given the monopoly of the fruit machines. Over half of all wage-earners got less than a dollar a day, while the great mass of farm labourers could only find work for six weeks in the year, during the sugar-cane harvest. During that time the regime's profiteers amassed millions of dollars. Havana became the capital of prostitution in Latin America. In 1956 there were 270 registered brothels, over a hundred 'specialist houses' and almost a thousand bars where dozens of 'hostesses' were forced to act as prostitutes when required. The centre of this pleasure-factory was la Rampa, between the old Hilton Hotel (since 1959 the *Habana libre*) and the Vedado district.

*

Havana, though a paradise for tourists, became a hell for anyone who opposed the regime. The SIM (Military Intelligence Service), the BRAC (Bureau for Suppressing Communist Activities), the secret police and the regular police behaved in ways that made Trujillo's police look like sensitive and scrupulous artists by comparison. Ventura and Senator Masferrer, skilled executioners, gouged out prisoners' eyes, pulled out their fingernails and cut off their genitals before finally killing them. It might have been thought that the President would not want all this bloodshed and torture, all those thousands of victims; that it might perhaps have been doing him a good turn to tell him that one student killed during a demonstration in 1953 was called Ruben Batista – the name of one of his own sons – and that he had unwittingly let himself be drawn into this chain of hideous repression. But the fact is that he concealed, tolerated and actually encouraged the atrocities.

In 1958 American businessmen controlled 90 per cent of the mines and *haciendas*, 40 per cent of the sugar industry, 80 per cent of the public services, 50 per cent of the railways, and, together with English firms, the whole of the oil industry. That same year the increase in the profits of Standard Oil in Cuba was larger than the United States' aid to the whole of Latin America. It is also true that the U.S. was buying Cuban sugar at a price above that of the world rate. Thus, indirectly, the U.S. was giving aid worth 250 million dollars a year. Did the one make up for the other? Hardly, for the U.S. could change their quota of imports at will. In exchange for the extra two cents the Americans paid for Cuban sugar, they supplied the island with 75 per cent of its imports, thus holding its economy in the palm of their hand.

With an economy disastrously dependent on the United States and a succession of corrupt regimes quite unable to tackle the country's real problems, the movement of 26 July was first and foremost a protest against injustice and an affirmation of human dignity.

On 26 July 1953 machine-gun fire shattered the early morning silence in Santiago de Cuba, the capital of Oriente province. The Cuban revolution was beginning. The Cubans have always loved panache and the grand gesture. But only madmen would have attacked the Moncada barracks where a thousand troops were quartered: the assailants were only a handful of people divided into three assault groups. They were mainly students, trained by three leaders, Fidel Castro, his brother Raúl, and Abel Santamaría who was to be killed. And in fact their madness met with disaster: the attackers were repelled, made prisoners or summarily shot. Fidel Castro got away, and hid for four days among the wild country of the Sierra Maestra, but was finally found, and two months later brought to trial. They thought they were dealing with a straightforward gang leader, but in fact he was a brilliant advocate, who spoke to his judges in their own language, and pronounced a speech of accusations which was also the political programme for the revolution.

Fidel was condemned to fifteen years' imprisonment. It could have been far worse – Batista underestimated the man. More foolishly still he was to grant him a pardon after less than two years in the penitentiary on the sinister and feared Ila de Pinos. Having been elected for a further four-year term on 1 November 1953 Batista agreed to show proof of his clemency! Castro and his comrades, set free in May 1955, left for Mexico two months later. It took them no longer than eighteen months to collect enough money, weapons and volunteers, and on 15 November 1956 Fidel was ready to make another attempt on the Moncada. This one began almost as badly as the first one had: H-hour for the landing near Santiago de Cuba was to be on the 30 November during the daytime. On 2 December the ship bringing the assault party had the greatest difficulty in getting to shore at all because of a violent storm. Though eighty-two men landed, Fidel had no more than fifteen living in hiding with him in the Sierra Maestra at the end of 1956.

*

This fragile body became well organized, escaped all those who first tried to find them, and began a long series of marches and counter-marches, and of ambushes designed to create alarm among the regular troops sent out by the Batista government. In 1953 Batista had underestimated Castro, the young lawyer whose programme-dissertation to the court, 'History will absolve me', had already become a political declaration arousing excitement in the universities. Once again, in these first months, he underestimated the guerrilla *foco*; after all it was a thousand kilometres from Havana, and no one really knew much about it.

The rebels' first successes against the army – whose soldiers certainly demonstrated very little fighting spirit – enabled them to gather fresh recruits, some from towns, and others from the country, lured by the promise of agrarian reform. Urban support-networks were formed and grew gradually stronger. A 'students committee', a revolutionary body parallel to Castro's 26 July Movement was set up in the capital, and a second guerilla front was established in the Sierra del Escambray in the centre of the island. In the spring of 1958 some American journalists managed to spend a few days in Castro's base camp, and they disclosed to the world the existence of these romantic bearded guarrellis whom the dictatorship thought it had disposed of. American opinion had sided with José Martí against Spain in the nineteenth century; it now became enthusiastically pro-Castro, and sections of the press began to criticize Washington's support of Batista.

In May 1958 the dictator determined to put down this insolent and rapidly spreading rebellion. Reinforcements were sent to the troops in the Sierra Maestra so that the whole area could be thoroughly flushed out and the air force began bombing there. The secret police carried out even more searches and arrests in an attempt to dismantle the liaison networks. The 'pacification' operation failed and in August it was Fidel's turn to move onto the offensive. A second front, organized by Raúl Castro, was opened north of Santiago, and two rebel columns led by Che Guevara and Camilo Cienfuegos were ordered to move gradually west to link up with the Las Villas province and the Sierra del Escambray. Having overcome endless obstacles and come close to disaster the two columns achieved their breakthrough and completed their 'long march' across the open plains of the island. On Christmas Day 1958 Che Guevara's column captured the town of Santa Clara after wiping out an armoured train of government troops. Near Havana itself groups of partisans blew up military installations. On 1 January at 2 a.m. Batista decided to make his escape to Santo Domingo. On 4 January Che Guevara entered the city, to be followed on the 8th by Castro, who had marched there in triumph from Santiago. Wherever they went the victors were welcomed enthusiastically by the people. The excesses of the dictatorship, combined with the heroic quality of the venture undertaken by the barbudos,* contributed much to the support given by the vast majority of Cubans to the revolutionary regime which thus began on a wave of popular fervour.

'Fidel has always been outstanding in all literary subjects. He has very fine qualities. He is a real athlete, and has al-

* Bearded men.

ways played for the school with courage and pride. He has won the admiration and affection of all. He intends to make the law his career, and we have no doubt he will fill the pages of the book of his life brilliantly. Fidel is made of very fine stuff, nor does he lack artistic qualities'. This amazingly laudatory assessment by the Jesuits of Belén college, where Fidel got his *bachillerato* in 1945, tells us much of the personality of the future revolutionary. He had read the works of José Martí before reading Marx and Hegel. His revolution, a revolt against corruption, thievery and oppression, was first and foremost humanistic. Thus it naturally received the approval of liberals, humanists and socialists. When it opted for Marxist-Leninism and declared Cuba the 'first free territory in America', the disappointed liberals spoke in terms of treason, the humanists explained this 'deterioration' by the 'mistaken policy of the United States', and Marxists congratulated themselves on 'this concrete and inevitable application of Marxist theory'.

In his first Moncada speech Castro spoke of: 'Restoring civil liberties and democracy, agrarian reform, industrialization, construction, getting rid of unemployment, planning for education and public health'; on 13 March 1967 he declared: 'It is impossible that a man, having a revolutionary vocation and the qualities and conditions that go with it, should not finally become a Marxist'. Between these two statements we see the entire development of the Cuban revolution from 1959 to 1968.

On 4 January 1959 Dr Urrutia was inaugurated as president of the republic. He appointed Miró Cardona as his Prime Minister. Since March 1958 the leaders of the 26 July Movement had been planning to place the government in the hands of this judge from Santiago, well known for his integrity and his courageous opposition to the dictatorship. The Miró Cardona regime represented the lower and middle middle class, who were delighted at the overthrow of the dictatorship. But the true power was in the streets where people were demanding that Batista's 'war criminals' be hunted down. On 15 February Fidel became Prime Minister and his first measures were radical in the extreme: price control and a forceful attack on the gaming-houses of Havana – that symbol of Batista's corruption. The first sign of any break between the Cuban revolution and the kind of Latin American reformism supported by Washington was Castro's spectacular trip to Caracas (where Pérez Jiménez' military dictatorship had been overthrown a year earlier) which led the Venezuelan leadership to take a cooler attitude towards the new regime in Havana. The tremendous popular success with which the leader of the Cuban *barbudos* was welcomed in Caracas disturbed Rómulo Betancourt. There was a generation between the two men: Fidel was beginning something new, in the heat of victory and with the illusions of youth. Betancourt, still considered by the Venezuelan middle class as a dangerous revolutionary agitator, was only concerned with securing the victory he had won so dearly from Pérez Jiménez. Fidel wanted to overthrow everything. Betancourt wanted simply to hold on. It is clear that at that point Castro was not yet a dogmatist. Whose method of government would he opt for? The communists, a minority despite their extraordinary degree of organization, only aligned themselves with the 26 July Movement at a late date. In July 1958 the Popular Socialist party (i.e. communist) was still refusing to join the united front being formed by all the anti-Batista groups. Carlos Rafael Rodríguez, a member of the Central Committee, only joined the guerrillas three months before Batista's overthrow. It was to be more than two years before any Cuban communists got major jobs in the government. The revolution began by settling a number of old scores: the first executions took place in Oriente province. The trials in Havana were followed by thousands of Cubans in the Sports Stadium as well as by horrified and scandalized

American reporters: by the end of January 1959 almost 300 condemned men had been shot.

*

The Cuban way was not to be one of total cooperation with the United States. But it had not yet become one of hostility to the United States nor of friendship with Russia. In April 1959 Fidel tried to explain the direction of his movement. He summed up his programme in these terms:

Neither freedom without food nor food without freedom. Neither dictatorship by the people, nor dictatorship by one class. Freedom with food, without fear. That is humanism.

And he added, further,

... Between the two political and economic ideologies at present being debated in the world we have taken up our own position. We have called it humanism, because we want to set men free of all fears, oppressions and dogmatisms. We are revolutionizing society without enslaving it or terrorizing it. The dreadful problem the world is facing is that it is now so placed that it must choose between capitalism – in which the poor starve – and communism, which solves the problems of the economy but suppresses the freedoms man most needs. Cubans and Latin Americans want, and are trying to bring about, a revolution which can satisfy their material needs without sacrificing those freedoms. Should we succeed in this by democratic means then the Cuban revolution will stand out as a classic example in the history of the world. Our notion of freedom is different from that of the reactionaries, who talk of elections rather than of social justice. Without social justice there can be no such thing as democracy, for people are then slaves to poverty. That is why we have said that we are one step ahead of both right and left, and that ours is a humanist revolution. It takes away nothing essential to man, but makes him its major object. Capitalism sacrifices man; the communist state because of its totalitarian nature sacrifices the rights of man. That is why we can take neither side. Every people must develop its own political pattern to suit its needs, a pattern neither imposed from outside nor copied from anyone else. Ours is an autonomous Cuban revolution – as Cuban as our music. Why should all peoples everywhere listen to the same music? That is why I say that our revolution is not red, but olive green, for olive green is the colour for us, the colour of the revolution brought by the rebel army from the heart of the Sierra Maestra.

This lyrical definition of Cuban neutralism in 1959 failed to carry conviction in Washington. To counter this movement, whose gradual hardening disturbed them, the Americans began by using economic weapons. In April 1959 Castro was in Washington and New York where he said: 'We are not communists. Our revolution is inspired by the democratic principle: no dictatorship of men, no dictatorship by one class. Freedom with food and without fear: that is humanism.' And he added: 'Our trade with the United States can increase to our mutual advantage; it is quite impossible for us to make any progress if we are not in agreement with the United States.' On 2 May, in Buenos Aires, at the meeting of the Economic Council of the OAS, he made this still clearer: 'Latin America must try to obtain capital from the only country which is sufficiently economically developed to provide it: the United States.' But on 17 May 1959 Castro decreed his agrarian reform. 40 per cent of all property became socialist owned and the former landlords were indemnified in bonds that would fall due in twenty years. In Guatemala Arbenz Guzmán's progressive regime was condemned by the U.S. in 1954 because its agrarian reform affected the interests of the powerful United Fruit Co. In 1959 the troubles of the Cuban revolution also began when it started to interfere in the question of land ownership.

Cuban conservatives were anxious. 'North American monopolies are a threat to Latin America,' said Castro.

*

1959 was the year of the agrarian reform. Before his judges in Santiago in 1953 Fidel had declared the need for such a reform. In the Sierra Maestra he had it put into effect in every area as it became liberated by his men. He did not rest content with *wanting* to change a system whose archaism and inefficiency was accepted by almost everybody as a plain fact. It was the peasants who formed the fighting mass of the rebel army, who helped, informed, hid, and looked after the *barbudos* of the two assault columns – Guevara's and Cienfuegos' – who set out on that decisive march across the island at the end of the summer of 1958. They got no help from the reserved, careful or terrified town-dwellers.

In 1959, Fidel still mistrusted Havana, where the revolution's various calls to a general strike – especially on 9 April 1958 – had met with no response. He still had his reservations about the towns inland, even Santiago, where he had never received all the help he might have hoped for. Only the peasants had responded with enthusiasm and self-denial to the appeal of the first shots from the Sierra Maestra which were to awaken all Cuba from its long sleep. In 1953 Castro said

In this county there are 500,000 farm labourers living in ramshackle huts, getting only four months' work in a year, and racked with hunger the rest of the time; sharing their poverty with their children, without a yard of ground to cultivate, living in conditions which the most hardened heart could not fail to pity. There are 100,000 small farmers who live and die working land that is not theirs, who, like feudal serfs, have to pay for the privilege of using that land by giving up part of every harvest ... who dare not plant an orange or lemon tree because they never know when the commissioner or rural guard will drive them away from their home.

According to the reform law promulgated on 17 May 1959 all peasants in theory were given the right to a *caballería* (about 13 hectares). Experts reckoned that a farmer could feed a family of three children on one third of that. The National Institute for Agrarian Reform (INRA), one of the most central organizations of the Castro regime, set to work. By about the middle of 1962 nearly 45,000 title-deeds had been issued. But between 1959 and 1962 the redistribution into private hands of the expropriated land had barely moved forward at all. The reform quickly developed in the direction of cooperatives and people's farms and in 1962 these were working at least half of all the cultivated land in Cuba. On the people's farms farm labourers were in effect state employees. Thus there was an almost direct transition from the *latifundium* to communal farming. This speeding up of an undoubtedly necessary movement, this translation into practical terms of a lyrical sense of socialism, was not without its setbacks and confusions. The French expert, René Dumont, adviser to the Cuban government on agricultural affairs, has described the weaknesses, the mistakes, and the dangers involved in this unprecedented undertaking. He considered in particular that the calculations of the Cuban experts were far too optimistic. According to him, '27 hectares of very ordinary pastureland and poor scrubland was not really a great deal'. However, in the very first year of the reform, agricultural production went up. The improvement in the living standard of the peasants since 1959 was clear to see, and led to a parallel rise in general consumption. Was this the only reason for the food rationing so suddenly brought in by the government in March 1962? From 19 March 1962 every Cuban was allotted a kilo of fat per month, three of rice, three pounds of beef, 1 chicken, 5 eggs, a pound of fish, 125 grammes of butter, six litres of milk, 1 cake of toilet soap and one of scrubbing soap. The increase in the purchasing power of the rural masses combined with an exceptionally bad drought were not really enough to account for these restrictions – which inevitably led to the development of a black market and a lot of injustice. They were due also to the inexperience of an enthusiastic but not wholly efficient revolutionary government and the non-cooperation of certain categories of agricultural workers.

The agrarian reform helped to strengthen the clique of malcontents always to be found in any situation. To the big industrialists, the representatives of the huge sugar companies, the large landowners, the embittered and unemployed police and troops of Batista now retired on half pay, there was added by the end of 1959 a small group of peasants, small landowners who had never been exploited, and who only stood to lose by the 17 May reforms. From mid-1959 onwards there was an anti-revolutionary front in Cuba and in order to get rid of it, Fidel hardened the revolution still further. In July he dismissed the President, Manuel Urrutia, felt to be too moderate and known to favour the slowing down of agrarian reform, and replaced him with Osvaldo Dórticos.

*

The radicalizing movement took on a further impetus in October 1959. On the 25th a working-class district in Havana was bombed by two planes based in Florida. They were piloted by 'free' Cubans, one of whom, Pedro Díaz Lanz, was a defector from the revolution. Two people were killed and 45 wounded. Before half a million Cubans who gathered on the 26th outside the presidential palace Castro won overwhelming support for fresh draconian measures: the re-establishment of revolutionary tribunals, the setting up of workers' and peasants' militias, and death for terrorists.

Commandant Hubert Matos, a former comrade accused of treason, was arrested in Camagüey province by Camilo Cienfuegos himself. (The latter was to disappear a few days later while his plane was on its way back to Havana.)

Most of the men who embarked on the *Granma* in the Mexican port of Tuxpan in November 1956 for the great adventure were not Marxist. Those who were, like Che Guevara, an Argentinian doctor and life-long revolutionary, were more interested in guerrilla tactics than ultimate ideological choices. Time would tell. Contact with harsh reality, the need to tackle Cuba's problems head on, to choose a method, to follow a coherent path, to foresee events – in brief, to govern – naturally and rapidly divided the *barbudos* into differing groups: opportunists, adventurers, prudent reformists, every shade of opinion up to and including the most extreme. Two factors tended to make that olive-green uniform of the Sierra Maestra grow redder: first, the internal logic and chain of events within the revolution, and second, America's determination to destroy Castro's regime.

1959 saw the beginning of agrarian reform. 1961 was education year. The battle against illiteracy was begun with the same enthusiasm, the same unplanned haste, the same outrageous speeches that had marked the revolution itself. 'Not one person left illiterate by the end of 1961' – such was the word of command. A centre for the crash training of young volunteer teachers in the 'literacy brigades' was established at Varadero, a fashionable seaside resort 200 kilometres from Havana, which Batista had turned into a luxury harbour for use by Cuban and foreign millionaires. After a week's training there the brigade leaders, boys and girls of sixteen to twenty, would set off for the most isolated and unknown villages in the countryside with whatever equipment they could muster and the most fervent faith. In 1958 45 per cent of Cuban peasants could neither read nor write, and signed documents with their thumb-print. In Havana until 1958 the Columbia military camp was the dictatorship's fortress: 10,000 crack troops trained there to ensure that there should be no failures among the repression's machine. It was from Columbia that Batista flew at dawn after a night of watching and waiting to seek asylum in the Dominican Republic. Now the barracks of Columbia were re-painted, aired and turned into model classrooms where 10,000 children from the poorest parts of Havana could learn to read. In Santiago de Cuba the Moncada barracks – Castro's first object of attack – also became an educational complex.

*

Land for the peasants, blackboards in barns and barracks – then came the five-year plan. Only three years after their victory the revolutionary leaders decided to industrialize this island which lay caressed by the tropical sun, smelling of rum and covered in fields of sugar cane. 1962 was planning year. But socialization had in fact begun in 1959 with the seizure of most of the sugar refineries and the telephone and electricity companies. In 1960 came the nationalization of the Standard Oil and Shell oil refineries. At the end of 1960, 600 Cuban or foreign firms – 80 per cent of all industry – were controlled by the State. Agrarian reform had provoked a certain murmur of opposition. This large and rapid extension of public ownership aroused criticism and anxiety even in Fidel's own entourage. It was certainly vital to industrialize Cuba: first, to get away from the disastrous situation of having sugar as a single-product economy, and second, to avoid having to buy everything from abroad. In 1958 Cuba produced sugar, molasses, beer, candles, cigars, and a few perfumes – but not a nail, not a needle. Even the smallest manufactured articles had to be imported from the United States, as well of course as all cars, television sets, air conditioners, refrigerators and slot-machines. The 1962 planning man was Che Guevara, decreed a Cuban citizen in 1959, but still as cold, ironic, secretive, fanatical and intransigent as ever. Che, first director of the National Bank, then became Minister of Industry – though the change of job did not bring any change of method. He preferred to work at night. His objectives were anything but modest: he wanted to double the production of electricity by 1965, double the production of cement, increase steel production to half a million tons. Textile factories were to be established with help from East Germany, and naval shipyards with help from Poland.

*

To diversify the economy by establishing light industry is one thing; to establish heavy industry overnight on an island, four-fifths of whose activity has always been agricultural, looks like madness. The Moncada style was still in force. To all criticisms the Cubans would reply with conviction that that style had proved its worth. Yet countries with a far better balance of natural resources, like Colombia, Chile and Peru, had not yet got to the point of creating their own heavy industry. For instance, neither the Colombian steelworks nor the Peruvian industrial complex are actually paying propositions. The Soviet plans for factories and dams in India, Egypt or Guinea, have never been completed within the time limits set by the leaders of those countries. There was certainly no reason why Cuba should be any better off. Cuba lacked qualified workers, technicians and engineers; it lacked capital – the millions of dollars it used to get from its sales of sugar to the U.S. had not been replaced, since Russia, China, and the people's democracies which bought Cuban sugar for political rather than economic reasons were paying the ordinary world price (in other words, not the 'extra two cents' per pound), and only a small proportion (20 per cent of the total) of that was in dollars. Payment was now made in kind: machines, tools, tractors and industrial equipment instead of money. Before the revolution tourists used to bring 100 million dollars into the country every year, but Fidel's puritanism had closed the brothels and got rid of the prostitutes, shut down gaming-houses and casinos, and stopped other forms of gambling.

On 5 February 1960 Mr Mikoyan was in Havana and his

visit led to a restoration of diplomatic relations between Russia and Cuba, and the signing of a trade agreement. On 4 March the French cargo-ship *La Coubre* blew up in Havana harbour – to Cuban leaders this disaster, which involved many deaths, could only be 'the work of the CIA'. The atmosphere soon deteriorated. To America's decision on 11 May to stop giving technical aid to Cuba there corresponded a new agreement with Russia for industrializing the island. Since American firms would not refine Soviet oil the Cuban government seized Texaco and sequestrated Standard Oil and Shell. On 5 July the American Senate decided to give up buying any Cuban sugar and on 6 July Cuba in reprisal seized all American property on the island. This step was followed in August by the nationalization and expropriation of the goods seized. By September, after the OAS meeting which resolved to exclude Cuba (Mexico alone preserving diplomatic relations with Havana by 1968), the break was complete. The symbolic presence of an American diplomatic mission in Havana came to an end in January 1961.

On 17 April 1961 the fiasco of the Bay of Pigs landing coincided almost to the day with Castro's first reference to 'the socialist revolution'. The 2,000 mercenaries landed by the American navy were wiped out within forty-eight hours.

*

It was the Eisenhower administration which planned 'Operation Fish', an attempt to overthrow the Castro regime by force. Thousands of anti-Castroist volunteers or mercenaries spent months training in the jungle of Petén in Guatemala and also in Nicaragua. Washington only had to provide logistical support and air coverage. The body which coordinated the whole operation was the CIA, directed then by Allen Dulles, the brother of the former Secretary of State. In 1954 the CIA had planned and successfully carried out the Guatemala operation. This had been christened the

'Master Plan'; the Cuban operation was christened 'Must Go'. The same technique was used: the attack was to be actually carried out as far as possible by exiled nationals.

When he came to the White House at the end of January 1961 Kennedy found himself in a quandary and asked the advice of his experts. The State Department was resolutely against any kind of military intervention in Cuba; but the CIA, the Pentagon, and several of the most important members of the President's Brains Trust were for it. In June 1954 the attack on Guatemala had been preceded by the announcement in Washington that cargoes of Czechoslovak arms had arrived in Puerto Barrios, the banana republic's Atlantic port. The 1961 Bay of Pigs landing was justified by the announcement that 180 Soviet jets had arrived in Havana – a piece of news afterwards officially denied, but by then it was too late. D-day was to be the 17 April. Gossip among the leaders of the many anti-Castro organizations exiled in Miami was so rife, and the preparations in Guatemala and Nicaragua so obvious, that though he did not know the spot chosen for the landing, Fidel certainly knew the date. The first assault wave was held in check by a hundred peasant-militiamen, who died to the last man while waiting for reinforcement. The 2,000 attackers were fully armed and equipped. The three boats from which they landed were carrying 5 tanks, a number of armoured cars, and 18 anti-tank guns. In three days Soviet T34s and the Cubans' own heavy machine guns had crushed the invasion. There were hundreds of dead and 1,500 prisoners. Adlai Stevenson, Washington's delegate to the United Nations, spent some uncomfortable hours working out his reply to the speech of Raúl Roa, the Cuban Foreign Minister. A wave of anger against the U.S., not unlike the feeling against England and France during the Suez landing in 1956, swept the world.

The CIA leadership and some of the top men in the Pentagon lost their jobs over this ill-planned, ill-conceived, and ill-executed operation. The prime mistake of the American intelligence services was counting on a massive uprising of the Cuban people against Castro. It indicated both that they had received false information and that they totally lacked any psychology. This resounding failure led Kennedy to try a different tactic: a war of attrition. Washington's purpose was no longer to overthrow Castro directly but to isolate him totally from the rest of Latin America and then await results. This trial of force was thus also a trial of patience. The U.S. refused Cuba the dollars they were ready to give the last of the classic Latin American dictatorships under the banner of the Alliance for Progress. They counted on increasing economic and financial problems hitting the regime harder than any bombing of Havana or attacks from anti-Castro guerrillas.

Between November 1960 and November 1961 the Soviet Union delivered 100 heavy tanks and other military equipment to Cuba. Soviet performers, dancers from other eastern-bloc countries, Chinese theatre companies, all came to Havana in succession. Instead of American films the Cubans began seeing Russian ones. For thirty years the Cuban communist party had been one of the best organized and most powerful in all Latin America but it had never managed to play a really decisive role, and some of its most active members had even made compromises with the Batista regime. Now Cuban communists got some of the key economic and political jobs in the country.

Back in 1961 the 26 July Movement (Castroist), the Revolutionary Directorate and the PSP (communist party) had merged within the ORI (Integrated Revolutionary Organizations). In 1962 the ORI became the PURS (United Party for Socialist Revolution), but the establishment of a real communist party in Cuba was a slow and laborious business. One of the reasons for the slowness was the dispute – in several stages, so to say – between the original Fidelists and the leaders of the communist Old Guard who had aligned themselves with the revolution somewhat later. In March 1962 Castro denounced 'sectarianism' and dismissed Aníbal Escalante, a former PSP leader, and secretary of the ORI. The struggle against 'bureaucratism' broke out again in 1964 with the trial of Marco Rodríguez, the second Escalante affair in January 1968, and the elimination of what the Cuban leaders called the 'pro-Soviet micro-fraction'. Throughout all these *sub rosa* disputes the basic problem remained the same: Fidel Castro, leader of the new Cuban communist party, must not let himself be overwhelmed by any communists – whether former PSP activists or new members – who might be tempted to depart from the determinedly independent line of Fidelism.

That line, described since 1967 as the 'third way' in the socialist camp, made its appearance in the autumn of 1962 on the occasion of the rocket crisis. The establishment of firing bases for Soviet rockets on Cuban soil, first of all denied by both Havana and Moscow, led to a major international crisis and the unilateral withdrawal of the Soviets who agreed to dismantle the bases. This decision caused bitterness among the Cubans. Havana, where a secret conference of all the Latin American communist parties took place in December 1964 was in fact, from 1965 onwards, one of the capitals of the revolutionary 'Third World'. It was there that the delegates to the first Tricontinental Conference met (Africa, Asia and Latin America); and in August 1967 the first conference on the solidarity of the peoples of Latin America (OLAS) – marked by brushes between 'young Castroist revolutionaries' and 'orthodox communists' – confirmed Havana in this role. By 1968 the Cuban revolution was being watched from far beyond the frontiers of the Third World.

Yet the Cubans felt themselves in a very lonely position to deal with any dangers that might eventually threaten them. A certain coolness creeping into their relations with Russia, the political and trade dispute with China that came to the surface in 1966, persecution by the American bloc despite periodical rumours that relations with the U.S. were being 'normalized' – these were no doubt among the factors that led Fidel to say: 'We must learn to get used to the idea that we shall be fighting alone.'

This declaration was the logical conclusion of a development which began in 1962 after the rocket crisis; even then the 'treason' of the Russians was bitterly resented. In the university the wave of anger against Russia became so powerful that Fidel himself had to go and calm down the students. Fidel himself complained in private on several occasions of not having been consulted over Moscow's withdrawal of the rockets. Havana began to return to the theme of 'permanent and necessary guerrilla warfare' as the only way for socialism to triumph in under-developed countries. And up to March 1963 Fidel took great care not to come down on either side in the ideological dispute between the Russians and Chinese.

On 27 April 1963 it was learnt that Fidel had made a surprise visit to Russia. He was received in Murmansk by Mr Mikoyan and was present at the May Day celebrations in Red Square; for a month he was Khrushchev's star guest. The day before he left he received the medal of a Hero of the Soviet Union. The significance of this journey was plain: Fidel was making it spectacularly clear that he supported the Russians as against the Chinese, but as a revolutionary, the symbol of a Third World that must be won over, he received in exchange a fresh economic and financial agreement which was greatly to Cuba's advantage. When it came to choosing between the dreams of a total revolution all over South America cherished by the more idealistic Cuban leaders and the need to consolidate the Cuban regime under threat of death by starvation, Fidel could not be in two minds, nor was he.

But this attitude involved the need to make careful

attempts to improve relations with the U.S. – an improvement which the Russians themselves urged upon him. Between May and November 1963 Fidel intimated his good will to President Kennedy through various different intermediaries (sometimes too through self-appointed emissaries who hoped to worm their way into positions of importance by the back stairs, so to say). It is possible that a relatively favourable atmosphere was gradually being built up which made such discreet negotiations possible. The assassination of Kennedy put an end to any such hope. Kennedy had begun to make a serious attempt to stop the activities of the anti-Castro commandos in the U.S. and in the Caribbean. He personally intervened in the odd business of the sabotaging of Cuban sugar destined for Russia. The CIA was called to order by the State Department. But all too soon the Cubans realized that America under Johnson would be a very different place. The pragmatic Johnson once more gave free rein to the many organizations 'intending to liberate Cuba from the Castroist terror'. The anti-Castro lobby in Washington once again reared its head and raids on the island began to occur more frequently than ever, while air reconnaissance over Cuba was intensified.

Fidel still made his good will clear in no uncertain terms in an interview in the New York Times in July 1964. Never before had he stated so publicly his wish to normalize relations with the U.S. He offered to give up all 'Fidelist subversion in Latin America' (which it was perhaps tactless to mention, since it was an admission of how large a part he had been playing there), and asked the U.S. for their part to give up supporting the 'counter-revolutionaries' (possibly an admission of his own disquiet).

In any case his invitation met with no response. But by the end of 1964 and beginning of 1965 the temperature had dropped a few degrees between Havana and Washington. American opinion, hitherto so apparently obsessed with the 'Cuban threat', was naturally distracted from it by the continuing escalation of the Vietnam crisis. At the same time Fidel made it clear that he wanted to remain 'Cuban' while still being a 'Marxist-Leninist'. After their determination to industrialize at all costs Fidelist economists came back to the less romantic but more effective concept of sugar cane. Sugar production, which had been going down and down since 1959, began to increase enormously from 1963 onwards.

A very favourable agreement signed with Russia for the increasing sale of a large part of Cuba's production made it possible for the Havana government to make some plans for the future. The improvement in techniques of production, especially through mechanization where possible, resulted in the recovery of the production rate which fell disastrously twice, between 1961 and 1967, as the result of hurricanes, The departure of Guevara, former Minister of Industry in 1965, was interpreted as a recognition that his economic plans were not suited to the situation, and a determination to continue producing the 'material stimuli' denounced by him. Yet in fact from August 1967 onwards it was Che's ideas which won the day – though he himself was by then leading a guerrilla struggle in Bolivia. 'I am against material stimuli', declared Castro in August 1967 'because I consider them incompatible with socialism. In the society we are creating the enthusiasm with which a man works should not depend on how much or how little payment he receives.' He added: 'What we want is to de-mythologize money – not to rehabilitate it. Our ultimate objective is to do away with it altogether.'

The last private firms in Havana were nationalized in 1968. Within a few days 4,311 businesses in the capital were confiscated and the operation was extended to the rest of the country. A 'Revolutionary offensive' was also opened all over the island and the way it was carried out led a number of observers to compare it with the Chinese cultural revolution, the Committees for Defence of the Revolution being the Cuban equivalent of the 'red guards'. The theme was: 'Let the worker watch out for those in business firms and in the streets who spread intrigue, and create disorder and discontent.'

The official target was made 10 million tons by 1970, and from 3·8 million in 1963 (the worst year of all because of weather conditions and the mistakes made over industrialization), production rose to 4·5 million in 1964. The target for 1965, six million tons, was very slightly exceeded (6,050,532 tons) by mobilizing all the energies of the country. However in 1966 production again fell to 4·45 million tons; in 1967 it was up again to 6·12 million. The eight million tons hoped for in 1968 looked like being extremely hard to achieve because of a lengthy drought in Oriente province where a third of all Cuban sugar is produced. There are a number of factors to explain the difficulty of achieving regular and rapid expansion: the need to modernize some 152 processing plants and to increase the number of days for production, a lack of properly qualified labour, since volunteers could obviously not make up for the dearth of professional *macheteros*, inadequate fuel supplies, the antiquity of a considerable part of the transport equipment, yields being too low, the impossibility in many areas of modernizing cutting methods (Soviet combine-harvesters were virtually given up and a Cuban machine, *la libertadora*, was tested out in the winter of 1967 with some success). But the task was enormous, and the efforts made by the Cubans did not go uncriticized by their new sugar customers.

In Cuba itself criticism by orthodox communists of the methods used for planning and extending sugar production helped to aggravate the dispute between the 'old-style' communists and the Cuban leadership. In 1968, in the report presented by Raúl Castro against the 'micro-fraction' it was stated that the older communists were continually criticizing the methods of Fidel Castro, 'patterned on those of Che

Guevara, who established technocracy, and brought in Trotskyist Latin American technicians'.

Relations between the leaders of the 'first socialist republic in the Americas' and the headquarters of the existing Latin American communist parties were at least as ambiguous as those existing from 1956 to 1962 between communists and Fidelists in Cuba. The secret conference in December 1964 of all the Latin American communist parties – including of course the new communist party of Cuba – marked the high point of a collaboration whose obstacles became publicly obvious during the first conference of the solidarity of Latin American, Asian and African peoples in Havana in January 1966. The representatives from pro-Soviet communist parties among the various Latin American delegations undoubtedly supported the priority of the armed struggle in achieving power, but they did not, generally speaking, control their delegations, and their reservations were quite evident. The vicissitudes of the armed struggle in Latin America and the Soviet Union's policy of economic penetration in the subcontinent (resulting in agreements to trade and cooperate with several governments which the Cubans considered 'counter-revolutionary') explain the acerbity of the arguments during the Latin American solidarity conference of August 1967 in Havana. The resolutions adopted in the end had to take into account the criticisms of the communists who supported the 'Soviet line': it was admitted for the first time that conditions were not necessarily identical all over Latin America. In March 1967 Fidel Castro had already made a violent public attack on what he called the 'defeatism of the right-wing leadership of the Venezuelan Communist Party'. He accused them of 'wanting to abandon the armed struggle'. On the other hand he spoke in defence of the guerrilla leader Douglas Bravo and declared that 'the true communists are the people who are fighting'. This public admission of a dispute which had up to then been kept hidden between the Cuban leaders who exalted the 'revolutionary armed struggle in Latin America' and the communist leaders who thought 'the armed struggle was only one form of the struggle against imperialism' had its effect at the OLAS conference which barely escaped breaking up completely when it came to voting on a statement condemning 'Russia's commercial policy in Latin America'. Fidel Castro had been careful not to involve Russia directly in his dispute with the '*mafia* of the Latin American communist parties'. The death of Guevara in Bolivia and the publication of his Campaign Diary gave Castro the opportunity of denouncing 'the treason of the Bolivian communists' who were accused of having knowingly sabotaged Che's revolutionary movement. Castro's 'style' no doubt made it possible for him to continue on good terms with the Soviet Union (whose military and economic aid were far from negligible) while still urging a revolutionary line wholly at variance with any kind of peaceful coexistence. Eight years after breaking with the United States and joining forces with the socialist camp Castroism still opted for a 'third way' involving a denunciation both of American imperialism and of 'ill-adapted' communism. Vigorously demanding 'new action' and 'a revision of the out-of-date vocabulary of Marxism', Castroism in 1968 was in danger of being killed by isolation, while still hoping to remain a spokesman for all Third World revolutionaries.

Cuba, the socialist republic of the Caribbean, remains unlike any other country. And everything still depends on this one man, bearded, in his olive-green uniform, speaking in his soft voice to the Cubans who gather once a year in the Plaza de la Revolución.

List of Abbreviations

AD	Democratic Action Party (Venezuela) (Acción Democrática)
AID	Agency for International Development
APRA	Popular Revolutionary Alliance (Peru) (Alianza Popular Revolucionaria Americana)
BID	Interamerican Development Bank (Banco Interamericano de Desarrollo)
BRAC	Bureau for Suppressing Communist Activities (Cuba) (Buro para la Represión de Actividades Comunistas)
CDC	Christian Democrat Community (Bolivia) (Comunidad Democrática Cristiana)
CEPAL	Economic Commission for Latin America (Comisión Económica para la América Latina)
CIA	Central Intelligence Agency
CID	Democratic Institutional Coalition (Ecuador) (Concentración Institucional Democrática)
COPEI	Christian Social Party (Venezuela)
CORA	Agrarian Reform Corporation (Chile) (Corporación Reforma Agraria)
CUT	Central Workers' Organization (Chile) Central Unica de Trabajadores
CVP	Venezuelan Petroleum Corporation (Corporación Venezolana de Petróleo)
FAO	Food and Agriculture Organization

FCU	Federation of University Centres (Venezuela) (Federación de Centros Universitarios)
FDP	Democratic Popular Front (Venezuela) (Frente Democrático Popular)
FALN	Armed Forces for National Liberation (Venezuela) (Fuerzas Armardas de Liberación Nacional)
FOC	Chilean Workers' Federation (Federación de Obreros Chilenos)
FRAP	Popular Action Front (Chile) (Frente Acción Popular)
FRB	Bolivian Revolutionary Front (Frente Revolucionario Boliviano)
IAN	National Agrarian Institute (Venezuela) (Instituto Agrario Nacional)
IBRD	International Bank for Reconstruction and Development
IMF	International Monetary Fund
INDAP	Agricultural Development Institute (Chile) (Instituto de Desarrollo Agropecuario)
INRA	National Institute for Agrarian Reform (Cuba) (Instituto Nacional de Reforma Agraria)
MEP	Electoral People's Movement (Venezuela) (Movimiento Electoral Popular)
MIR	Movement of the Revolutionary Left (Chile, Peru, Venezuela) (Movimiento Izquierdista Revolucionario)
MNR	National Revolutionary Movement (Bolivia) (Movimento Nacional Revolucionario)
MOEC	Movement of Workers, Students and Peasants (Colombia) (Movimiento de Obreros, Estudiantes y Campesinos)
OAS	Organization of American States
OLAS	Organization for Latin American Solidarity (Organización Latino Americana de Solidaridad)

OPEP	Organization of Petroleum-Exporting Countries (Organización de Países Exportadores de Petróleo)
ORI	Integrated Revolutionary Organization (Cuba) (Organización Revolucionaria Integrada)
ORIT	Inter-American Regional Organization (Organización Regional Inter-Americana de Trabajadores)
POR	Workers' Revolutionary Party (Bolivia) (Partido Obrero Revolucionario)
PRA	Authentic Revolutionary Party (Bolivia) (Partido Revolucionario Auténtico)
PRIN	National Liberation Front (Bolivia) (Partido Revolucionario Izquierdista Nacional)
PRD	Dominican Revolutionary Party (Partido Revolucionario Democrático)
PSP	Cuban Communist Party (Partido Socialista Popular)
PURS	United Party for Socialist Revolution (Cuba) (Partido Unido para la Revolución Socialista)
SIM	Military Intelligence Service (Cuba) (Servicio de Inteligencia Militar)
URD	Democratic Republican Union (Venezuela) (Union Republicana Democrática)
YPFB	State Oil Deposits of Bolivia (Yacimientos Petrolíferos Fiscales Bolivianos)

Index

DR – Dominican Republic, LA – Latin America
NA – North America, SA – South America, mh – main heading

More about Penguins and Pelicans

Penguinews, which appears every month, contains details of all the new books issued by Penguins as they are published. From time to time it is supplemented by *Penguins in Print*, which is a complete list of all books published by Penguins which are in print. (There are well over three thousand of these.)

A specimen copy of *Penguinews* will be sent to you free on request, and you can become a subscriber for the price of the postage. For a year's issues (including the complete lists) please send 30p if you live in the United Kingdom, or 60p if you live elsewhere. Just write to Dept EP, Penguin Books Ltd, Harmondsworth, Middlesex, enclosing a cheque or postal order, and your name will be added to the mailing list.

Some other books published by Penguins are described on the following pages.

Note: *Penguinews* and *Penguins in Print* are not available in the U.S.A. or Canada

Political Leaders of Latin America

Richard Bourne

Latin American politics are of increasing importance in world affairs. This volume contains portraits of six political leaders of the region: individually they stress the diversity that lies between caudillo and Communist; together they may be taken to typify the face of Latin American government and the special problems confronting it.

Che Guevara	The Argentinian revolutionary who conquered in Cuba and died in Bolivia
Eduardo Frei	The President of Chile and the first Christian-Democratic president in Latin America
Alfredo Stroessner	The Army dictator of Paraguay
Juscelino Kubitschek	The President of Brazil from 1956 to 1960 and founder of Brasilia
Carlos Lacerda	who has helped to overthrow three Brazilian presidents
Evita Perón	The glamorous wife of the Argentinian dictator who combined military and labour supporters in a powerful nationalist movement

The Pelican Latin American Library

The Twenty Latin Americas, Volume 1

Marcel Niedergang

This volume deals with Brazil, Argentina, Uruguay, Paraguay, Mexico, Guatemala, Honduras, El Salvador, Nicaragua, Costa Rica and Panama.

Capitalism and Underdevelopment in Latin America*

Andre Gunder Frank

'It is capitalism, both world and national which produced underdevelopment in the past and which still generates underdevelopment in the present.'

For the Liberation of Brazil

Carlos Marighela

A collection of writings by the man who, more than any other, shifted guerilla opposition to Brazil's fascist regime into the towns.

Guatemala - Another Vietnam?*

Thomas and Marjorie Melville

Through ignorance and a monstrous lack of understanding the United States is creating the conditions for peasant war throughout Latin America. In this book two missionaries describe the way in which the U.S. government engineered the now notorious coup which brought an oppressive right-wing junta to power.

*Not for sale in the U.S.A.